THE
PADRE

Jennifer O'Leary is an award-winning investigative reporter for *Spotlight*, BBC Northern Ireland's flagship current affairs programme. In that role, she has reported on a diverse range of investigations including money laundering by the powerful mafia group, the 'Ndrangheta, a criminal conspiracy to export horses unfit for human consumption into the food chain, and the secret intelligence war between the state and the IRA.

THE

PADRE

The True Story of the Irish Priest
Who Armed the IRA with Gaddafi's Money

JENNIFER O'LEARY

MERRION
PRESS

First published in 2023 by
Merrion Press
10 George's Street
Newbridge
Co. Kildare
Ireland
www.merrionpress.ie

978 1 78537 461 6 (Paper)
978 1 78537 464 7 (Ebook)

A CIP catalogue record for this book is
available from the British Library.

Typeset in Sabon LT Std 11/17 pt

Cover design by riverdesignbooks.com

Back cover image courtesy of Eamonn Farrell/RollingNews.ie

Merrion Press is a member of Publishing Ireland.

To John and Angela

CONTENTS

PROLOGUE

The women huddled around a table overflowing with cups of froth-laden coffee, baby wipes and iPhones. They had cause to sit shoulder to shoulder; the din of chatter in the café, nestled on the first floor of a large lifestyle store close to the village of Rathcoole in south-west Dublin, was rising. Snippets of conversation bounced off the large windows framing an aspirational walled garden below.

The verdant scene outside was completed by the green and white marbled ivy that had begun to creep over a red-brick wall outside. Sloping fields, still untouched by the sprawl of suburbia, added a rural texture to the view beyond, and two chestnut-coloured horses could be seen nuzzling at grass before lazily moving out of sight.

The women sitting around the table were mostly smiling; relieved, perhaps to have made it to what looked like a mother-and-baby group. Each infant was only a few months old and a sturdy few were being held aloft like trophies. No mother looked at another's child with the ferocity with which she gazed upon her own – it was primal, not personal. The cadence of the chat amongst the group was largely soothing, momentarily allaying the deep-rooted fear that haunted the subconscious of some of these mothers – the dread that death would be visited upon their children.

Around them, the paraphernalia of parenthood expanded beyond the circumference of the table, blocking the path to a free table on the far side of the café. An elderly man following a younger woman holding a tray were trying to navigate their way through the busy space.

The thin, angular-cheeked man who looked to be in his late eighties was dressed all in black; his gait was slow but sure-footed. As soon as he caught their eye, some of the mothers at the table began to jolt their chairs out of the way. Appreciative of the minor kerfuffle, he smiled and slowly lifted his right hand with a dramatic flourish. The gesture made him appear as if was steadying himself to bestow a blessing on the mothers and babies assembled in front of him. Indeed, he could have done so. Decades earlier, parents would solemnly bow their heads to pray as he carefully poured holy water on the heads of their infant children. *I baptise you in the name of the Father, and of the Son, and of the Holy Spirit.*

In Ireland, Catholicism was, for decades, not only a religious ideology, but also a fundamental force that shaped and limited almost every aspect of people's lives. Achieving Irish independence from Britain had been a violent and divisive process, but once attained, the new Republic became a highly conservative state where the Catholic Church came to be the dominant force in social life. Catholic priests were the arbiters of the Church's monopoly on morality, and few dared defy the men wearing the clerical collars.

The man was of the generation where a religious vocation brought with it education, power and great status. As the second-eldest son reared on a small farm in County Tipperary, he had made his mother proud. 'A bull in the field, a pump in the yard and a priest in the family' were, according to him, the most impressive indicators of social status in the rural Ireland of his day. He was ordained in 1954 and worked for years as a missionary priest in East Africa before becoming the assistant curate of a parish in East London in the 1960s. However, the trajectory of his life would change in 1969, when the bloodshed that had marked the early years of Northern Ireland returned.

In August that year, British troops were sent to Northern Ireland in response to the growing disorder surrounding civil-rights protests and an increase in sectarian violence between Catholics and Protestants. It soon became clear that the violence was not going to end. The very presence of the British Army aggravated Irish republican militants, who believed the time was ripe for armed rebellion against the state. The Provisional Irish Republican Army (IRA), formed in 1969, increased levels of violence against the police and army, while loyalist paramilitary groups, intent on keeping Northern Ireland part of the UK, also stepped up their campaign of sectarian violence.

The conflict, which became known as 'the Troubles', would run across four decades and claim the lives of over 3,500 people, just over half of whom were civilians. Claudy, Warrenpoint, Kingsmills, Enniskillen, Teebane and the Shankill Road are among the long list of locations that became synonymous with the death and destruction. And in the summer of 1969, this conflict would lead the man who had once devoted his life to God and the service of the Catholic Church and its teachings to turn his attention to a very different dogma, one that ultimately led to the spilling of blood and the taking of lives on the streets of Northern Ireland and beyond.

Two of the mothers stood up and made a better attempt at clearing a path for the elderly man and his companion. He thanked them and paused to squeeze the shoulder of one whose dark-circled eyes made her appear particularly weary. Her exhaustion had not gone unnoticed.

'I must say that you look tired but beautiful on this sunny morning. God bless you.'

His remark elicited delight from all those who heard it. But his blessing was truly in disguise. In the absence of a Roman collar, those who heard his pronouncement had no idea that the man standing before them had once been ordained with an authority to administer all seven sacraments of the Catholic Church. Penitents seeking absolution for their sins had knelt in dark confessionals and whispered their secrets to him. Then a much younger man, he would lean one side of his face against the grille and listen carefully for the transgressions that were left unsaid. He quickly discovered that a simple question, gently posed, could release a flood of human failings. They would come unfurled on the back of a hurried breath. But the now-octogenarian had many secrets of his own.

The mothers who smiled at the man were completely unaware that his cunning had brought messages of death to many, delivered most often by someone in uniform at a family's home or in a hospital corridor. Solemn words that caused knees to buckle and hearts to break at the unfathomable loss of a daughter or son killed by bullets fired or bombs planted by members of the IRA.

The elderly man moving in the midst of the mothers and babies was Patrick Ryan. A person of deep contradictions along with an uncompromising pursuit of whatever orthodoxy he turned his attention to. After reaching the quiet corner table in the café that morning – the very table at which he and the woman now sitting across from him had spoken at many times previously – Ryan, for the first time, began to share his life story.

The moment was years in the making. It began on the back of a throwaway remark to me by a source – 'If you want a story about the IRA that's never been told by the main player himself, there's a Ryan you need to speak to, but I doubt he'll talk' – which became a name with a question mark written in the corner of a notebook, soon replaced with subsequent notebooks filled with details of other investigations and deadlines that demanded attention until, some two years later, I knocked on a stranger's door. A cold call that eventually culminated in many meetings with the elusive Ryan.

My source had been correct; Ryan did have a story to tell.

It started well. As a missionary priest he had built schools and health clinics in East Africa. Such was his enthusiasm that he had even obtained a pilot's licence in order to deliver vital medicine to clinics hundreds of miles apart. 'I had to learn how to fly a plane,' he said, 'because one of those journeys could take ten or twelve hours by road and you'd have sore bones for the rest of the week. I could fly a two-seater myself and deliver the medicine to the doctors, and for a time on the journey, I would gaze down on the beautiful wild animals in the Serengeti.'

However, the diligence that Patrick Ryan demonstrated in the pursuit of saving lives was later equally applied with the opposite intent. His technical ingenuity, honed in East Africa while drilling for water and learning to fly an aeroplane, came full circle when he re-engineered a simple parking timer for use in explosive devices, single-handedly increasing the IRA's ability to affect carnage in scores of bombings from the early 1970s onwards. Yet this outwardly radical transformation did not seem to prompt any introspection from Ryan: 'I was approached by some of the IRA leaders [to see] if perchance I could work for them, and I did.'

Patrick Ryan would stop at nothing to achieve his aims. He criss-crossed Europe and travelled even further afield on a singular mission: 'I set out to go around the world and discover the enemy of my enemy, the Brits, and make their enemy my friend.' His diplomatic skills and manipulative ability quickly yielded results and he became one of the IRA's most significant intermediaries for money, as well as the main contact for many years between the IRA and one of its main sources of weaponry and finance – Colonel Gaddafi's Libyan regime.

The mothers in the café that morning were smiling at a man whose very existence and role in the IRA was known, for some time, only to an elite few. IRA bomb-makers carefully constructed increasingly sophisticated devices without ever knowing that a one-time priest, a so-called man of God, had sourced the key components that were used to maximum effect.

For almost two decades, Ryan appeared to evade intelligence agencies across Europe. He was also, at a time, one of the most wanted men in Britain, given his connection to a series of bombings, including the one that came very close to assassinating British Prime Minister Margaret Thatcher. She narrowly escaped death in the attack on the Grand Hotel, Brighton, in October 1984. Five others were not so lucky.

Decades on from the carnage at Brighton, sitting in a café on the outskirts of Dublin, Patrick Ryan was unrepentant. 'I had a hand in the IRA's bomb at Brighton and many other IRA bombings. My only regret is that I wasn't more effective.'

Patrick Ryan had never given away any details about his ruthless zealotry in pursuit of money, weapons and assistance for the IRA's campaign of violence – until he spoke to me.

ONE

THE SHOWDOWN IN RHODES

The Palace of the Grand Masters on the Greek island of Rhodes, built in the early fourteenth century by the Knights of St John, a military religious order, had long harboured the secrets and political ambitions of those who had occupied its triple circuit of walls.

After the Ottoman Empire captured the eastern Mediterranean island in 1522, the palace was used as a command centre and fortress, until centuries later, in 1912, another invading force, the Italians, whose army had also invaded Libya, defeated the Turks. Under Italian occupation, the palace was reconstructed as a summer residence for the King of Italy, Victor Emmanuel III, and later for Italy's fascist dictator, Benito Mussolini, yet, ironically, neither the King nor Il Duce ever stayed there.

On 3 December 1988 a rain-laden sky blocked a low winter sun from casting long shadows across the Palace's sand-speckled stone. The visitors inside were invited guests of a Greek government keen to showcase the magnificent location to the assembled television crews and reporters from across Europe. The Palace was the venue for a meeting of the European Council, an institution of what was then named the European Economic Community (EEC), a political union forged with the aim of fostering economic co-operation and preventing a return to totalitarian regimes following the Second World War.

In 1988 European land borders redrawn in the wake of the war between the Axis and Allied powers remained in place. Germany was still divided into West and East by the Berlin Wall, although the Cold War division between the Soviet Union and western countries was thawing out. The continent was largely at peace, with the exception of what was then Europe's most ferocious conflict, the Troubles in Northern Ireland.

In Rhodes, European heads of government, along with a coterie of ambitious advisors and civil servants, walked through the enormous, marble-tiled inner courtyard of the Palace to begin another round of diplomatic machinations and deal-making. Time pressures and the wet weather discouraged the visitors from stopping to marvel at the imposing sculptures of Roman emperors, excavated from the ancient Odeon on the nearby Greek island of Kos. A night of storms and high winds, which blew in from the Aegean Sea, had been the harbinger of a day of thundering downpours, unforgiving in their ferocity.

A political storm was also brewing. Twelve European leaders were meeting, but just two of them were dominating the headlines, with warnings of a looming row and 'bitter showdown' between the British Prime Minister, Margaret Thatcher, and her Irish counterpart, Taoiseach Charles Haughey.[1]

There was little sign of this inside the walls of the palace, where dust particles danced in the shafts of light that broke through, and, for a short time, a lazy winter light lingered on a floor paved with an ancient Byzantine mosaic. Few of the political leaders or bureaucrats rushing between meetings in Rhodes that day would have known that the Palace of the Grand Masters stood testament to the art of restoration – the reconstruction of the castle by its Italian conquerors took place decades after it was destroyed in 1856 by an explosion of gunpowder hidden in a basement. Fewer still had experienced the explosive and shattering force of a bomb, while, at the same time, knowing they were its intended target. The British Prime Minister, however, had first-hand experience.

* * *

Four years earlier, Margaret Thatcher had survived an IRA assassination attempt; as she herself later put it, 'those who had sought to kill me had placed the bomb in the wrong place'.[2] The IRA had long held an ambition to assassinate Thatcher, and the British security service had been forewarned. For some years, MI5 had been reporting intelligence that the IRA intended to bomb one of the annual Conservative Party conferences.[3] In the early hours of Friday, 12 October 1984, that intelligence was borne out.

On 15 September a man using the pseudonym Roy Walsh had checked into the Grand Hotel in the English coastal town of Brighton and paid £180 in cash for a three-night stay. The resort was a frequent location for the autumn season of British political party conferences on account of its conference facilities, as well as the plentiful availability of cheap accommodation at the end of the summer holiday season. The front-desk receptionist allocated Walsh Room 629 as it had a nice view across the English Channel.

The man's name was a brazen alias. Roy Walsh was the name of an IRA bomber serving a life sentence in HM Prison Parkhurst for planting a bomb outside the Old Bailey in 1973 that injured 200 people. The man who had actually signed the hotel registration card was Patrick Magee, an experienced IRA operative; he was there to plant a bomb behind a bath-panel in his room, some five floors above the hotel's VIP suites.

The IRA operation was ruthless in its execution. The Grand Hotel was being guarded during the Conservative Party conference week by plain-clothes and uniformed Sussex police officers, as well as members of the Metropolitan Police Close Protection Unit. Patrick Magee carefully circumvented these security measures with deadly precision by planting the bomb, packed with a commercial nitroglycerine-based gelignite explosive,[4] on 17 September and setting its long-delay timing mechanism to count down 24 days, 6 hours and 36 minutes to detonation. The IRA intended for Margaret Thatcher, along with her cabinet, to die in the early hours of 12 October.

Early that morning the Prime Minister was working on her party conference speech in the first floor Napoleon suite of the Grand Hotel. 'I had just finished doing something when I looked at the clock. It was a quarter to three and I started on another paper. My husband was in bed.'[5] At 2.54 a.m. the bomb in Room 629 exploded with terrible results. Tons of rubble came crashing through seven floors of the elegant, off-white Victorian building, knocking down walls and filling hallways and stairwells with dust and smoke. The windows of the Prime Minister's suite were blown in and her bathroom, according to her husband, Denis, looked as 'if it had been blitzed'.[6] Only a few moments earlier, Mrs Thatcher had been in the bathroom, which had suffered such damage that nobody in it at the time of the blast would have survived the impact.

'The air was full of thick cement dust: it was in my mouth and covered my clothes as I clambered over discarded belongings and broken furniture towards the back entrance of the hotel,' Mrs Thatcher later recalled in her memoir. 'It still never occurred to me that anyone would have died.'[7]

The search for survivors intensified as the sun rose that morning. Millions of viewers of British breakfast-time television watched in horror as the Minister for Trade, Norman Tebbit, injured and moaning in agony, was rescued from the rubble where he had been buried for four hours. His wife, Margaret, was paralysed for life, and many others were injured by the IRA bomb intended to assassinate the Prime Minister and destroy the British government. Four people were killed in the explosion: Roberta Wakeham, Jeanne Shattock, Eric Taylor and Sir Anthony Berry MP. Muriel Maclean, who had been sleeping in room 629 where the bomb was planted, later died in hospital from her injuries.

Nine hours after the attack, the IRA claimed responsibility. The statement chillingly added: 'Today we were unlucky. But remember we only have to be lucky once. You will have to be lucky always. Give Ireland peace and there will be no war.'

The search for evidence resulted in crime-scene investigators collecting close to 900 tons of debris over a number of weeks, but despite the sheer volume of material that needed to be carefully analysed, as well as the challenge of forensically searching an unstable building, on 27 October an anti-terrorist squad detective made a crucial discovery. In the S-bend of a toilet in room 329, Detective Constable Ian Macleod uncovered part of the explosive device.

'I recognised it straight away,' he said. 'It was one of the two plates from a Memo Park Timer.'[8] Memo Park timers were small gadgets used by motorists in parts of Europe to remind them that the time on a parking meter was about to expire. This seemingly innocuous device had been adopted by the IRA as a reliable and accurate bomb detonation timer, with devastating results. Its adaptation for such a malevolent purpose was a result of the cunning and technical nous of one man: Father Patrick Ryan. It was Ryan who had conceived of the redesign a decade earlier, and who purchased the timers in bulk in Europe to ensure that IRA bomb-makers were never short of what he described as the 'little timers that made all the difference'. Without these timers, and Ryan's template to convert them into reliable detonation mechanisms, the IRA's ability to plant a device on a long-delay timer, as happened at Brighton, would simply not have been possible.

* * *

By December 1988, in a year that was defined by a fury of bloodshed, the death toll in Northern Ireland had long surpassed 2,000. Over fourteen days during March alone, escalating violence culminated in some of the most infamous imagery to emerge from the Troubles.

On 6 March British special forces killed three members of the IRA – Sean Savage, Daniel 'Danny' McCann and Mairéad Farrell – who were planning a bomb attack in Gibraltar. At their funerals at west Belfast's Milltown Cemetery, ten days later, lone loyalist gunman Michael Stone launched a frenzied gun and grenade attack on the mourners, killing three and wounding more than fifty.

Three days later, as one of Stone's victims was being buried in west Belfast, two plain-clothed British Army soldiers drove into the path of the funeral cortège as it proceeded along the Andersonstown Road towards Milltown Cemetery. Corporal David Howes and Corporal Derek Wood were pulled from their car by an angry crowd and beaten before being dragged to a nearby sports ground and beaten again, stripped down to their underpants and socks, and searched. The men were then thrown over a wall with a nine-foot drop, where they were bundled into a black taxi and driven to waste ground to be shot dead by the IRA.

The graphic violence of the entire episode was filmed by an army helicopter with a live 'heli-teli' feed to a nearby police and army control room, while the initial stages of the attack were captured by television crews and broadcast in TV bulletins around the world. Corporal Wood's grandmother, who helped bring him up after the death of his mother when he was twelve, had watched the attack on television, unaware that her grandson was one of those being brutally killed by the IRA.[9]

Another image from the day's horror was seared into the public consciousness: that of Tipperary-born Redemptorist priest Father Alec Reid administering the last rites over the bloodied, near-naked body of Corporal Howes, who was lying on the ground with his arms and legs spread wide. In the split-second moment that the priest looked in the direction of the photographer's lens, the expression on his bloodstained face was a freeze-frame of compassion amidst the horror of what he had witnessed. 'I walked up to this area of waste ground. There was nobody else there, just the two bodies. I went up to the one on the right. He was still breathing so I tried to give him the kiss of life. Then after a while a man came in and stood behind me and said, "Look, Father, that man is dead." I anointed him and went over to anoint the man who was lying three yards away. Then two women came along with a coat and put it over his head and said, "He was somebody's son."'[10]

It was against this backdrop of horrifying violence that Margaret Thatcher prepared to meet with her Irish counterpart, Taoiseach Charles Haughey, in the British delegation room in the Palace of the Grand Masters. The relationship between Haughey and Thatcher at this time was at an all-time low, a sharp contrast to their very first meeting as leaders eight years earlier, which had appeared to hold genuine diplomatic promise.

* * *

On 21 May 1980 Haughey made his way into the Cabinet room of 10 Downing Street, the very room where Irish nationalist leaders had negotiated for Ireland's independence close to sixty years previously. He presented Thatcher with a Georgian silver teapot, along with a silver tea-strainer inscribed with the words attributed to St Francis of Assisi that Thatcher had recited on her first day in Downing Street: 'Where there is discord, may we bring harmony.'

'That will knock her back a bit,' Haughey had told a confidant on the eve of this, their first Downing Street meeting.[11] The gesture was well received; Thatcher's private secretary, Lord Powell, recounted that 'there was a glint' in Haughey's eye that Thatcher 'found attractive'. Three days after the summit Haughey told the British Ambassador to Ireland, Robin Haydon, that the atmosphere had been 'wonderful' and that, 'to be honest', he had been surprised everything had gone so well.[12]

Following the Downing Street encounter, relations between London and Dublin appeared at their most cordial in several years. Ireland's Ambassador to London, Eamon Kennedy, wrote to the Prime Minister expressing thanks for the 'elusive blend of warmth and elegance' displayed at the luncheon. 'We all felt that new and encouraging vistas of co-operation in friendship had been opened between us, and that the two islands were coming closer together,' said Kennedy, who followed up with a gift of orchids. Writing from Chequers, the official country residence of British prime ministers, a few days later, Thatcher replied, 'I am glad that you enjoyed the lunch. So did I. The orchids are quite lovely. I have had them brought down to Chequers and they are by me as I write.'[13]

However, the warm relationship did not see out the summer. Just two months later an official of the British Embassy in Dublin was describing the connection between the two leaders and their respective countries as a 'love/hate relationship'.[14]

In the years that followed, the IRA's continuing campaign of violence infuriated Thatcher, who had signed up to the Anglo-Irish Agreement in 1985 in the belief that it would improve co-operation with the Republic in security matters. Thatcher had long sought increased security co-operation between Britain and Ireland, and in particular, the extradition of terrorist suspects from the Republic to Northern Ireland for trial. However, from the outbreak of the Troubles, successive Irish governments feared that public perception that they were giving in to British security requests could precipitate an upsurge in nationalist sentiment, which, in turn, could destabilise the Republic. In the early 1980s a senior garda briefed the Irish government that 'if the state were to accede to the British demand for enhanced security cooperation and, in particular, if extradition procedures were to be implemented' there would be outright conflict with the IRA. 'The state might not be able to hold the line.'[15]

It was the horror of the Enniskillen bomb on Remembrance Day that forced the acceleration of the enactment of extradition legislation in the Republic. On the evening of 8 November 1987 the brutal aftermath of this atrocity visited almost every home with a television in Ireland. Amateur video footage, recorded just minutes after an IRA bomb had blown up without warning at 10.43 a.m. at the town's cenotaph, next to people remembering their dead, was broadcast in news reports. Many of the victims, who had gathered to commemorate the British military war dead, were elderly. Eleven civilians were killed and scores injured, including children. The dead included three married couples, a retired policeman and a nurse.

Days after the attack, Dermot Gallagher, a senior Irish government diplomat, wrote a confidential note on a lunch meeting with the Prime Minister's press secretary, Bernard Ingham. 'There was a deep sense of shock in No. 10,' he said. 'The PM's office warned it would be difficult to manage Dublin's call for new extradition laws to be deferred in the wake of the atrocity. Enniskillen has hardened Mrs Thatcher's heart, Ingham said.'[16]

In the aftermath of the carnage at Enniskillen, Charles Haughey agreed to enact legislation to allow for the extradition of terrorist suspects to Britain, but under pressure from his party he inserted a 'safeguard' that each application would have to be examined and approved by the Irish Attorney General. The safeguard annoyed the British Prime Minister, who believed it effectively rendered the bill unworkable.

Ongoing security concerns had dominated two previous meetings between the leaders in 1988, both of which, like the meeting in Rhodes, had taken place on the margins of a European summit. In February, in Brussels, the Taoiseach had also complained about the rejection by the Court of Appeal in London of a plea by the so-called Birmingham Six to have their convictions for the 1974 Birmingham pub bombings overturned.[17] When Haughey emphasised that 'a very keen sense of injustice [was] rampant in Ireland', Mrs Thatcher asked for how long these emotions had lasted. The Taoiseach said, '700 years in our country.'[18]

Fractious exchanges also characterised the next meeting, in Hanover on 28 June, where Thatcher complained that the Irish government was not delivering on security and was scathing about An Garda Síochána (the Irish police). 'We do not get intelligence from the gardaí,' she said. 'They are not the most professional force,' Mr Haughey replied, then went on to point out, 'You had Lisburn. You had Enniskillen. These are not failings of our making.' Less than two weeks earlier, an IRA bomb had killed six soldiers at a fun run in Lisburn. 'These are things which happen within Northern Ireland where your security forces operate,' said the Taoiseach. 'If the gardaí are not 100% effective, then neither are the RUC 100% successful.'[19] Thatcher retorted, 'I have one objective: that is to beat the IRA. For that we need the latest intelligence.'

By December 1988, in the minutes before the Taoiseach and the British Prime Minister met in the Palace of the Grand Masters of Rhodes, Thatcher could not hide her disdain for Haughey. It was widely perceived that the latter had already won the first round of political jostling after he'd cancelled a meeting with Thatcher the previous day for reasons, it was said, of personal convenience. As they stood side by side during the traditional photocall of summit leaders, the Prime Minister gave the Taoiseach the cold shoulder. On this occasion, Thatcher was furious for a specific reason: twelve months after the signing of the extradition legislation, her concerns about it were being borne out and she was incensed that Irish authorities were continuing to delay the extradition of an Irish priest wanted in London for questioning about IRA bomb attacks.

Father Patrick Ryan had been arrested in Brussels months earlier, after the IRA had killed three off-duty British servicemen in two separate incidents in the Netherlands. The British authorities immediately requested his extradition, but the Belgian government refused the request, claiming that charges against him were too vague. Instead, they flew him to Dublin on a military plane, taking care to avoid British airspace. The controversy sparked a major diplomatic row between Ireland and Britain. As the two leaders sat facing each other in Rhodes, Ryan had been back on Irish soil for ten days as a free man. The time had come for Thatcher to look Haughey in the eye and be unsparingly blunt.

'I will go straight to the point,' said Thatcher. 'We are at the receiving end of a vicious campaign of terrorism. The IRA are not letting up on their campaign. You have heard what I said about the Ryan case. Ryan is a really bad egg.'[20] The Prime Minister looked down at the briefing paper before her. 'He is largely responsible for the Libyan money. Very large sums have been traced to his account from the Libyans – money like £700,000 and £150,000. He has also been caught with bombing devices of the sort that were nearly used on over eleven of our seaside towns. We stopped that. That was one of our successes.'

According to Thatcher, the Irish authorities were 'quibbling' over commas and duplications in the British documents seeking the extradition of Ryan: 'I know that the Bow Street clerk didn't put the date in and there were other things like that. But the important point is that, yes, we are worried about Ryan. You had three days to take out a provisional warrant and back ours. That should have been enough time for you to have been able to decide. But you didn't. Your Attorney General wouldn't take a request from ours.'

Thatcher's anger was not solely on account of her frustrations over the implementation of cross-border security policy, it was also personal. 'We are at the receiving end of this terrorism,' she told Haughey. 'I and my soldiers – we are at the receiving end.'

When the coffins of Corporals David Howes and Derek Wood, draped in Union flags, were carried from a Hercules transport plane at RAF Northolt, the Prime Minister had been at the airfield standing next to their families. She stated, 'I will never forget receiving the bodies of those two soldiers murdered in Belfast before the television cameras. Those films were seen by their relatives; that was a terrible experience. I have ensured that these people will not be allowed to appear on TV in future. I have been criticised for this decision. I am asked, where is the freedom of the press? My reply is the words of the mother of one of these murdered boys: she said, "Where is my son?"'

Haughey did not interrupt Thatcher as she continued: 'Ryan is a very dangerous man. Both the Belgians and our services know this. He is at liberty still. I do not know what will happen in Knightsbridge or Oxford Street at Christmas. People like Ryan with contacts with Libya, with expert knowledge of bombing – they can skip – I feel so strongly on this and feel so badly let down. I have said my say. What do you think?'

The Taoiseach looked across at Thatcher, the heady days of his 'teapot diplomacy' charm offensive long faded: 'First, we cannot,

under our law, issue a warrant in anticipation of a person's arrival
in this State. We must wait until the person comes into the country.
There was time for the preparation and perfection of warrants. This
time was not used – and it was not our fault. It is a pity that every
time you and I meet we have one of these difficult issues on something
that is marginal between us. We can never get to the major questions
which you should be discussing – like the possibility of progress with
the North, how Northern Ireland is to be governed, relations with
the Unionists, and such like matters. Last time it was the Gardaí and
different intelligence. I don't know how we can get away from this
constant bickering, attacking each other after each incident. At the
moment, Fr Ryan is the villain of the piece.'

Haughey claimed that, prior to Ryan's arrival in Ireland, his government had no knowledge of any reason why he should be extradited. 'We never heard of this man until he appeared in Belgium,' he
protested. 'Your police asked the Belgians that he be kept under observation and then at the end of June he was arrested. I don't think your
people asked for that arrest. Certainly, we didn't hear that they had.'

'You amaze me,' Thatcher responded. 'From 1973 to 1984 he
[Ryan] was the main channel of contact with the Libyans. He has
had meetings with at least two prominent Libyan ministers. Between
1973 and 1976 he was connected to two sterling sub-machine guns.
He has links with the Oxford Street, Brighton and Dulwich bombs. He
is also known to the Belgian police.' She paused. 'He has had money
in his accounts from the Libyans amounting to over £740,000.'

An exasperated Haughey replied, 'If we had a straightforward
case like the Harrods or Enniskillen bombs we would have no
difficulty; but every damn case now has some twist to it. Ryan is an
extraordinary case. You have a mad priest careering around Europe,
arrested in Belgium and then flown to us in a military plane, avoiding
British airspace.'

'Yes,' said Thatcher, 'he avoided our airspace. There is the conspiracy case. But he was also the source of Libyan money to the IRA and was involved in arms and bombs. These people are very hard to catch. They moved from country to country and they are very careful.'

Before the meeting concluded, Thatcher reminded Haughey that on the day that the British election was called in 1979, Irish republicans murdered her Conservative Party colleague and mentor Airey Neave. 'Their viciousness, their savagery is unbelievable. And they torture people dreadfully. There is no substitute for worthwhile extradition arrangements.'

Summing up the meeting, Irish civil servant Dermot Nally wrote that while the Prime Minister had talked 'with considerable warmth on many subjects, her general attitude, in the end, was cordial. She spoke a great deal of the time more in sorrow than in anger.' The joint statement issued afterwards was terse: 'The regular meeting between the Taoiseach and the British Prime Minister took place at the end of the European Council. There was a frank exchange of views on a number of issues including extradition, fair employment, security co-operation and the review of the Anglo-Irish Agreement.'[21]

At a press conference afterwards, Margaret Thatcher stated that she had made her views about 'the Ryan matter' very clear to Charles Haughey. 'I think that he can understand why ... we regard it as a very grave matter ... It is our police,' she said, 'it is our soldiers – who may I say defend the whole of Europe as well – our civilians and our people who are on the end of being bombed, maimed or killed and therefore, we expect there to be efficient procedures so that those people who are charged with offences can be detained – if necessary extradited – and brought before a court to decide the matter of guilt or innocence – and I think he understands that.'[22]

The Taoiseach, meanwhile, gave away little in public of the specifics of what had been said during his meeting with the British

Prime Minister in Rhodes. 'The convention is now established that the details of these discussions are not publicised,' Haughey said in a statement to the Dáil. 'The discussion took place in a realistic atmosphere and views were exchanged openly and frankly. On extradition, I expressed disquiet at the fact that each case now seems to become politicised, and this affects the whole background and is a matter of serious concern in its effects on the legal process and the rights of individuals.'[23]

Thatcher reserved her fury for Wilfried Martens, the Belgian Prime Minister whose government had refused to extradite Patrick Ryan to Britain. During their meeting in Rhodes, the pair 'hardly shared a common subject' and parted on bitter terms when Thatcher terminated the meeting by saying, 'We have nothing further to talk about, you and I', whereupon she 'grabbed' her handbag and 'stormed out, leaving Martens sitting there'.[24] She later wrote about Ryan, 'a non-practising Catholic priest, well known in security service circles as a terrorist', who 'for some time ... played a significant role in the Provisional IRA's links with Libya', and recalled her meeting with Martens in Rhodes. 'I was unconvinced and unmoved by M. Martens' explanations. His Government had clearly taken its decision in contradiction to and in defiance of legal advice ... But as a Belgian government under the same M. Martens later showed at the time of the Gulf War,[25] it would take more than this to provide them with a spine. And Patrick Ryan is still at large.'[26]

How had a man who had once committed his life to God become such a sought-after target for the British government?

TWO

A MOTHER'S LOVE

The darkness amplified every sound. Mary Ann Carroll shifted her body weight from side to side as she stood guard, not far from her family home in Upperchurch, County Tipperary, in the mid-west of Ireland. A low whistle preceded a gust of wind that rolled like a furious wave across the lower hills of the nearby Slieve Felim mountains before it crashed against the high scrub of blackthorn bordering both sides of the boreen.[1] The shudder and snapping of brambles intensified the twelve-year-old's focus on her task at hand: to stay alert for the boots of the new British recruits, the 'Black and Tans'. It was 1920; the second year of the Irish War of Independence against Britain, the climax of a struggle for control of Ireland that had seen many revolts against British rule in the centuries since the Norman invasion of 1169.

Her shoulders were beginning to slouch, so Mary Ann straightened her back and tilted her chin towards the cloud-covered sky. The North Star was obscured from view, but she instinctively knew the direction in which to turn and pivoted on her heels to face south towards the Tipperary townland of Soloheadbeg, the very spot where the opening shots of the war had been fired.

Even in daylight, the spindly hedges that cushioned the boreen largely blocked Mary Ann's view of the valley; in the black of the night, the hedges made her feel like she was in a dark tunnel as she listened for any sound that signalled danger. She could barely see beyond the shape of her small hands, yet, from where she was standing, she knew by heart the number of steps it would take for her to push open the door of her family's home and raise the alarm. Mary Ann had long learned which curves of the hedge to lean away from in order to avoid being scratched by protruding thorns. In the absence of any encroaching soldiers, there was nothing to do but stay alert and try not to dwell on the spine-tingling stories of a seanchaí she sometimes overheard by firelight in her grandmother's home.[2] She was not afraid of the restless spirits who supposedly shuffled along the valley's lonely lanes; there was more to fear from the living.

The memories of those long, lonely nights of standing guard in the boreen never left Mary Ann. Even decades later, she would close her eyes and purposefully count out the number of steps to the door of her parents' house; her children recognised the chant as a sign that their mother, often following gentle encouragement, was about to recount the story of her role in the Irish War of Independence.

As a wife and mother, Mary Ann was Mrs Ryan, and proudly so. The wise word of a matchmaker and the handover of a modest dowry had seen her marry Simon Ryan from the parish of Rossmore, County Tipperary. Matchmaking was central to marriage in rural Ireland in the 1920s; romance was of no regard compared to the importance of maintaining the pattern of farm succession among 'respectable' families. An inheriting son was matched to a woman with an appropriate dowry and the process involved assessing 'the relative status of the families and any possible barriers to the union, such as consanguinity, insanity, or notorious crime in past ancestry'.[3]

For Mary Ann, the match was fortuitous. Simon Ryan was an honest, hard-working farmer, who drew delight during the evenings from his wife speaking at length about what she had done to keep the

Black and Tans from her family's door. He would smile and quietly observe their six children sitting in absolute thrall to their mother. Their second-eldest son, Patrick, never failed to listen intently. 'The family lore was what my mother did as a youngster, and I was captivated by her stories; it was like I was back there with her, watching and listening out for the enemy. The house would grow very quiet when she spoke about that time. All she wanted was for us to listen, and we did.' Alongside Patrick sat his brothers, Simon, John and Joseph, and his sisters, Mary and Kitty. 'All you had to do was mention the subject and she was off, it was in her bones.'

Mary Ann Ryan's formative experiences defined her deeply held patriotism for the rest of her days. Even at a young age, she sensed the urgency in the hurried conversations she picked up following the events of 21 January 1919, an historic day defined by the ballot box and gun. That afternoon in Dublin, the first public meeting of Dáil Éireann took place in the Round Room of the city's Mansion House. Proceedings got underway at 3.30 p.m. when newly elected Members of Parliament (MPs) who had pledged not to sit in Westminster gathered to proclaim the Dáil as an independent legislative assembly for Ireland. Absent from the Mansion House gathering were Unionist MPs and MPs from the Irish Parliamentary Party, which favoured devolved Home Rule. The room was crammed with onlookers and journalists, who watched as Dáil members adopted a constitution and issued a declaration of independence. The declaration ratified the Irish Republic that had been proclaimed on Easter Monday 1916 and ordained 'that the elected Representatives of the Irish people alone have power to make laws binding on the people of Ireland, and that the Irish Parliament is the only Parliament to which that people will give its allegiance'.[4]

The first meeting of the Dáil was the manifestation of the pursuit of Irish independence from Britain by constitutional political means.

However, blood had already been spilled earlier that day by those who saw armed conflict as a necessary prerequisite to that independence. In a narrow country lane, about 120 miles south-west of the Mansion House, eight men from the Third Tipperary Brigade of the Irish Volunteers were lying in wait to ambush a convoy carrying a quantity of gelignite from Tipperary Military Barracks to Soloheadbeg quarry, where it was intended for use in blasting rock. The Volunteers, still rebuilding after the 1916 Easter Rising, had no explosives of their own and were not going to let an opportunity to obtain gelignite to pass them by. Such was their need that the ambush party had been waiting for five days from early dawn until late afternoon for the gelignite to be moved and Séumas Robinson, the brigade's officer commanding, was growing increasingly nervous. 'I thought long, deeply and anxiously and I almost panicked when I saw the date of the Dáil meeting drawing near and no sign of the gelignite coming ... Luckily (is there such a thing as luck?) the cart arrived on the 21st ...'[5]

The consignment of gelignite was on a horse-drawn cart, led by two council workers and guarded by two Royal Irish Constabulary (RIC) policemen, James McDonnell and Patrick O'Connell. It was between 12.30 and 1 p.m. when the convoy reached a bend in the road and the ambush party jumped over a roadside fence nearby and shouted, 'Hands up!' Both of the policemen were shot dead for failing to drop their rifles. One of the Soloheadbeg ambushers, Dan Breen, recalled in his statement to Ireland's Bureau of Military History, 'The only regret we had, following the ambush, was that there were only two policemen in it instead of the six we expected, because we felt that six dead policemen would have impressed the country more than a mere two.'[6]

The Soloheadbeg ambush is generally accepted as marking the start of the Irish War of Independence. Ten days later the Irish Volunteers' newspaper, *An tÓglach*, declared that every Volunteer had a duty 'to use all legitimate methods of warfare against the soldiers and policemen of the English usurper and to slay them if it is necessary to do so in order to overcome their resistance'. The message was interpreted by many as nothing less than a declaration of war, and for three years a strategy of military confrontation with the RIC and British forces would be borne out in blood and deed.

Mary Ann Carroll was close to playing her part in helping militant Irish republicans who were operating under a new name, the Irish Republican Army (IRA). As violence and shootings increased, isolated rural police barracks were abandoned, as were the ranks of the RIC, with growing numbers of resignations and falling numbers of recruits. With Ireland edging closer to becoming unpoliceable, the RIC needed to bolster its numbers and turned to the large numbers of unemployed First World War veterans in Britain, young men with both military training and combat experience. The recruitment advertisement seeking recruits asked: 'Do you want a job? You can join the RIC: the finest constabulary force in the world.'

After only a few weeks' training, the first recruits of this reserve police force arrived in Ireland on 25 March 1920. A shortage of police uniforms saw the new recruits issued with clothing that included khaki tunics and black trousers, which earned them the pejorative nickname the 'Black and Tans', the distinctive colours of the pack of beagles used in the Scarteen Hunt in Limerick. Despite their irregular uniforms, the new recruits lived and worked in barracks with Irish policemen and spent much of their time on patrol, which made them frequent victims of the IRA's guerrilla campaign of attacks, ambushes and assassinations. Before long they earned a brutal reputation for violent reprisal attacks; burning and looting towns and destroying businesses, and, as a result, many in the RIC strongly resented their new workmates, whom they regarded as professionally and morally reprehensible.

Mary Ann Ryan wanted her children to learn from the events of those days. As he listened, Patrick took in every detail his mother recounted. 'In her area of north Tipperary, the local lads gave the Black and Tans a tough time and, in that situation, they brought in the military, who camped a couple of miles from where my mother lived.' The IRA grew increasingly dependent on the support of local people to help them evade capture. The Carroll home was known as a safe house for those fighting the Black and Tans, and Mary Ann took pride in both her family's reputation in their locality as supporters of the IRA and her own contribution to the cause in standing guard.

One lifelong lesson she passed down to her second eldest son was that any effort to keep an enemy at bay, however seemingly insignificant the action, was a risk worth taking: 'There would be a knock on the window and she'd get out of her bed and give it to one or two of the lads looking for a bed, and then spend the night outside the house watching until daylight, because if the local police had any idea where these lads were, they were able to guide the Tans to your house, where the lads would be shot and the house burned. On a couple of occasions, my mother was able to tip them off and they would skip off through the back window and get away.'

By early 1921 the IRA had stepped up its campaign of attacks and the Liberal British Prime Minister, David Lloyd George, was under increasing pressure to quell the rebellion. Following military advice, additional counties of Ireland were subjected to martial law and the whole of Munster, including Tipperary, came under British Army rule, leading the IRA in turn to increase its use of flying columns – forces of highly mobile volunteers able to carry out ambushes across the countryside.

By then, a man who had fought for the British Army in the First World War, rising to the rank of sergeant, had turned his gun on those with whom he would once have stood shoulder to shoulder in the trenches of Mesopotamia. In 1920 Tom Barry joined the Third (West) Cork Brigade of the IRA and became one of the most ruthless and revered of all the flying column leaders. 'My mother spoke as well about how local lads were under severe pressure, so they sent word to Tom Barry in Cork of their plight, could he send up some men, which he did, but in those days they couldn't go on the railways because the Brits controlled the railways, so it was walking and bicycles. They had a list of houses on the way up to be avoided because they were pro-British; when they came to the parish of Upperchurch they knew that my mother's family home was a safe house. She remembered every detail of standing guard in the boreen to protect Tom Barry's men.'

Two of the IRA men dispatched to north Tipperary by Barry took shelter inside the Carroll family home, where Mary Ann's watchfulness while they slept would determine if they lived to see another day. She knew first-hand the consequences of failure to spot a Black-and-Tan raid. She had smelled the acrid smoke from burning houses as it drifted across the valley. She also knew what had happened to neighbours in her parish of Upperchurch, where in one instance two brothers were hauled out of their home at midnight by the Tans and only survived by making a run for their lives.

The guns fell silent at midday on 11 July 1921. After two and a half years and more than 2,000 dead, a truce between the IRA and the British government ended the War of Independence. It was a stalemate. The IRA agreed to stop all attacks on Crown forces and property, and the British agreed to halt offensive actions against republicans and withdraw to barracks. The way was open for negotiations, which ultimately led to the creation of a separate Irish state. The Anglo-Irish Treaty was signed by British and Irish delegates in the early hours of 6 December 1921 in the cabinet room of 10 Downing Street. The partition of the island of Ireland was confirmed, leading to the creation of the twenty-six-county Irish Free State in 1922, with the separate six-county Northern Ireland established by the Government of Ireland Act of 1920 remaining under British control.

The Anglo-Irish Treaty did not, however, end the violence. Within a year, many of those who fought on the Irish republican side in the War of Independence would be fighting one another over whether to accept the compromise offered by the British. The Treaty's opponents, including Mary Carroll's family, were led by Éamon de Valera, who felt it did not go far enough; its supporters, led by Michael Collins and Arthur Griffith, both signatories of the document, argued that it offered a pathway to full independence and the reunification of Ireland. The Civil War that broke out between the pro- and anti-Treaty factions ended with a ceasefire rather than a decisive victory; the anti-Treaty IRA leadership, knowing they could not win, ordered their forces to stand down on 30 April 1923.

In telling her story, Mary Ann Ryan passed on her Irish republican lineage to her flesh and blood. Nature and nurture conspired to ensure that the second son she gave birth to on 6 June 1930, in particular, inherited her deeply held republicanism, as well as a ruthless singlemindedness. 'That was the background in which my mother was reared and brought up, and she retained that anti-British sentiment all her life.'

Patience was another character trait that Patrick Ryan inherited from his mother. In the summer he would often lie chest-down at the edge of a lush, dew-heavy bank of the Multeen river near the village of Rossmore and put his hands down into the cold water to feel the fish flitting by. He was never able to grab one of the yellow-bellied brown trout or salmon swimming upriver, but the fish were not necessarily getting away – the thrill was that they were swimming towards the net he had laid further upstream. 'There was quite a share of fish in the local river, and the countryside was full of rabbits and pheasants, and by eight years of age I had become an irredeemable addict of poaching all these things. So much so that the family would often be praying for me, feeling that because I was gone for so long, I was probably drowned in the river.'

Ryan's stroll back to the farmhouse with a full bag of fish, in the gloaming of the summer's evening, was never hastened by the knowledge that his family's nerves were half-shattered because they feared the worst. 'I'd arrive back after having spent hours standing in the shallows of the local river and as I'd walk towards the door of the house, I'd slow down to hear them chanting the Mysteries of the Rosary so that I'd come back alive. Sure, I always did.'

The family's reciting of the Mysteries of the Rosary, a set of prayers split into five events of the life of Jesus, was not false piety but born from a deep faith in the Catholic Church. Mary Ann was a devout Catholic, who not only ensured that her children knew their prayers by heart, but also that they said them aloud every morning and night. In the same way that she had instilled Irish nationalist political values in her children, Mary Ann Ryan passed down her Catholic faith, predicated on a devotion and loyalty to an institutional Church that dominated Irish society. The Ryan children learned from an early age that the principle of patriotism and prayer went hand in hand.

The family were continuing a centuries-old tradition of faith and Irish nationalist identity, which had been indelibly bound together after the Irish Penal Laws of 1695 denied Catholics religious freedom and education. Other legislation prohibited Catholics from practising law, teaching or running schools, holding office in government and the right to bear arms. They were also excluded from parliament, the army and the navy. By 1728 they had completely lost the right to vote.

The laws aimed at keeping Catholics out of power were, in turn, extended to those who led Catholic worship: the clergy. The introduction of the Banishment Act of 1697 required all Catholic clergy and bishops, and those exercising ecclesiastical jurisdiction, to leave Ireland, which prompted some priests to go underground while others fled abroad. Over time the law became less stringently enforced, and Catholic priests were allowed to stay if they registered with the authorities. Unregistered clergy were to be sought out by mercenary 'priest hunters' for a cash bounty.

The most impactful anti-Catholic rules were those surrounding the ownership of land. The Popery Act of 1703 forbade Catholics from passing down their land to their eldest son and instead required landowners to distribute the land equally among all sons.[7] In the century in which the full rigour of the Penal Laws operated, Catholic land ownership plummeted from 14 per cent in 1702 to 5 per cent in 1776, which forced many to emigrate. Those who remained, however, gained a sense of unity, thereby sowing the early seeds of the connection between Irish nationalism and Catholicism, a religious faith that had been elevated in the eyes of many as a form of rebellion against British rule.

This soldering of Catholicism and Irish nationalism was first harnessed by 'The Liberator', Daniel O'Connell, who for thirty years led a national movement to campaign for Catholic emancipation. He achieved a landmark measure in 1829, the Catholic Emancipation Act, which finally repealed the Penal Laws and enabled Catholics to sit once again in the British Parliament. O'Connell was less successful in his Repeal movement, which advocated for the revoking of the Act of Union that united Ireland with Britain, but by the time of his death in 1847, he had laid the foundations of the cause of a non-violent, constitutional Catholic nationalism.

Soon the Catholic Church would become a singular power bloc in Ireland. Under the leadership of Paul Cullen, who became Ireland's first cardinal in 1867, the Irish Catholic Church was characterised by a strong allegiance to Rome. As an Ultramontane, Cullen was in favour of improving clerical discipline under papal authority in matters of faith and discipline; at the Vatican's request, he organised a national synod at Thurles, County Tipperary, through which efforts were made to standardise the administrative and religious practices of the Church along Roman lines.

From then, the entire Irish Church was reshaped in discipline and devotion. Traditional practices, such as gatherings at shrines and services in private homes, were discouraged and, instead, Catholics were told they must attend Mass at church every Sunday, go to Confession regularly and take Communion – practices that brought them in line with the Vatican's thinking. Cullen also introduced the custom of priests wearing the Roman collar and being called 'Father', thus making them stand out from ordinary people and giving them a greater sense of authority.

After the founding of the Irish Free State, the Catholic Church was more confident than at any previous time, and its hierarchy played a more conspicuous role in Irish political life than it had in the era of British rule. The deference early Irish governments showed to the Church hierarchy was demonstrated by the first leader of the Irish Free State government, W.T. Cosgrave, when he suggested in 1921 that a 'Theological Board' should be added to the upper house of the Dáil to ensure that the Irish government would not pass any legislation 'contrary to Faith and Morals or not' of the Catholic Church. His fellow cabinet members deemed the proposal a step too far but, nevertheless, such was the power and authority of the Church that when it encouraged the government to bring censorship legislation on to statute as soon as possible, in an attempt to prevent images contained in Hollywood films from corrupting Irish people's morals, the Censorship of Films Act in 1923 became one of the first acts passed by the new Dáil. Laws curtailing the consumption of alcoholic drink were also soon introduced at the prompting of bishops. Celebrations in June 1929 to mark the centenary of Catholic Emancipation culminated in Dublin with a Pontifical High Mass in the Phoenix Park attended by 300,000 people, which allowed the Free State to project 'an image of a country that was united, Irish, Catholic and free'.[8]

Simon and Mary Ann Ryan's children were born into an Ireland where the Catholic Church had an institutional monopoly on morality, operated through an extensive organisational infrastructure in the realms of education, health and welfare. The 1926 census revealed that Catholics comprised 93 per cent of the population;[9] before partition they had accounted for 73 per cent.[10] By the time Taoiseach Éamon de Valera wrote, and Ireland enacted, a new constitution in 1937, the Catholic religion was guaranteed a special role in society.

Like his siblings, Patrick Ryan's childhood was dominated by Catholic rituals: saying the Rosary every night, going to Mass on Sunday, fasting from midnight before receiving Holy Communion, not eating meat on Fridays, and going to Confession once a month. Every public observance of Catholic sacraments, every prayer said aloud, demonstrated his willingness to conform, alongside his siblings, to the norms of society.

What marked him apart from his siblings was his self-professed devotion to poaching: 'I was different to my brothers and sisters because of all the rabbits and pheasants I killed, so many of them. I was a veteran killer of rabbits – skinning them and preparing them for the pot – so much so that in the family I was nicknamed "Paddy the Skinner". A total addict.' He was not squeamish and embraced the brutal techniques needed to prepare rabbits for the pot. He found that it was easier to separate the skin from the flesh of the freshly killed. This callous detachment from the more unpleasant aspects of poaching, which manifested in his childhood, was an early indication of the ruthlessness that would define Ryan's character as an adult.

* * *

The Ryan family home, nestled into a hill in Turraheen in the parish of Rossmore, was, for a number of years, a home of few worries. The children were content, studiously learning and helping out on the farm. Patrick and his siblings knew well that their eldest brother, Simon, was the most academically gifted. 'He was the brightest of us all in school. He had a bicycle to get him to the local railway station at Goold's Cross and from there he would board a train that would take him into the town of Thurles, where he had started his secondary education at the Christian Brothers.'

But this home of happy contentment was later overtaken by sadness, and despair slowly took root in the Ryan household. Mary Ann could only watch as rheumatoid arthritis took hold of her husband's physicality; there was nothing she could do to stop it and there was no standing guard against the invisible enemy that ravaged Simon's nerve endings from within. What first manifested as a seemingly inoffensive but recurring pain in the joints of his fingers soon convulsed his entire body.

'When it started, my father drove a horse and cart to a local doctor in Thurles once a month for some sort of an injection – it was clouded in mystery.' However, the monthly injections could not slow down the painful march of a disease that spread with a steady pace akin to that Simon Ryan endeavoured to maintain when he drove his horse-drawn cart in the days before his hands stiffened up and went out of shape. 'Eventually every joint of my father's body was in pain. Even if you put a spoon between his fingers, he couldn't move them. The house was visited by a heaviness that never really left and it was a tragedy that a man who took so much pride in his hard work was confined to his bed.'

Rheumatoid arthritis eventually rendered Patrick's father too weak with pain to move beyond the bed he once determinedly jumped out of every morning to work the land. His misfortune left his first-born son with no choice but to leave school early and abandon any hopes he had of studying into his teenage years. In rural Ireland, the importance of keeping the farm intact and land in family ownership overrode personal ambition. The stifling of the eldest son's education was merely an acceleration of what was already mapped out for him – birth order and a trauma of Irish history had already conspired to determine his future.

* * *

In 1841 Ireland's eight million people lived in a land where half the farms were under five acres in size – a direct result of the widespread practice of subdividing the holding when a son got married, which meant that many farms had become so small that the only food source that could be grown in a sufficient quantity to feed a family was a basic crop like potatoes. An overdependence on the potato spelled disaster in 1845. What became known as the Great Hunger started to manifest mysteriously that summer, as leaves on potato plants suddenly turned black and curled. Much worse was hiding in the tubers beneath. Potatoes dug out of the soil at first looked edible but shrivelled and rotted within days. The potatoes had been attacked by the same fungus, *Phytophthora infestans*, that had destroyed the leaves above ground. The arrival of the potato blight in Ireland caused alarm in London. 'If the potato fails … famine becomes a fatal certainty,' declared Sir James Graham, the Home Secretary of the day.

In October the main potato harvest was taken out of the ground. A stench of decay permeated the air; the crop had rotted in the fields. The harvest across the island only reaped shock and despair. 'In Cork, men wept openly as half-ruined potatoes were lifted from the ground. In Limerick, shovels dropped and labourers soaked through to the skin with rain filed out of the fields like mourners ... Men sprinkled holy water on their potatoes; they buried them with religious medallions and pictures of Christ and the Virgin Mother. Nothing worked. God had turned away.'[11] The London *Spectator* reported that 'Ireland is threatened with a thing that is read of in history and in distant countries, but scarcely in our own land and time – a famine.'[12] Within months that prediction had become a reality.

The potato blight returned in 1846 with much more severe effects on the crop, creating a catastrophe that lasted another three years. Horror shadowed the trail of hunger and disease, with dead babies at their mothers' breasts, skeletons walking, people lying dead on the roadsides with grass and nettles in their mouths to try to keep the hunger at bay. In May 1844 an American Quaker, Asenath Hatch Nicholson, had left New York for what would be a fifteen-month trip to Ireland to 'personally investigate the condition of the Irish poor'. When she returned during the famine, she did so as a relief worker and wrote of what she witnessed, including an account of an island off the Donegal coast: 'Six men, beside Mr. Griffith, crossed with me in an open boat, and we landed, not buoyantly, upon the once pretty island. The first that [*sic*] called my attention was the death-like stillness – nothing of life was seen or heard, excepting occasionally a dog. These looked so unlike all others I had seen among the poor – I unwittingly said – "How can the dogs look so fat and shining here, where there is no food for the people?" "Shall I tell her?" said the pilot to Mr. Griffith, not supposing that I heard him. This was enough: if anything were wanting to make the horrors of a famine complete, this supplied the deficiency.'[13]

The Famine led to the deaths of over a million people between 1845 and 1851. For the living, the choice became clear: emigrate or face destitution or death. By 1849 Ireland had lost a further million people to emigration and a million more by 1855. What remained was a legacy of bitterness towards the British, whose policies were blamed for contributing to the massive loss of life.

The trauma of the Great Hunger, though rarely spoken of, prompted a major readjustment in the family system; the sub-division of land was abandoned and replaced by the practice of passing a holding to the eldest son alone. The options for family members who did not inherit were more limited and, in reality, this system meant emigration or entering religious life. So, by birth order, Simon Ryan's future was predestined – he would inherit the land. His brother Patrick decided on a vocation: 'I'd wanted to be a priest since I was ten years of age and at fourteen years of age I joined a congregation of clergy called the Pallottine Fathers in Thurles and began my studies to become a priest.'

By 1948, the year the Free State officially declared itself a republic and cut formal ties with Britain, Patrick Ryan, as a seminary student of eighteen years of age, was on track to elevate his family's standing in society. 'Having a priest in the family was a very important marker of respectability in Ireland at that time because it automatically marked you apart. My mother had reared a priest, but what she didn't realise was where I was going to end up working.'

THREE

MISSION TO AFRICA

The staccato crackles of the fire had competition. The night sounds of the East African bush grew louder in pitch and intensity as the darkness closed in. A continuous chorus of nocturnal insects and bird calls was complemented by the deep rumbling of a family of elephants grazing in the distance. Bats fluttered on the back of a soft wind as glowing seams of red-tinged embers lit up the faces of the men standing around the fire pit at the Irish Catholic mission in Tanganyika.

Named after a combination of two words in Swahili, 'Tanga' (to sail) and 'Nyika' (uninhabited plains or wilderness), the territory of Tanganyika, situated between the Great Lakes of Central Africa and the Indian Ocean, had been part of the colony of German East Africa. Wars in Europe then redrew boundaries in Africa: in 1925, after Germany's defeat in the First World War, the League of Nations confiscated the territory, located just south of the equator, and gave the British a mandate of control.[1] It remained that way until after the Second World War, when the United Nations converted the British mandate into a trusteeship. Nonetheless, the territory remained under British control.

For African nationalists agitating for independence from colonial rule, the post-war world was a period of hope and, for some, impatience, given that British territories in India were granted independence in 1947 and divided into India and Pakistan. It was in this political climate in the 1940s that Irish missionary orders of priests and nuns first arrived in Tanganyika.

The missionary zeal of the Irish Catholic Church accelerated in the post-independence era; an outworking of a strand of Irish nationalism keen to assert Ireland's difference from Britain. The large number of vocations in a fervently religious nation created a surplus of priests and nuns, who could extend Ireland's thriving 'spiritual empire' abroad. The Catholic faithful back home were kept informed of the effort to convert souls in the 'pagan world'; accounts of Irish missionaries' work were widely distributed throughout Ireland in magazines and pamphlets.

That night in Tanganyika, in 1956, the missionary priest, Father Patrick Ryan, threw some more wood into the fire pit for his guests, four British Army officers. The men had travelled south from Kenya and crossed the border into Tanganyika for a week-long game-hunting tour. 'We gave them shelter at our mission. You'd come across some of them doing a tour while they had some time off, and they'd come in and have a cup of tea with us.' The strangers were welcome to stay in the Pallottine mission's basic guest accommodation if they wished. 'We had an outside building. I'd say, "Lads, you can bunk in there for the night if you wish," and some did take up the offer of safe shelter. If they wanted food, I'd make some dinner for them, but I'd nearly always light a fire and we'd be sitting down around it gossiping and talking.'

Father Ryan felt no animosity towards his guests, only curiosity. He was impressed by their innate assuredness and poise, characteristics he assumed were accentuated by their rank within the British Army. He noted how they appeared to see beyond his religious vocation; they conversed with him in a straightforward manner and not as those who expected a fawning display of faux piety in conversation and company.

However, Ryan also found the British Army officers' self-confidence disconcerting. They openly spoke of where they grew up, the private schools and tutors who had shaped their outlook, as well as their training at the Royal Military Academy, Sandhurst. The twenty-six-year-old priest had little experience of such matter-of-fact conversations carried out in the absence of self-consciousness – Ryan's years of study in a seminary were defined by a strict hierarchy, even in seemingly benign conversation – but he quickly realised that his guests were simply being themselves, as they possessed a certainty that whatever they set out to accomplish, they would. But there was one particular activity where he could match their confidence head-on – the one hobby that all of the men around the fire had in common was the thrill of a hunt.

Ryan's poaching skills, honed in the fields and rivers near his family's home in County Tipperary, had another outlet in East Africa, albeit on a much larger scale. 'I was a good hunter and there I was, almost on the equator, at an altitude of about 6,000 feet above sea level, dry, low humidity, one of the loveliest climates on the whole planet and all these wild animals, right on the edge of the Serengeti.'

The British Army officers had purposely crossed the border to hunt because, unlike neighbouring Kenya and Uganda, Tanganyika's wildlife offered more opportunities for big-game hunting, augmented by a lack of rules pertaining to the European hunting of elephants and other animals. The white man was given free rein to hunt as he pleased.

The officers were only following in the footsteps of their fellow countrymen. The opportunity to earn a fortune from ivory hunting had attracted the Englishman George Gilman Rushby to Tanganyika in the 1930s. Rushby went on to become infamous for tracking down and killing the man-eating lions of Njombe in Tanganyika, and his skills made him one of the most proficient elephant hunters of the twentieth century. By 1956 the widely lauded poacher had turned game ranger, and Rushby retired as Deputy Game Warden of Tanganyika.

In East Africa, Father Patrick Ryan learned that ivory was a valuable commodity that could help to expand his missionary ambitions. 'I remember one time, I went out with a couple of locals who were great trackers,' he recalled. 'It was around a hundred miles east of the diocese, way into the bush, and I shot one, he was eight tons, and we built a school out of the money we got for his tusks.' Weighing around 14,000 pounds, elephants posed a threat to local crops. 'Another time, the elephant came to us; he was part of a family raiding a garden of maize nearby, so the locals came to me and I shot him cleanly through the heart. In all, I shot three elephants.' Ryan was a good hunter but regrets his actions now: 'It was elephant country before any man or woman.'

It was natural that Ryan and the officers would discuss their hunting efforts, but soon enough conversation around the firepit turned to Kenya, where the British Army had been deployed to counter an insurgency. In 1956 the uprising against British rule in Kenya was into its fourth year. Armed fighters, known as the Mau Mau, were mainly drawn from Kenya's major ethnic grouping, the Kikuyu, who had lost land during colonisation. Although the Mau Mau had been banned by British authorities, a campaign of sabotage and assassination was attributed to them and the British Kenya government declared a state of emergency in 1952, moving army reinforcements into the country.

British military operations started to concentrate on areas where the Mau Mau were most active. These included 'Operation Anvil' in Nairobi in April 1954, which saw the mass screening, arrest and detention of huge numbers of Mau Mau fighters and supporters. Although the declared state of emergency was to continue until 1960, British military operations effectively ceased in November 1955. By this point, thousands of Mau Mau had been detained and they had suffered over 10,000 casualties.

Around the fire pit, Ryan listened to the officers' whispered accounts of the violence in Kenya with the same concentration he had applied to his mother's stories of the Irish War of Independence. 'I wasn't quizzing them about the Mau Mau, but the men would just start quietly talking about what was happening themselves; they must have felt safe because it was like they forgot they were in company.' Ryan noticed that while the officers had a presence that demanded attention, he had a particular skill for listening to what was being said, but, equally, what was being left unspoken. He also observed the officers' facial expressions to establish who might have been privately troubled by the detention camps in which many Mau Mau suspects were placed.

Ryan's shrewdness was honed by watching. He never asked probing questions, but rather allowed space for the men to talk. 'I had already picked up reports that the war over the border was brutal – there was talk of detention camps and torture. It came as no surprise to me that the uprising in Kenya was being pushed back in a savage way and I could tell that it troubled some of the visitors.' The internal conflict and unease he picked up from some of the officers' tones of voice did not come as a revelation; Ryan's study of history in preparation for the priesthood had taught him that empire-building was often a blood-soaked affair, with little attention paid to violence and its effects on the colonised and, equally, the colonisers. 'In the seminary, I had studied the history of colonisation around the world. Look at what the Spanish *conquistadores* did, or the French in Algeria, or worst of all, the Belgians and what they did in the Congo – a brutal reign that killed millions of Congolese and had a flair for skinning people alive, that was the depth of their cruelty, and the Belgians have never faced up to what they did.'

The open fire was dying out; its flames had long receded and the logs had burned down to crumbled embers that were slowly turning into white and black speckled ash when Father Ryan reminded the officers that they would be most welcome to stay at the Pallottine mission again, should they return to the area to hunt. 'I got on very well with the Brits, they were no trouble and it was no bother to let them bed down in the outside building if that's what they wanted to do. After a while talking, they'd usually go quiet and I'd say good night and good luck to them.'

As the fire dimmed, the darkness accentuated the vast sky above; constellations competed with the glowing swathe of the Milky Way in the wide-open, East-African night sky. The astral delight on show was determined by the tilt of the planet, but the world's political axis was also slowly turning and would later transform the course of Patrick Ryan's life. 'I was a long way from my own country, but the world was changing and in the years after World War Two, people were rebelling against being colonised. At that stage in Tanganyika there was an anti-colonial leader called Julius Nyerere who was agitating for change, but I was getting on with my missionary work of drilling for water, building medical clinics and schools. In all of my days in Africa, I had no notion whatsoever of what lay in store for me.'

* * *

The Second World War had not yet ended when Patrick Ryan began his path to the priesthood. He joined the Society of the Catholic Apostolate, the Pallottine Fathers, as a postulant in 1944. Named after its founder, Vincent Pallotti, an Italian ecclesiastic and saint, the Pallottine College in Thurles served as a seminary, with students also being schooled in nearby St Patrick's College in theology and philosophy. 'I was fourteen years old when I joined the junior seminary and left the world as I knew it behind.'

His mother's devotion to Catholicism had been rewarded. Mary Ann was secure in the knowledge that her firstborn son would stay at home to look after her and the farm, while her second-born had chosen to train for the priesthood. 'I don't recall the day I decided to enter the college to study to become a priest, but I do know that it was my decision; nothing was ever decided for me in any part of my life. I was very young, but it wasn't unusual in those days for boys to enter seminaries at that age, or likewise, for girls to enter convents.'

Ryan's decision to dedicate his life to the service of the Catholic Church was made with the knowledge that his family could afford to pay for his education. 'It cost £40 a year until I became a novice, which was much more than what most people at the time could afford. I was very lucky because we lived off good land and my father had saved money from cattle he always had to sell.'

In entering the junior seminary at the age of fourteen, Ryan's childhood effectively ended overnight. Gone were his days of freedom and benign mischief with his siblings. The teenager had been handed a burden of responsibility to see out his priestly destiny. 'It was a lonely time at first, but I suppose it wasn't too bad because home was only twelve miles away. Later, I didn't get out a whole lot, but when I did, the excitement of going home was something else. I'd race back to take a break from the books and go out fishing or poaching.'

As a child, Ryan was brought up in the belief that to die with a mortal sin on his soul would see him forfeit heaven and be condemned to the fires of hell for all eternity. He was also taught that sinners could be forgiven by those ordained to impart sacramental absolution: priests. During Mass he closely watched this figure of power wearing his elaborate vestments and taking charge on the altar. It was the priest who would open the tabernacle, remove the locked box in which the Eucharist – consecrated Communion hosts – was safely stored and then raise the host, prompting the congregation to kneel and pray before they received Holy Communion in a state of grace.

A vocation to the priesthood afforded possibilities aside from a guarantee of status in Irish society. Being able to study away from home meant that Ryan could focus on his education. As a postulant, a candidate for the priesthood, the teenager was allowed to continue his secondary-school studies at the Christian Brothers school in Thurles, where he excelled in mathematical order. For hours after his lessons, he would sit alone and study Euclid's theorems in his geometry book.

Like most boys of his generation, Ryan was being taught a Christian Brothers education; a curriculum which included an explicitly Catholic and patriotic emphasis. The school, which opened in 1816, was a continuation of the Catholic ethos of Edmund Ignatius Rice, who founded the order of Christian Brothers in Waterford in 1802 to educate boys. Rice sent Brothers to start schools in many parts of Ireland, opening up secondary education to thousands of families who could not otherwise afford it.

The boys the Christian Brothers educated became some of the men who fought for Irish independence. Of the sixteen men executed for leading the Easter Rising, the majority were Brothers alumni.[2] In their schools, the Brothers were the educators of the new Republic's civil servants, teachers, administrators and politicians. Speaking at the annual dinner of the Past Pupils' Union of Christian Brothers College in 1957, Éamon de Valera, the Easter Rising leader who was then Taoiseach, said the Brothers had justified their right to the title Christian and Irish. 'Throughout their meritorious career they have always placed first things first,' he said. 'They believe that the youth of the country should be brought up true to the Faith which they hold dear, and to the national traditions and culture transmitted to them by their forebears.'[3]

During his education, it helped that Patrick Ryan was gifted at learning – this allowed him to evade the brutal beatings or ritual humiliations some Christian Brothers meted out to those less fortunate. Three years after entering the junior seminary, his education became singularly focused on theological formation and, instead of sitting his Leaving Certificate exam at the age of seventeen, Ryan formally became a priest in training.

In Tipperary there was a multitude of families with the Ryan surname, as well as sons who were christened Patrick, so in the seminary he was known as 'Paddy Ryan Simon' in an effort to mark him apart from others of the same name. His first year as a novitiate was dedicated to hard labour in the form of farm work. He then undertook six years of study in St Patrick's College, a short walk from the Pallottine seminary, where the study of philosophy, in particular, equipped him with an intellectual rigour and vocabulary for deconstructing reason and rationalising human virtues. 'Philosophy was something I'd never learned about before, but once I started, there was never a day that was too long.'

As a priest, Ryan would be expected to counsel his congregation on aspects of virtue and sin. The study of philosophy opened his mind to the human condition, its frailties and goodness, but also its depravities. 'I would say that at the time I didn't really appreciate how good my training in philosophy was. Did I have a strong faith? I suppose I must have had at that age, but the very essence of faith is that it's difficult to define. I know, because I was taught how the Bible defined faith: *est autem fides sperandorum substantia rerum argumentum non parentum*. That definition, that faith was the substance of things we all hope for, an argument in favour of the things that never appear to anyone, left me as wise at the end as I was at the beginning. I had a definition of my own and it was following my own path.'

Away from the books, 'Paddy Ryan Simon' applied himself on the pitch when playing for the Pallottine College hurling team. The fast-paced ancient Gaelic field game, played with a wooden stick called a hurley and a small ball known as a sliotar, had become a sporting expression of Irish nationalism from the turn of the twentieth century. On 1 November 1884 Tipperary native Maurice Davin and County Clare man Michael Cusack called a meeting in Hayes' Hotel, Thurles. Cusack in particular believed that the spread of English games like cricket and rugby was undermining Ireland's national identity. A letter signed by both men and published in the national press invited readers to the meeting 'to form an association for the preservation and cultivation of our national pastimes and for providing national amusements for the Irish people during their leisure hours'.[4] That day the Gaelic Athletic Association for the Cultivation and Preservation of National Pastimes – a title later shortened to the Gaelic Athletic Association (GAA) – was founded, aimed at reviving traditional Irish games of hurling and Gaelic football.

On the Pallottine College hurling team, Ryan played defence. Timing was key – reading the game while working on getting close enough to the attacker to prevent a score being taken but waiting for the right moment to make a tackle. The sharpness he developed, while running on a pitch and chasing a sliotar with a hurley, were skills that he would apply, years later, to a different end.

Few got past 'Paddy Ryan Simon' on the day his team recorded nine goals and six points against a team from St Patrick's College, who scored a meagre one goal and two points. Father Phil Barry from Thurles, who had also entered the junior seminary at a young age, played on Pallottine College team alongside him. He recalled that 'Paddy Ryan Simon was tough on the pitch. He played defence and was ferocious in trying to stop any opposing team scoring points. There were only thirteen of us on the team that defeated St Patrick's, but it was some day.'

The team photograph shows Ryan standing straight-backed in the back line, standing apart from his peers, his arms crossed and, unlike most of the team, staring directly at the camera lens. His posture is indicative of his then role in the college: student prefect. 'It was very strict,' recalls Barry. 'There was a list of rules we had to follow, such as absolute silence after supper until the following morning, and Paddy Ryan Simon was the student prefect one year. I remember him making sure we all obeyed the rules, walking along the corridors listening, making sure none of us were smoking. He was fair but strict, but he had to be, it was all very strict in those days.'

* * *

In June 1954 Patrick Ryan held a lit candle aloft in his right hand as he waited in line for his name to be called in the Cathedral of the Assumption in Thurles. The vestments of the Pallottine Order were draped on his left forearm and standing alongside him were the other candidates, who, like him, were in clerical dress and all of whom had given seven years of preparation to become priests of the Catholic Church. The flame of the candle he was holding was burning high and straight, in contrast to those of some of the other candidates, whose flickering candle flames appeared to be locked in a duel with their trembling wrists. Ryan felt light-headed. The Cathedral was packed with the Catholic hierarchy and proud families, including his own, but the stifling heat along with the continuous chanting of prayers combined to make the air feel almost treacly. A sudden roll call of names jolted him back from blacking out and he looked at

Archbishop Jeremiah Kinane, who was sitting on a silk-cushioned chair in front of the white marble altar inlaid with precious stones.

Ryan had already forged an opinion of the archbishop – his mother's upbringing once again influencing his judgement. Growing up, the families of Kinane and Carroll were neighbours in the parish of Upperchurch. 'My mother remembered him because during the War of Independence the men who were fighting the Black and Tans around their area had the name of one house in the parish of Upperchurch that was to be avoided. That house was the family home of Jeremiah Kinane, who later became the Archbishop of Cashel & Emly.'

Kinane was not shy about making his views of the IRA known. In an edict read aloud to congregations by priests in the Diocese of Waterford on Sunday, 6 January 1935, the then Bishop Kinane banned every Catholic in his diocese from joining the IRA, describing it as a sinful, irreligious organisation that young men should cease to join. Speaking 'as the divinely constituted teacher of faith and morals', Kinane cited the condemnation of the IRA by the bishops in Ireland four years earlier and said that that condemnation continued.[5]

Decades later, Mary Ann Ryan would keep her own counsel about Archbishop Kinane. His family home may have been a cold house for IRA men on the run from the Black and Tans, but in the Cathedral in Thurles that day, the Archbishop was the arbiter of the divine and about to ordain her beloved second-born son through the sacrament of Holy Orders.

On hearing the roll call, Archbishop Kinane observed each candidate who stepped forward in turn and replied '*adsum*' (present), a formal expression of their call to serve the Church. Patrick Ryan waited his turn. 'I remember looking around that day at the mothers and thinking that it must have been a proud day for them all, dressed in their best and wiping away their tears. Looking back, I suppose it was more of a sad day for them. They had already lost their sons to the seminary, but, you see, the very point of ordination is to set you apart, to elevate you from everyone else in society, and I suppose the mothers were saying goodbye in a formal sense. The sons they had given birth to were now priests; a different type of being altogether.'

Patrick Ryan stepped forward to genuflect and bow his head in front of the Archbishop before he kneeled in the semicircle of candidates that had formed around the sanctuary of altar. The Archbishop turned to speak to them before he too knelt down in front of the altar. In perfect unison the *ordinandi* laid themselves prostrate on the sanctuary as a sign of their unworthiness before God, while the choir chanted the 'Litany of the Saints'. It was only when the choir fell silent that the candidates rose and knelt in preparation for the most solemn moment of the ordination. The Archbishop laid both hands on the head of each candidate, indicating each person to whom the power of the Sacrament of Holy Orders was being conferred. The act and prayer of consecration turned an ordinary man into a priest.

The same laying-on of hands was done by the other priests who were present, but it was merely ceremonial, a gesture of acceptance into the ranks of priesthood. The newly ordained Father Patrick Ryan was now part of a clerical elite and in turn had elevated the social status of his family. 'The upside was that, in taking the vow, many of us transformed the standing of our families in our localities because they now had a priest in the family. A lot of the time, newly ordained priests would start off in a parish relatively nearby, at the most within a day's travel. What my mother didn't know was that I was about to be packed off to East Africa. She had no clue where I was headed. I was about to be sent off to do some good for mankind.'

* * *

Two months later, Father Ryan set off on his journey. The twenty-four-year-old, who had never travelled outside the country of his birth, was about to cross continents and the equator to follow in the path of Irish Pallottine priests who first made their way to Tanganyika some fourteen years earlier.

The mailboat from Dún Laoghaire to Holyhead in Wales was packed with men and women of Ryan's generation and younger. Holyhead's geographical position, jutting out into the Irish Sea, made it a natural endpoint for the sixty-mile sea crossing, and once the boat safely docked, the crowds swiftly departed in the direction of the Irish Mail Train destined for London's Euston station. Some of the smartly dressed young men on board whispered curses over the weight of the bulging suitcases their forlorn mothers had packed for them, while others grudgingly held on to noticeably smaller satchels containing most of their worldly possessions.

In the 1950s some 40,000 people left Ireland every year to emigrate to Britain. The land was failing the young – agriculture still accounted for some two-fifths of the working population, but the small-farm rural economy, particularly in the west of Ireland, was in irreversible decline. The 1955 Commission on Emigration stated that emigration was 'a part of the generally accepted pattern of life'.[6] Some of those who left on the mailboat may not have intended to see out the rest of their days in London – their ambition was to work hard, save money and return prosperous. But for others there was a freedom in earning a wage and living away from prying eyes and Catholic Ireland's stifling religious moralism. In the crowded Irish Saturday-night dances of the ballrooms, such as the Hammersmith Palais, Garryowen and the Galtymore in Cricklewood, many of the 'mail-boat generation' found partners, married and raised families in a city far from home.

Standing on the upper deck, Father Ryan watched a group of young men furiously wave white handkerchiefs as the mailboat passed the head of Dún Laoghaire's East Pier and its lighthouse. Others had already turned their back on a state that had failed them. Many of those leaving were of a generation silently broken in mind by the brutal conditions they had endured while incarcerated in industrial schools predominantly managed by Catholic religious congregations. On their sixteenth birthdays state payments ceased and the boys were released into a world that was often completely foreign and ultimately unwelcoming. With no family connections and little opportunity to build a life in their country of birth, many had no option but to emigrate.

On the mailboat some carried their secrets like a heavy suitcase they could never let go of and mingled self-consciously with the well-heeled men, who included Patrick Ryan. His clerical collar marked him out as a member of the elite of Irish society. Unlike those who had been turfed out of industrial schools or orphanages, Ryan was not leaving in an effort to break free from a stigma associated with his past, or to avoid economic troubles. Instead, he was taking flight to help spread Ireland's spiritual empire, secure in the knowledge that he would only ever be made to feel welcome on his return.

The new priest's five-day-long trek across borders on trains and aeroplanes eventually came to an end in Nairobi, the capital of Kenya. 'When I got off that plane, the first thing that hit me like a wall was the heat. It was unlike anything I had ever experienced.' County Tipperary's temperate climate was a world away, and Ryan next had to endure a day-long journey in the cab of a lorry in order to get to the house of a bishop in Tanganyika. There he rested for a couple of days before a further 100-mile-long trip to his destination, a single-storey thatched house in the diocese of the semi-arid region of Singida, in central Tanganyika.

In East Africa Ryan quickly learned that the seasons were cleaved into two distinct phases: the long dry season from April to November and the short rainy season from December to March. 'It was a place I could never have prepared for, but I wasn't homesick; by nature, I was extremely adaptable to any situation. English was not the spoken language, it was Swahili, so from day one you had to begin to learn that because if you couldn't speak it, you could die from thirst from not being able to ask for water.'

Practicalities aside, speaking Swahili was also a powerful tool to distinguish the missionary priests from government officials. Embracing the language marked Ryan out from the coloniser and demonstrated a willingness to be part of the local community amongst whom he was living. 'My missionary work was all mainly outside, building schools and hospital clinics, and drilling and working on the land. I was a priest, so I was supposed to be teaching the catechism, but that was the part of my role where I was conflicted. You see, we were out there to produce healthy minds in healthy bodies, and that's all well and good, but I had a philosophy of my own, because I preferred to get stuck in to the building and some of the clergy would frown on me because I was more interested in doing that than in standing around with a catechism in my hand all day.'

In Tanganyika, nuns of the Medical Missionaries of Mary order had been providing health services since they were first invited to open a hospital in 1945 by Monsignor Patrick Winters, who wanted the Irish missionary nuns to run health clinics in his diocese. By the time Father Ryan arrived in Singida, Monsignor Winters was consecrated a bishop and the Medical Missionaries of Mary had established four hospitals across the territory.[7] 'The Medical Missionaries of Mary had dispensaries in the area and beyond, and I'd help out driving the doctors or nurses between the dispensaries. It was a tremendous challenge to cover the distances of hundreds of miles between the dispensaries by land. We were in an area that was deemed a "diocese", but the area was as big as Ireland, so distances were a big problem because the roads were so poor – in those days they were only clay roads.' No matter the time of year, the bumpy hurtling and tumbling of a four-wheel chassis along basic roads was a guarantee of sore bones for days afterwards. 'In the warm season the land would be dry but hard to drive over, and in the rainy season, a journey that should take half a day to a dispensary could end up taking several days.'

In 1958 a letter arrived. Ryan recognised his mother's handwriting on the envelope. He could picture her sitting at the kitchen table in Rossmore writing out neat curves, with a near-perfect equidistance between each word, to the rhythm of the ticking clock on the wall. He sensed that the contents of the envelope bore bad news. Although there was no physical difference in its shape or size to mark it out from previous letters he had received from home, holding it he felt there was an innate heaviness to this particular envelope that set it apart. He knew before he carefully opened it that his father was dead and buried. 'I was ten years waiting for that letter. You see, he'd been confined to bed for years with an extreme form of arthritis, a man who had taken pride in hard work, but his quality of life had failed him long before he drew his last breath.'

Simon Ryan was indeed dead; his heart had long grown weary and eventually surrendered to the disease that left him bed-bound and aching in pain for nearly three decades. Ryan knew that his father's funeral Mass would have been well attended and that some locals, in pious judgement, may have exchanged words or a knowing side glance about the missing son who should have led the prayers from the altar but was instead tending to the poor in Africa. He carefully folded the letter away. What struck him the most was that his father's disease had for decades denied him the opportunity to enjoy sunlight and fresh air, and when he did finally leave his home in Rossmore, he was only able to do so because he was carried out in a coffin.

It was another twelve months before Ryan could return to Rossmore and pay his respects at his father's grave. At home, he noticed how his mother appeared physically shrunken and much older than she actually was – it wasn't merely that she was aging naturally, it was almost as if she had finally relented and given herself over to the exhaustion she had kept at bay for years in a misplaced hope that her husband's arthritis would someday release its grip and the man she married might return to her. She was pleased to see the safe return of her second son, and proud to hear of his travels and plans for his missionary endeavours in Tanganyika, but Ryan noticed how, at times, she appeared distracted and often sought comfort in reminiscing about his father.

On a walk to the nearby village early one morning, Ryan was forced to dart into a ditch for safety as a motorbike sped past him. When he later spied the same two-wheeler parked outside the village post office, he waited for its owner to return, not to admonish him, but to find out from where he had sourced such a spectacular machine. His patience was rewarded – the motorbike belonged to a schoolteacher in the next parish who had purchased surplus Birmingham Small Arms Company (BSA) M20 motorcycles from a military camp in County Kildare. As Ryan admired the M20, he hatched a plan. 'In the course of our chat about the motorbike, the schoolteacher talked about there being crates available to order, and that's what we agreed on. I arranged to give him the money and before I returned to East Africa, I had already ordered a crate of motorbikes to be exported out. It was many months before the crate arrived, but the M20s were hardy machines and much more suited to the dirt roads of Tanganyika than coasting around the boreens of Tipperary.'

There was no time for Ryan to give in to grief for his father, as he had an ambition to accomplish in the weeks he had left at home in

Rossmore. He set up a number of appointments at a local flying club outside of Tipperary town, gaining enough flying hours to see him return to East Africa as a qualified pilot. 'I did my exams in Dublin, although I had to redo some of my exams in Africa because I was flying at a far higher altitude, but I studied and passed and there was no stopping me and I dug out an airstrip near our base.'

Bishop Winters was so keen on the ambition of his confrère to fly doctors between dispensaries and hospitals by air that he requested money from his Pallottine superiors to purchase a two-seater aeroplane, encouraged to do so by Ryan. 'It made sense. I would bring a doctor to a clinic within an hour and be back safely the same day. I was very careful, I wasn't a qualified engineer, so I'd stick strictly to the book and once a year bring the plane to Nairobi where I'd have it legally serviced.' This was not the only innovation that Ryan would introduce that would improve the lives of both the missionaries and locals.

* * *

The course of political change in Tanganyika came to a head as midnight approached on 9 December 1961. In the capital Dar es Salaam's National Stadium, the Governor, Sir Richard Turnball, and Prime Minister, Julius Nyerere, stood before a huge flagstaff with the Union Jack spotlighted at the top: 75,000 people were crammed into the stadium along with an array of dignitaries including the Duke of Edinburgh, who watched on as a band played 'God Save the Queen'.

At the stroke of midnight the stadium lights were dramatically switched off and, after a moment of silence, on again while the new flag of Tanganyika – green for the land, black for the people and gold for its mineral wealth – was raised to the music of the new national anthem, 'Mungu Ibariki [God Bless] Tanganyika', as a firework display lit the skies.[8] That was it. Tanganyika was a sovereign independent state.

The political change heralded an unexpected but prized gift for Father Patrick Ryan. 'An Afrikaner gave me his water-drilling machine as he had decided to leave Tanganyika before the locals took over.' Ryan shadowed the man for six weeks before he returned to South Africa. In between taking instructions on how to use and fix the equipment, Ryan asked the man why he felt the need to flee Tanganyika and return home. 'He was threatened by the change, but no matter, I got a drilling machine and I was then able to drill a thousand feet for water and that was a game changer. I was able to put water into houses, clinics and the schools, and I could do the whole thing free of charge because otherwise it wouldn't be done.'

As a pilot, Ryan experienced a sense of freedom and accomplishment he could never have attained had he not set himself the challenge of learning to fly. There was simply no sensation like lifting off the ground, however bumpy and uneven the rudimentary airstrip was in parts, and there was nothing to match the feeling of looking down at the vastness of the East African terrain while listening to the steady hum of the plane's engine. 'It was all going so well until the Bishop got it into his head that he wanted to become a pilot himself. I quickly discovered he was unteachable, and on one occasion, I nearly lost my life over him.'

The small plane Ryan piloted was kitted out with the very minimum of interior comforts: two small, low-back seats, a rudder lever, two throttles, a pair of joysticks and brake pedals. By its very design, the plane proved almost impossible for training the ambitious Bishop; the basic flight instruments were mostly obscured from the view of the person in the rear seat, where Winters would sit. 'He'd be sitting behind me and he was small in stature, so I always gave him a couple of cushions to give him a lift on his seat. One time I was coming in to land but didn't the high cushion he had supporting him block a cord that was connected to the tail, so when I pulled the cord, it locked. I had to very quickly put my hand down to release the cord and it saved our lives.'

Ryan soon resented what he was being asked to do and became convinced that Winters' inherent clumsiness could be the death of them both. 'There had been a succession of these near-disaster events, so I thought it over for a while and decided that the safest option was to leave East Africa.'

FOUR

OUT OF AFRICA

They marched through their city without saying a word. The only sounds were the muffled remarks of curious onlookers amid the steady thuds of the marchers' footsteps on the rain-sodden streets. A biting-cold wind blew up from the fast-flowing River Foyle that cleaved the city into an east and west bank; yet history had also determined the divide between its inhabitants.

The city through which the marchers were making their way had derived its name, Derry, from the Irish word *Doire*, meaning 'oak grove', but in 1613 it was renamed Londonderry in recognition of its connections with City of London livery companies during the Plantation of Ulster in the 1600s, when Scottish and English Protestants loyal to the British monarch settled on land confiscated from the Gaelic Irish. In 1689 the city was at the heart of an epic clash between Catholics and Protestants for the crown of England, when it withstood a siege of 105 days to protect its Protestant liberties and keep out the Catholic Irish supporters of King James II. 'The Siege of Derry' was a pivotal moment in the history of Ireland and Britain, and, centuries later, the city was once again on the cusp of another historic moment – it would soon become the crucible of Northern Ireland's civil rights movement.

The march on 28 January 1964 was silent, but not without a

blatant expression of intent. Men and women held aloft placards, which read: 'OUR LIVES IN YOUR HANDS', 'NOBODY WANTS US', 'I AM GOOD ENOUGH TO SERVE IN THE ARMY BUT NOT GOOD ENOUGH TO HAVE A HOME FOR MY CHILDREN', 'SPRINGTOWN, DERRY'S LITTLE ROCK'. The marchers, over 200 in all, were residents of Springtown Camp, a former United States naval barracks built on the outskirts of the city. When the American forces left at the end of the Second World War, desperate families, who could not get adequate housing in the city, moved in. The military base had over 300 small tin huts, but they were never intended for long-term accommodation and had no running water, electricity or any means of heating. After a public outcry, the unionist-majority Corporation granted temporary rentals to the new residents of the camp and charged rent as part of an agreement that was to see the families allocated proper housing after six months. The agreement failed, and two decades on conditions in the camp had further deteriorated: the tin huts were damp and in disrepair, and the residents were seeking better housing for their families.

The marchers included Wilfred Brennan, who was living in a hut with seventeen people including his elderly widowed mother and other members of his family, as well as another family. Another resident, George McLaughlin, a father of seven, was worried about the health of his children. 'When you come in at night and put those youngsters to bed at seven o'clock, they are lying in the cold and dampness. It's bound to be affecting their health because I see the wife often having to get a towel in the morning to dry their hair from the dampness and frost in the huts. I think it's inhuman.'[1]

As the group reached Strand Road in the city, some locals applauded from the sidelines. They knew why the Springtown residents had cause to take to the streets: housing was a scarce resource in Derry, and even more so for Catholic families.

Despite the city's large Catholic voting majority, the voting wards were split to preserve majority representation for Protestants in terms of the number of seats on the local council. Unionist control of local government led to accusations of discrimination against the Catholic population in the allocation of council jobs and housing, and the protest march in January 1964 was reported in the *Derry Journal* days later under the headline 'Derry's Little Rock Calls for Fair Play'.[2]

Another three winters would pass before the residents of Springtown Camp were finally allocated new homes in 1967, some twenty-one years after their first request for better housing. However, on that cold and wet January day in 1964, a marker had been put down – taking to the streets in an effort to demand fairness and equality had the potential to effect change, albeit slow. The Springtown Camp silent protest was a precursor of the civil rights protests to come.

* * *

In County Tipperary, reports of Catholic discrimination in the allocation of housing in Derry in 1964 were of no concern or interest to Father Patrick Ryan, who travelled home that year. 'I was on my second visit home since my posting to Tanganyika and whatever was going on in the North at that time was not something I was aware of.'

Ryan was not alone in his ignorance. That summer, a team of journalists from the Irish documentary film series *Radharc* visited Derry to report on accusations of discrimination against the Catholic population in housing and political representation. The subsequent programme, which included contributions from Frank McCauley of the Catholic Registration Association and schoolteacher Paddy Friel (father of playwright Brian Friel), never made it to air after it was deemed too sensitive to broadcast on Raidió Teilifís Éireann

(RTÉ), Ireland's national public state broadcaster. 'The reason given was that it would be inopportune to show it when the Taoiseach was meeting the Prime Minister of Northern Ireland for the first time,' said the film-maker, Father Joe Dunn.[3]

Back in Rossmore that summer, Ryan was focused on demonstrating his technical ingenuity in his birthplace. 'My mother still lived in the home. In the years since I'd been gone, my older brother Simon had acquired his own farm, so my younger brother John was running the farm at home. I wanted to be of help and came up with a notion of how I could be.'

The apparent eccentricities of the missionary priest back home on respite were observed by some of the locals in the townland. The eagle-eyed first noticed a dig of some sort underway in a field that was part of John Ryan's farm; as they stepped out of the parish church after Mass and looked straight ahead at the hill across the valley, they could make out the neat line of a mound of earth running parallel to a trench that was taking shape a couple of fields below the Ryan homestead. Their initial curiosity turned into intrigue, and over a number of successive Sundays, elbows were sharpened and locals who appeared blind to what was going on were nudged and openly encouraged to look towards the trench in Ryan's field. *What was going on?*

At the same time, Patrick Ryan was watching the watchers. He quietly observed the Mass-goers squinting their eyes at the dig in the distance and found it both infuriating and thrilling that his neighbours hesitated to ask him outright what he was up to. His patience was augmented by a fervent surety that a local would eventually break. 'One Sunday morning one of the locals enquired, "Father Paddy, what are you up to with the trench? What are you building it for?"' Ryan savoured a brief few seconds of silence before he outlined exactly what he was up to. There was always something to be learned from observing how a person's facial muscles would instinctively betray their gut reaction, even if what they gave voice to was the very opposite of what they appeared to be thinking. 'I told him the truth. "I am going to make water flow up the hill to the mother's house."'

The man hurriedly inhaled, in an effort to stifle his laughter, but he wasn't fast enough to suppress a startling snort that set his shoulders shaking in absolute glee. *Father Ryan, did you say that you're going to make water flow up a hill?* 'Well, you'd want to have seen the faces on the rest of them. Of course they didn't want to laugh in my face because I was a priest, but I knew fine well what they thought of me.'

Mary Ann Ryan's second-born son, the boy who had been blessed with parents who were able to finance his studies for the priesthood, was apparently trying to defy a law of physics. But Ryan's stated ambition to thwart the rules of gravity was not a boast. 'The news spread that I had lost my marbles, that the sun in Africa had destroyed my brain. "Oh, the poor creature," they used to say, "whoever heard of water flowing up a hill, he must think he can work miracles," but I had a plan, and they underestimated my ability to see it through.'

His plan would deliver a miracle, of sorts. Houses with piped running water in rural Ireland were then very much in the minority. The 1961 census recorded that of 374,971 dwellings in rural areas, almost 75 per cent got their water from a 'well, fountain, pump' or other non-piped source. In Ryan's county of Tipperary, just over one-third of private dwellings had a flushing toilet.[4] A house with, at the very least, a running water tap would be of particular benefit to a mother who had already given years to carrying buckets of water from a well to her home.

Ryan continued his dig. It was winter and the soil was stubbornly hard to shift. The land itself was of superb quality, free-draining with a limestone base and, given its location just seven miles north-west of the Rock of Cashel, the stronghold of the kings of Munster for several hundred years prior to the Norman invasion, the area was commonly referred to as the 'land of the Kings'. However, Ryan's work with a shovel was far from regal; winter was a time of supposed rest and not the season to try and gouge out the earth with a shovel.

It was boredom that was the catalyst for Ryan's technical ambition. The winter days in Tipperary passed much more slowly than he remembered, and the shorter hours of daylight taunted him more than he wished to admit. He wasn't needed at home on the farm to work the land, he wasn't needed to build clinics or schools like he was in East Africa, and such were the political machinations between local parish priests that he wasn't even required to carry out religious duties while back home, so, initially, he took to the road.

Every morning he would head out for a walk around the valley. He enjoyed strolling along the briary lanes and twisty roads while trying to come up with a strategy that might steer Bishop Winters away from his ambition of also becoming a pilot in Tanganyika. Ryan was concentrating on such matters when he came across a challenge which, were he to overcome it, would leave a mark on the land long after his return to East Africa.

'There was water coming out of the ground in a spring, it flowed down a fall of ground and formed a little stream alongside a ditch. It was flowing there probably a thousand years.' The sound of the water springing forth so easily from the earth stopped Ryan in his tracks; he was literally stepping over the very element he'd soon be back drilling for under the hot African sun. There, as the drill bit tore noisily through dirt and rock, the locals helping him to set the machine in place would repeatedly warn him, 'Stay out of the sun after midday, Father Paddy, you might die of sunstroke.'

In Tipperary there was no fear of keeling over from a scorching sun, and the water underneath the ground, much like the rain in the weary grey clouds above him, was far closer to the surface. 'I had never noticed it before, but my work in the missions had opened my eyes to the importance of water, and here I was at home and it was springing up freely out of the ground. I became obsessed with it.'

Ryan's daily strolls immediately came to a halt. For three weeks he sat on a low stone wall along the ditch and looked at water bubbles coming out of the ground. The challenge would be getting the water up the hill so his mother would, for the very first time, have a piped water supply in her home. Sitting in a near meditative state, he soon arrived at one conclusion: praying would be unproductive; only physics could solve the puzzle. 'I got a hunch of something that would work – a hydraulic ram can be powered by the water that it pumps, but it needs a type of waterfall to give power to the water coming into it. The difficulty is that the higher the water has to be lifted, the greater the height of the waterfall needed. The breakthrough would be to achieve the effect of a waterfall, without building a dam.'

He now had a purpose for his visit. In the evenings Ryan sat studiously at the kitchen table and wrote out algebraic equations; a logical combination of numbers and Greek letters could unlock the solution. 'I reduced the problem to a mathematical formula, which I submitted to three different water bodies in the UK. I was interested to know, if I went through with the plan, would it work or was I wasting my time? They all wrote back and gave me the same answer; a novel idea but mathematically guaranteed to work.'

It took Ryan six weeks to dig a trench deep enough to protect the water pipe from the elements. His brother John left him to it, and his younger sibling's nonchalance incentivised Ryan to dig deeper – there was a fraternal one-upmanship to be gained from demonstrating that he had the physical will as well as the engineering nous to achieve his ambition for land he had no claim over. 'There was no building involved, just digging. I laid down a two-inch pipe along the bed of the stream where the water was flowing and when I reached a certain part of the field I put a turn on the pipe, a 10-foot difference in the height of a turn and that was the trick; the principle that water seeking its own level would push the water up the pipe, up the hill and arrive at a water tank I had put in at the back of the house.'

The days of hard labour helped crystallise a principle that would guide Ryan's self-philosophy in the years ahead: if nature could be manipulated by mathematical reasoning and application, the frailties of men and women would make them even more susceptible to subtle machinations of influence in order to achieve a particular outcome.

One of Ryan's main challenges in the years to come would be understanding a person's character and motivations, the hidden layers beneath their façade, and then to dig slowly in order to direct that person along a particular path. Water, like human nature, would always seek its own level. 'My work was impervious to hail, rain or snow and the pipe had no moving parts, just two little rubber valves and it pumped away day and night.'

There was also a lesson to be drawn from watching and waiting, as he had done while sitting on the stone wall, instinctively being aware that some of his neighbours had underestimated his resolve. 'I left the house with fresh-flowing water into the kitchen and into a toilet in the bathroom and from a tap in the bath and everything functioning. There wasn't another house in the parish that had it. My mother was thrilled and I was delighted that I had proved my point to those who had doubted me.'

* * *

Father Patrick Ryan's return to Africa in 1965 was his final posting as a missionary priest south of the Equator. His frustrations with Bishop Winters' insistence on learning to fly proved too overwhelming to navigate. 'I had to break the power of the Bishop. My plan was to go home for twelve months to start fundraising for the building of a hospital, then go back and become a citizen of Tanganyika so that I could buy a patch of ground outside the jurisdiction of the Bishop and set up the clinic that I wanted to. My dream was to have a little air ambulance.' However, Ryan's plan was thwarted when he requested the transfer, but rather than being allowed to return to Ireland, he was assigned instead to an East London parish as a curate in 1967. 'My superiors wanted to send me to America, but I ended up in London.'

St Thomas More church in Barking was where Ryan was sent. Built in 1935 for the Pallottine Order, the church was named in honour of the English lawyer Thomas More, a favourite of King Henry VIII until he failed to support the monarch's split with the Catholic Church and was beheaded for treason.

At the time Ryan was arriving in England, the Roman Catholic Church in Britain needed a constant supply of priests to cater for a growing membership built largely out of new arrivals from Ireland. Up to the early 1960s, Ireland was the main source of immigration into Britain and the generation of immigrants Ryan had observed on the mailboat from Dublin to Holyhead, like generations before and after them, had not abandoned their faith. Away from home, the Catholic Church became a natural focal point for Irish communities in Britain fearful of losing their cultural identity.

Father Ryan also found himself facing a loss. The freedom and independence he had carved out in East Africa were completely out of reach in a location where he was expected to serve the faithful through prayer instead of feats of construction or engineering. 'I was sent to the parish of Barking, which wasn't too far from the big Ford factory in Dagenham. I had no choice but to get on with it.'

Barking and neighbouring Dagenham in Essex were then the heartland of England's industrial south-east. In 1921 construction began on the Becontree Estate, once described as the largest public housing development in the world. David Lloyd George, Prime Minister at the time, had promised 'homes fit for heroes' to the mostly working-class men who returned home from the Great War. Some 27,000 new homes were built on 3,000 acres of compulsorily purchased market gardens, fields and lanes in Barking, Dagenham and Ilford. The houses, which had indoor toilets, hot and cold running water, and front and back gardens, were luxuries to families displaced from London's East End by post-war slum clearance.

At first, most Dagenham residents commuted to central London for work. Then the Ford motor plant opened in 1931. Such was the demand for labour that, in the 1940s, the plant recruited employees for heavy foundry work directly from Ireland.[5] By the time of Ryan's arrival in 1967, the plant employed some 55,000 workers. The man who had led a sheltered life, literally an equator away from the 1960s sexual revolution in London, was about to learn that the world had changed far beyond the reclaiming of borders in post-colonial Africa. 'I was a long, long way from the missions, that's for sure. One of the things that struck me was that I could never visit parishioners until after five in the evening, when the men were already home, because if you visited the house in the morning, they'd say you were after the wife. That will tell you how things worked – no respect.'

Ryan felt adrift. The seminary had prepared him for missionary work but not the mundane. In Barking he was expected to greet his congregation at the entrance to the church every Sunday before Mass, a custom he resented before he ever uttered his first salutation from the altar. 'I noticed that a lot of them would look at me as if they were doing me a favour by coming to church. I despised those that did.'

Gone were the days of excitedly taxiing a plane on a makeshift runway or travelling for days on dirt roads across the wilds of East Africa. As the months went by, Ryan grew increasingly bored of the congregation who sat in the church pews of St Thomas More church looking up at him. 'I didn't want to be there.' His experiences in London only magnified what he already knew about himself: he had no interest in trying to convert souls. 'The only worthwhile aspect of my time in London was meeting a young woman I would come to rely on for some help with my work for the IRA – she was particularly useful years later. But at that stage I'd had enough. I went back to Ireland at the first opportunity I got.'

It was Mary Ann Ryan's infirmity that answered her son's prayers and gave him the perfect excuse to flee from his religious duties in London in 1969. When he wrote to his ecclesiastical superiors one morning after saying Mass, the fundamentals of the proposition he put to paper were honest, in that it was true his mother was unwell. He carefully wrote of how he would like to return home to spend time caring for her, so that, ultimately, he would be able to administer the Last Rites as she passed away.

Ever practical in his cunning, he also suggested a role he would gladly undertake while home in Tipperary. 'The Pallottines always had somebody going around the country to collect the money out of the mission boxes. You'd see them on shop counters for people to throw in a few pennies for the missions in Africa and we had hundreds of these boxes out around the country, so I also asked if I could come home and start collecting the boxes.' His superiors acceded to his request and Ryan was again on the move, this time in a direction that personally suited him.

Back in Tipperary he could assume the social privileges of being a Catholic priest but without any of the responsibility of a parish to which he had to administer the faith, something he would never do again. The events that unfolded during the summer of 1969 went on to rule Patrick Ryan out of ever being assigned to another Catholic parish. While he was driving around Ireland collecting pennies and pounds for the Pallottine missions, what became the Troubles in Northern Ireland were set alight.

* * *

Community tensions in the North had been building. In October 1968 television pictures of the Royal Ulster Constabulary (RUC) baton-charging a civil rights demonstration in Derry were shown around the world. At that point, the Northern Ireland civil rights movement became international news. The march had been planned by the Derry Housing Action Committee (DHAC) with the support of the Northern Ireland Civil Rights Association (NICRA) to protest the unfair allocation of council houses and public sector jobs in the city, where the mainly Protestant and unionist-controlled local authority still discriminated against the majority nationalist and mainly Catholic population. NICRA also sought the introduction of one man-one vote in local council elections, rather than one vote per household, which was seen as discriminatory against Catholic homes with multiple occupancies, as well as an end to gerrymandering, the manipulation of ward boundaries in local elections to maintain a false unionist majority.

The following month the Stormont government tried to prevent the situation getting out of control by announcing a series of reforms, but the proposed changes did not go far enough for some civil rights campaigners, and divisions began to manifest within the movement. The moderate Derry Citizens Action Committee, of which John Hume was one of the leaders, mounted a series of non-violent protests. But the more militant People's Democracy, which developed out of student protests in Belfast, organised further marches, which were accompanied by rioting and violence.

Events in Northern Ireland continued to accelerate. The civil rights movement sought moderate political and economic reforms to end discrimination, but insecurity about the purpose of the campaign had prompted pre-emptive violence from the Ulster Volunteer Force (UVF), a loyalist paramilitary group. In early 1969 UVF members bombed a series of water and electricity installations in Northern Ireland in the hope that the attacks would be blamed on a dormant IRA – their plan was a success.

On 12 August 1969 Derry was on edge as the annual Apprentice Boys' march to commemorate the siege of Derry prepared to get underway. Tensions simmered following the deaths of two Catholic men in July. Francis McCloskey, an elderly farmer, was found unconscious on 13 July, following a police baton charge in Dungiven, County Derry. He died the next day. On 17 July Samuel Devenny died of a heart attack in hospital in Derry city. More than 20,000 people turned out for the funeral of the 42-year-old father of nine, who had been recovering in hospital for months after a brutal police assault in his home during rioting in the city.

As the two-mile-long Apprentice Boys' parade passed by the city's Catholic Bogside on 12 August, trouble flared, provoking a 700-strong RUC force to storm into the area. Petrol-bomb attacks, water cannon and baton charges, along with fierce running battles through the streets, went on for hours between local residents and the RUC, leaving the Bogside looking like a war-torn wasteland. Shortly before midnight the RUC began firing CS gas into the district, marking the first time that tear gas was used against such disturbances in Northern Ireland. The riots, which came to be known as the 'Battle of the Bogside', continued for almost three days and saw over 1,000 people injured. The violence soon spread to other cities and towns, and ultimately resulted in hundreds of injuries and a number of deaths.

In Dublin, Taoiseach Jack Lynch went on television to announce that the Irish government had contacted the British government to make a request to the United Nations for a peace-keeping force to be installed in Northern Ireland: 'It is evident, also, that the Stormont government is no longer in control of the situation. Indeed, the present situation is the inevitable outcome of the policies pursued for decades by successive Stormont governments. It is clear, also, that the Irish government can no longer stand by and see innocent people injured and perhaps worse.'[6]

It had become obvious that the RUC had lost control of the security of Northern Ireland. On 15 August the inspector general of the RUC wrote to the general officer commanding Northern Ireland: 'In view of the continued worsening of the situation in Londonderry city on this date as outlined in the attached copy of a warning message sent to the Home Office, London, and the fact that this situation has deteriorated further since the timing of the message to the Home Office, I now request the assistance of forces under your command in Londonderry City.'[7]

In an unprecedented step, the British Army was deployed on the streets of Northern Ireland for the first time to restore law and order. Troops entered Derry on 14 August and Belfast the following day. However, the warm welcome extended to them was short-lived, as was the government's intention to pull out the troops within days. It soon became clear that the violence was not going to end.

All changed utterly in parts of Belfast that until this point had been relatively mixed, with Catholics and Protestants often living side by side. As the violence spread, thousands of people fled their homes. Some were burned out, others had windows broken or faced intimidation, and many Catholic women and children fled south of the border to escape the violence.

As August progressed, Ryan found himself increasingly drawn to the newspaper stands, where reports of shootings and gun battles in Belfast were splashed across the front pages. 'Something deep had been unleashed and it could not be put back in a box. It had been my intention to return to Africa and to spend my life there doing good things, but then the war broke out and my dream turned to skittles. I wanted to help. How could I not, seeing women and children crossing the border after being burned out of their homes. So, at that stage anyway, I contributed financially [to republicans] as much help as I could from the mission boxes and redirected it to the situation up North.'

As the winter of 1969 closed in, Mary Ann's children took turns to sit at their mother's deathbed in the house where she had reared them. Besides Patrick and her two farmer sons, there was Mary, married to a local farmer, Joseph, who had a drapery business, and Kitty, the youngest, who had worked for a solicitor before emigrating to America, where she married a man from County Clare.

Mary Ann was not in any pain and was dying under her own roof; two comforts of a type. As her breathing changed before the moment of death, Father Patrick Ryan steadied himself to help administer the Last Rites alongside the local parish priest. 'She died on an evening in November and I led her funeral Mass in the days after. Simon was in his new farm, so my younger brother John got the homestead and the farm, but something much more important had already been passed down to me. A love for my country.'

As Mary Ann's coffin was lowered into a freshly dug hole in the graveyard in Rossmore, the second-born son who was leading prayers over it resolved never to let his mother down. 'I inherited a deep nationalism from my mother and just like her, I was prepared to do something about it.' A small group of mourners, including Patrick, shuddered in the cold as they waited for the grave to be covered over, before walking away still tightly clutching their Rosary beads.

Mary Ann Ryan died on her own terms, having lived a full life. Thousands of others would be denied that dignity in the decades of the Troubles still to unfold.

FIVE

THE SCULPTOR
AND THE COLONEL

The pilot had been forewarned. The path of the flight route he planned to follow from Iceland to Canada would see him fly directly into a low-pressure weather system, centred just north-east of Newfoundland. The risk was that the plane would run out of fuel. Strong headwinds blowing directly towards the front of the aircraft, a Douglas DC-3, would slow the ground speed of the plane, meaning the flying time would take longer and therefore the fuel reserve would run critically low.

The obvious danger was avoidable; the pilot could fly to Goose Bay or Gander instead of St John's, Newfoundland. The weather forecaster at Keflavik Airport in Iceland suggested the alternatives not just because both options covered a shorter distance, but also because on the routes to the north and west of the low-pressure system the pilot would encounter much lower headwinds, and possibly a tailwind in certain areas.[1]

It was 17 November 1972. Isaac Stefansky and his co-pilot, Harold Harrison, had a critical decision to make. The pair were on a refuelling stopover ahead of the final leg of their flight home to Canada from Ireland. As the nose of the DC-3 lifted off the airport runway, the pilot chose to ignore the forecaster's advice. Stefansky stuck to his original plan: based on his calculation of a ground speed of at least 150 knots, he estimated that the flight would take nine hours and thirty minutes for the distance of over 1,400 nautical miles. However, the low-pressure weather system manifested as predicted and the resulting headwinds considerably slowed the progress of the DC-3 over the North Atlantic, with the plane's ground speed averaging only 112 knots.

As the plane flew over the ocean, its fuel gauge indicated that the first portion of the flight was not progressing according to Stefansky's plan. The two Canadians still had time to ditch their original path and alter their flight route north of the low-pressure system, to an area of lesser winds. However, despite the increasing danger, Stefansky ploughed onwards. Other pilots checked in on their progress; position reports relayed through overflying jet aircrafts recorded that the men were 'overly optimistic' about their progress and 'did not accurately fix the aircraft's position at any time'. The stakes could not have been higher, but still the men stayed on course and continued toward St John's 'in the hope that the headwinds would subside'.[2]

For all their combined flying experience, Stefansky and Harrison made a fundamental error by choosing to ignore the advice of the Icelandic weather forecaster. Their determined hope in the face of a critically low fuel gauge may have been emboldened by a daring flying mission they had successfully completed days earlier: the delivery of twenty-five rocket-propelled grenade RPG-7 launchers and 496 warheads from Libya to Shannon Airport in County Clare. The Canadian pilots had made history – the DC-3's cargo was the first shipment of arms from the Libyan regime to the Provisional IRA.

* * *

It was some three years since the beginning of Operation Banner, the military operation put in place to assist the police when the Troubles flared up. It was also three years since differences about the tactics that should be used in response to the deployment of British troops to Northern Ireland had given rise to what became the Provisional IRA.

The remnants of the original IRA had continued to fight the partition of Ireland between the 1920s and 1960s, but with little success or even support. Their 'border campaign' of 1956–62, aimed at fighting 'until the invader is driven from our soil and victory is ours',[3] primarily focused on British Army patrols and border posts, but it had faded out due to a lack of popular support. A 1967 meeting of the IRA's leadership at a farmhouse in County Tipperary was told that the secret army had just over 200 active members and 'enough ammo for one good job'.[4]

In August 1969, as trouble flared in Northern Ireland, the IRA's southern-based leadership stood accused of running its military capacity down to a point of near uselessness. Traditionalists wanted to rebuild the IRA's military strength and return the organisation to its historical roots – the use of physical force against British oppressors to win independence for all of Ireland – and this led to a split. In December 1969 the first Provisional Army Council of the IRA was formed. As the violence continued to escalate, the Provisional IRA, which soon became known simply as the IRA, had no shortage of recruits, but there was a problem: money and weapons were in short supply.

At first, the IRA looked west for weaponry. Its gunrunning network in America was led by George Harrison, a native of County Mayo, who had emigrated to the US before the Second World War but maintained a deeply held devotion to the Irish republican cause. In 1971 Denis McInerney from Ennis in County Clare, the IRA's then quartermaster general (QMG), responsible for procuring arms and equipment, travelled to the US to meet with Harrison's

Irish-American gunrunning network. He recalled: 'We arranged for shipments to be smuggled into Ireland. This was achieved by procuring large boilers, opening them up and removing parts of their insides and loading in equipment. We would pad them so that the stuff would not rattle. We first sent M1 carbines and ammunition, and then we sent Garand rifles and, when they became available, M16 rifles and M60 machine guns.'[5]

By then, Father Patrick Ryan's collection of money from some missionary boxes had begun to prompt some concern within the Pallottine College – a recurring shortfall in public contributions to the Pallottine's missionary efforts overseas had become startlingly obvious. 'It came to my attention because the cheques got smaller,' said Father William Hanly.[6]

Ryan did not shirk from coming clean. 'I told them that I was giving it to another organisation. "Would you mind telling us who that is?" they asked me. You can imagine how my answer [the Provisionals] went down. They were appalled and needless to say, did not give me permission to keep going at it.' Father Hanly instead appointed a replacement fundraiser in Ireland to take Ryan's place, later recalling: 'He might have been spending more time working for others than for us. He was his own boss, free to come and go as he chose.'[7]

Still based in Tipperary, Ryan defied his ecclesiastical superiors, who encouraged him to return to England as a curate in Hastings. 'I chose to stay in Ireland because I didn't like what was happening up North. I wanted to shift the Brits out.'

A suggestion by Ryan that he should be sent to work in a parish north of the border was met with short shrift by the Pallottine Fathers. 'Paddy Ryan Simon asked if he could be dispatched up North,' recalls Father Phil Barry, 'but the Pallottines didn't serve any parishes over the border so that was a non-runner, and then, well, he just went to ground.'[8]

Father Donal McCarthy was Rector of the Students' House of the Pallottine Fathers in Thurles and knew Ryan when he was training for the priesthood. 'While he was with us, we could see a man who was zealous, hardworking and very orthodox. In many ways he could have been an idealist,' he said. 'He left working for us to devote himself to the behalf of these prisoners [in Northern Ireland]. Our superiors were not terribly happy about one of our priests being involved.'[9]

Ryan had no religious-like devotion for those behind bars. He was more concerned with assisting those who followed in their wake, men and women possessed with an enthusiasm and determination to point and fire a gun on behalf of the IRA. The zealotry he once applied to his missionary work was being redirected to a very different calling. 'My collecting of the money from the boxes was curtailed, but no matter, I started sending up weapons and ammunition. I was passing on gear to people I knew could get to the IRA.'

A local contact introduced Ryan to the IRA's then officer commanding (OC) in Munster, Tom O'Sullivan, who said, 'I was one of the first to work with Father Paddy Ryan.'[10] When the two men first met, O'Sullivan was astonished to hear a Catholic priest speak so plainly of his eagerness to assist the IRA in whatever way he could. 'We had people who wanted to help from all sorts of backgrounds, but he spoke out straight about it, he wanted to help. I was taken aback and I said to myself, sure what can you do only play it by ear, so we developed a connection.'

Wearing a clerical collar presented opportunities to Ryan that did not go unnoticed by the Tipperary-based IRA commander. 'His get-up helped, the collar opened doors,' O'Sullivan observed. 'Father Paddy was able to root out somebody who was willing to help in some direction or other, and the next thing he would arrive with a bit of gear.'

In a society subservient to the power of the Catholic Church, it mattered that few would dare challenge a Catholic priest on any issue, including the morality of sending guns to the IRA. 'Father Paddy had an arrogant touch about him, priests were trained in that way, and I was under no illusions about him, but the difference was that he was charismatic enough to get people to help.' Still, some in O'Sullivan's circle discouraged Ryan's flaunting of his priestly vocation for nefarious ends. 'There was one particular man, a Tan war veteran, who was not impressed. "Paddy," he said, "for God's sake, will you throw off the garb."'

In the same way that Ryan had applied himself to his missionary endeavours on behalf of the Pallottines in East Africa, he utilised the same determination to source weapons for the IRA. 'It turned out that I was good at ferreting out guns from around the country.' But Ryan's skills would soon be redirected to another mission outside of Ireland.

* * *

A sloppy operation in late 1971 had put the IRA's gunrunning from America under strain. The debacle unfolded when the luxury cruise liner *Queen Elizabeth II* arrived in Cobh, County Cork, in October. The disembarking passengers were all cleared by customs, but it soon transpired that six blue suitcases had been left behind. A customs official who tried to lift one of the cases became suspicious and, when they were opened, it was found that the cases contained hand grenades, automatic rifles, hand pistols and ammunition.

The IRA had been smuggling weapons into Southampton from New York on the Cunard liner, a route that had been put in place by the IRA's Belfast Brigade, but Denis McInerney had been kept in the dark about the shipment that landed in Cobh. 'I had to return to America to iron out the problems which arose from that incident.'

On McInerney's return from the US, the IRA's commander in Belfast informed him of a separate development by way of a Breton nationalist and sculptor living in Ireland. 'I was informed by Joe Cahill that contact had been made by Yann Goulet and he wanted to meet with me.' Born in Brittany in 1914, to a family of modest means, Goulet had won a scholarship to the prestigious École nationale supérieure des Beaux-Arts in Paris.[11] While still a student, he joined the Breton nationalist movement, agitating for independence for Brittany from France. When the Second World War broke out, Goulet, like other young men of his generation, was called up to fight. 'I thought that if I fought honestly for the French I would earn the right to express my views. I was a fool.'[12] Goulet was taken prisoner but, unlike other prisoners of war, was quickly released and returned home to Brittany where he went on to lead a paramilitary unit, the Strolladoù Stourm, who were allied to the Germans and open to taking advantage of any German willingness to support their cause. 'We were ready to use them, like some in Ireland were ready to use them. Do you not think, perhaps, that if the Germans occupied the British Isles, they might have given you the Six Counties? You would have taken things from there, as we would.'[13]

After the liberation of France, Goulet was sentenced to death *in absentia* for treason and collaboration with the Nazis. He fled to Ireland, where he became an Irish citizen and successful sculptor, winning commissions for public works commemorating, among other things, the IRA of the War of Independence and Civil War.

McInerney was keen to meet with him. 'I went to his house and he informed me that he had [had] contact from Libya and they wanted to make contact with the IRA. He did not have any idea of what was on offer.'

* * *

In 1972 Libya was just three years into the rule of Colonel Muammar Gaddafi, a man whose path to power was fuelled by a fervent Arab nationalism. Born into humble living conditions in the North African desert, Muammar Mohammed Abu Minyar Gaddafi was part of the generation who grew up under the rule of the first, and last, King of Libya, Muhammad Idris as-Senussi, who came to power after the country gained its independence in 1951. Forty years earlier Italy had invaded Libya, provoking twenty years of rebellion. One of Gaddafi's grandfathers was killed resisting the Italian invasion and, as a child, Gaddafi grew up listening to stories about the resistance against Italian colonialism and the brutality it brought with it. With the defeat of Italy in the Second World War, Libya passed to Allied administration before the United Nations recognised its independence as a monarchy in 1951.

In his youth, Gaddafi was an ardent admirer of the Egyptian leader Gamal Abdel Nasser, who championed Pan-Arab unity. In 1952 Nasser led a military coup against King Farouk to create an Egyptian republic free from foreign rule. Emulating his Egyptian idol, after finishing his schooling Gaddafi entered a military academy at Benghazi. On graduating he spent ten months in England, receiving training in 1966 at a British Army signals school, an experience that hardened his views against the West. When he returned to Libya, he began to organise his fellow officers into a clandestine cell system with the aim of overthrowing King Idris, whom he regarded as a corrupt, pro-Western monarch.

On 1 September 1969, when the King was in Turkey, the Revolutionary Command Council (RCC), made up of twelve young army officers under Colonel Muammar Gaddafi, took charge of the country. At just twenty-seven years of age, Gaddafi had seized power in a bloodless coup.

Gaddafi's brand of Arab nationalism soon manifested in anti-imperialist actions and a foreign policy that was vehemently anti-Western. One of his first acts in power was to demand the departure of the US military from its strategically vital Wheelus Air Force Base, located some 15 kilometres east of Tripoli. Gaddafi proclaimed that 'the armed forces which rose to express the people's revolution will not tolerate living in their shacks while the bases of imperialism exist in Libyan territory'.[14] In December 1969 it was announced in London that Britain had agreed with the RCC to withdraw all British forces from the El Adem/Tobruk RAF complex by 31 March 1970.

Gaddafi was not done with expunging any notion of colonial rule in Libya. Months later, he demonstrated the ruthlessness that would define his regime. In July 1970 a new RCC decree ordered the confiscation of property belonging to Italian citizens still living and working in Libya after the bloodless coup. It also ordered their expulsion by 7 October, along with the remaining Jewish community, whose assets were to be seized. All of Libya's Italians, about 20,000 people, fled or were deported. To celebrate, Gaddafi declared 7 October 'The Day of Vengeance', a new, annual, national holiday.

Gaddafi became obsessed with exporting revolution and taking his anti-imperialist campaign around the world. He began to fund and publicly support militant groups and resistance movements wherever he found them, including militant Palestinian splinter groups, and guerrilla movements based in the Philippines, Ethiopia, Somalia, Yemen, Chad, Morocco, Tunisia, Thailand and Panama.[15] By late 1971 the IRA was also on the brink of being financed by this oil-rich, anti-colonialist benefactor.

On hearing from Goulet that the Libyan regime wished to make contact with the IRA, Denis McInerney made his way to the Libyan Embassy in London for a tourist visa. 'I met the Ambassador. He instructed me that when I reached Libya I was to be called Mr. Blackwell and this was to be my code name.' McInerney travelled to Libya on his own passport, then followed the instructions he had been given to activate his code name – on his arrival at Tripoli Airport he asked the receptionist to announce that Mr Blackwell wished to meet his reception committee. However, he had overlooked the likelihood that his passport would concern the security agents tasked with meeting the supposed Mr Blackwell. 'I had to explain that I had no false passport. After they were happy with me, they took me to the Foreign Minister's house.'

In Tripoli, McInerney made his case for assistance in the form of weaponry and suggested an audacious form of transport to bring it to Ireland. 'I pointed out that we were very short of equipment and arms. We were particularly interested in heavy arms and rockets. I also asked if they would supply a submarine to transport the equipment to Ireland. He said that they would supply arms to the IRA, but we would have to supply our own transport. He also promised to supply the Army with finance.'

McInerney had returned to the US to work out the logistics for transporting the Libyan arms he had been promised, when, on 11 June 1972, Gaddafi publicly declared that Libya supported the IRA and was supplying it with money, arms and volunteers to fight British occupation forces in Northern Ireland. He made the admission in a speech marking the second anniversary of the evacuation of US forces from Wheelus Air Force Base.

In America, McInerney was introduced to Isaac Stefansky, a Canadian pilot. 'He had a friend, Harold Harrison, another Canadian Jew who was prepared to be the co-pilot. I brought seven thousand dollars across the US border to Canada to pay for the leasing of the plane. There was only one problem: both the pilot and co-pilot were afraid to go into Libya because they were Jewish. When I raised that point with the Libyan Foreign Minister, he said it was okay as long as they were not Israelis.'

The Canadian pilots flew the plane they had leased to Tripoli, where McInerney was waiting for their arrival and helped to strip out the interior of the DC-3 to accommodate the arms shipment that weighed over two and half tons. Despite concerns from some Libyan airport officials that such a heavy load would impact lift-off, Stefansky, Harrison and their IRA passenger departed for the south-west of Ireland. Their intended destination was Farranfoe, a local airport in County Kerry, but there was a problem. 'At that time the airport in Kerry had no runway lights and did not operate after dark,' McInerney recalled. 'As this was eight o'clock at night, we decided to fly on to Shannon Airport.'

As the DC-3 was taxiing up the runway at Shannon, the IRA's QMG took the opportunity to exit the plane in order to avoid being recognised by airport security. 'I instructed the pilot to inform the control tower that he had damaged the landing equipment and would need to have it looked at. He was then to pull into the aircraft repair facility at Shannon to have this done.' The move allowed IRA contacts in the repair hangar to take control of the aircraft and keep customs control at bay. Meanwhile two other IRA men, under the guise of a frozen food delivery, accessed the airport grounds. 'They proceeded into the hangar where the aircraft was, unloaded the weapons and drove out through the customs checkpoints, waving to those inside. They handed over their vans to two volunteers who drove them to the weapons dumps. The vans were cleaned and returned to the owner's yard and were ready for normal business the following morning.'

The delivery of twenty-five RPG-7s and 496 warheads in November 1972 boosted the IRA's capacity to kill on a larger scale. Yet even before the IRA had acquired its new arsenal, it had already demonstrated its violent intent. In 1972 Northern Ireland's descent into terror reached a brutal nadir: by the year's end 480 lay dead, nearly half at the hands of the IRA, and over ten times that were injured.

Before the Canadians departed Shannon for home, McInerney handed $5,000 to Stefansky. 'This money was to cover the cost of fuel for the next journey to Libya. We arranged a date when they would fly back to Libya and I would meet them there.'

* * *

As the DC-3 aircraft countered the headwinds which had been forecast north-east of Newfoundland, Stefansky made radio contact with St John's Tower. His earlier hopeful optimism had dissipated to despair – the plane was running dangerously low on fuel and he needed assistance. For twenty-five minutes the pilot remained in contact with the radio operators, who dispatched an air-sea rescue aircraft, but it was too late: both engines of the DC-3 were failing from fuel starvation.[16]

What had been predicted had come to pass. The fuel gauge dropped to empty. The wind was rising in gusts of 50 mph and the waves in the raging swell below were between 20 and 25 feet.[17] Stefansky called 'Mayday'.

Rescuers said that the plane disintegrated when it hit the sea. They eventually spotted one of the men they were searching for; his legs were tied to a life raft floating amongst debris and an oil stain. It was Stefansky. His was the only body recovered from the water off the coast of Newfoundland. Still in his pocket was the IRA's fuel money of $5,000.

Meanwhile, in a secret training camp outside the village of New Inn in County Tipperary, the IRA prepared to test one of its newly acquired rocket-propelled grenades. The training group included Brian Keenan, the then quartermaster of the Belfast Brigade, who had already developed a formidable reputation for planning bombings in Belfast and seeking out arms-smuggling contacts. When Marcus

Fogarty, who was tasked with supplying the camp with food every couple of days, arrived with supplies, he witnessed a problem that no one appeared to have anticipated – the instructions were in Chinese. He recalled that 'no one was able to read the Chinese markings. They didn't know how to use the RPG-7. They had a vice grip around the warhead, trying to prise it apart it at one stage; thanks be to God, they didn't succeed.'[18]

The training camp later went to the site of a disused mine near Ballynunty in County Tipperary. By then Paddy O'Kane, a former member of the British Army's Parachute Regiment turned IRA man, had travelled from Belfast to demonstrate to the group, including Fogarty and Keenan, how to correctly use a rocket-propelled grenade. The target was a derelict building already missing a roof. 'The first Libyan RPG-7 was fired at the gable end of a stone building at half past eight in the morning, and I know that because a lad I worked with was going to Mass in Killenaule and said there was a merciful bang as he was going into the church, but he did not know what the noise was.'

The IRA wasted no time in using its newly acquired arsenal. On 28 November 1972 fifteen rockets were fired at ten different targets across Northern Ireland. The first was directed at 9.35 a.m. at an RUC station in a border village of Belleek in County Fermanagh, killing RUC officer Constable Robert Keys when the rocket penetrated the ¾-inch armour plating in front of a window. Rockets were also fired at two army bases, a Saracen armoured personnel carrier in Belfast, and four police stations in various towns, injuring seven. One was also fired at an army post in a north Belfast school, 30 yards from 200 schoolchildren, but failed to explode.[19]

As he was getting to his feet in the House of Commons the next day, the Minister of State for Defence, Ian Gilmour, told parliament that he had just been informed of another attack: 'there was a further rocket attack in Belfast earlier this afternoon. It was against the Army post at Flax Street Mill. Fortunately there were no casualties.' The minister also confirmed that the IRA was using a new weapon: 'fragments of the rockets used and the one recovered are being examined. It appears to be an RPG7, which is a rocket type anti-tank weapon manufactured in several Warsaw Pact countries and supplied to various forces outside the Warsaw Pact. As the hon. Gentleman and the House will realise, the country of origin of this weapon is not necessarily the country of supply.'[20]

The actual country of supply, Libya, had already committed to providing ever-increasing amounts of weapons and cash, but, after the deaths of the Canadian pilots, the IRA needed a new way to smuggle arms. Denis McInerney put his mind to finding a solution. 'We were promised 100 tons of arms and equipment as well as one million pounds sterling by the Libyans. I did not want to miss this chance of arming the IRA for what I expected would be a long war. I decided that we should try and get a ship to collect what we were promised.'

SIX

'A BOOT UP THE TRANSOM'

Patrick Ryan was making his way to a courtyard garden in the heart of the Medina, Tripoli's old walled city. The midday sun had infused a heaviness in the air. Seagulls from the nearby port tore at debris dotted along the narrow, cobbled streets, pausing only to expel squawks that pierced the thrall of the market hum. A silk merchant clapped his hands in an effort to scare the birds back towards the sea. His exaggerated movements were a source of amusement to a metal craftsman, who had stopped banging on a piece of copper to smile at the spectacle.

A gust of wind lifted the birds and loosened rust-coloured sand from finials stacked side by side outside the copper workshop. Ryan squinted his eyes and wiped away the metal grit he could feel along his forearms. He was agitated. The shirt he was wearing was too formal and his trousers were too creased to afford him any chance of blending into the background. It wasn't that his attire made him appear dishevelled; he looked like he could not decide whether he was passing himself off as a businessman or a tourist. He rolled down the sleeves of his shirt and vowed to dress more decisively in future.

His annoyance was tempered when he remembered that it was only his second time away from the hotel; his first was a stroll to get a sense of the city's topography. In Tripoli, Ryan was taking care to avoid being seen in the company of the IRA's chief of staff, Joe Cahill, whom he had first met in Rome only days earlier. 'Word came through that I was being sent on a task abroad, my first for the IRA, and I was told to meet Joe Cahill in a hotel not too far from the Vatican. The IRA gave me the money for my fare from Dublin, but it was up to me to organise my flight.'

Ryan's sense of foreboding about Cahill had magnified with every passing day. As he saw it, the Belfast man was reckless, a character trait that ran contrary to an IRA operation where so much was at stake. Aside from trying to secure what the Libyans had materially promised, a breach of security had the potential to bring down at least one member of the IRA's governing body, the Army Council.

The IRA's QMG, the man with overall responsibility for obtaining weapons and explosives, had already made his way to Tripoli. Denis McInerney brought with him a formidable reputation and Ryan was impressed when he was introduced to him in a quiet corner of the hotel. 'He was the type of character who, if he couldn't get around a mountain, he would climb over it, and if he couldn't climb over it, he would drill a hole through it.' This was in stark contrast to Ryan's experience of Cahill, who had to be convinced by Ryan of the merits of feigning ignorance of each other on the flight from Rome to Tripoli. Cahill's apparent resistance to this precautionary measure had unsettled Ryan, who had advised Cahill of the need for minimal public contact between them for the duration of their time in Libya. The less interaction the better, thought Ryan, who also sensed that Libyan government officials would be making an independent assessment of every individual the IRA had sent out. It took two weeks for contact to be made, but his intuition about what might unfold was prescient.

Ryan's stroll to the courtyard garden was on the back of an approach by a sharply dressed Libyan man as he was finishing his daily breakfast of fruit and coffee. The man had been loitering in the hotel lobby for some time and, despite the crispness of his suit, carried himself with the passive acceptance of someone who knew he was merely a messenger. Ryan had noticed he was being observed and was surprised it had taken so long for the man to eventually introduce himself as a government official. His speech was quite deliberate as he informed Ryan of a location in the city's historic quarter where another government official was keen to meet with him. The invitation extended strictly to Ryan alone. The man repeated his specific instruction: no one else was invited, nor would it be wise to talk about the meeting with anyone. Ryan bowed his head to confirm that he understood what was being said.

As he walked under the main gateway off Tripoli's Green Square into the Medina, Ryan steadied himself for a sensory assault. To enter the Old City was to go back in time and glimpse a myriad of North African, Arab and Mediterranean influences. In the market, neat mounds of spices competed for visual attention with colourful Turkish tile-work. Ryan had never seen such an arresting display of red and yellow colours as those presented by the pyramids of saffron and turmeric. As he drank in the image, his concentration was interrupted by the din of clanging emanating from rows of workshops where craftsmen turned out metal plates, urns and trinkets.

Ryan looked at his watch before hurrying down a side street lined by a row of teahouses. He turned left and was instantly stilled by a view of the sea, where fishing boats were swaying in tandem in the Mediterranean swell. The port was also giving refuge to the IRA's vessel, a 298-ton coaster, the *Claudia*, which was waiting to be stocked with arms and ammunition.

Ryan had purposefully stayed away from the port. He would have been interested in catching a glimpse of the prized cargo, but he knew that Joe Cahill was down there. He could visualise Cahill elbowing the crew aside and barking orders in his sharp west Belfast accent. Ryan's experience of listening to the sins of men and women in dark confession boxes had gifted him with an innate ability to know who could best keep secrets. He feared Cahill's gleeful whoops in anticipation of the promised arms shipment would alert every British agent within earshot.

Ryan turned his back to the port and continued on the path that brought him to the gold market, Souq al-Siagha. He paused in wonder. Shafts of sunlight breached the joists between the wooden beams above, illuminating the glittering display of the goldsmiths' toil. Gold-infused rays of sunlight appeared to tilt towards a teahouse that sat on the corner of a small street leading away from the market. The tea room was near-empty, but even so, Ryan kept his gaze downwards until he reached a blue-painted door at the very back of the establishment.

The door opened onto a courtyard garden empty of other customers and staff. Ryan sat at a table in the shade of a pomegranate tree weighed down with crimson flowers. It was early March, and the city's market stalls were still months away from selling the tree's bounty. The sound of approaching footsteps soon signalled to him that his contact was about to arrive. The man who appeared and introduced himself as a government official was not a face Ryan recognised from the hotel lobby. After some small talk, the official eventually said, 'He [Gaddafi] is aware of you and why you are here.'

Ryan had read about the Libyan leader in a *Time* profile that came out just months into Gaddafi's reign. He mentioned this to his companion, and his recollection of the magazine article, along with his effusive praise of Gaddafi's brand of post-colonial Arab nationalism, appeared to impress the nameless government official, who was also particularly interested in Ryan's experiences as a missionary priest, as well as his fluency in French and Swahili. Then, 'There is a problem,' the official said. 'The boat is being loaded tonight. Your fellow travellers are expecting us to load well over 100 tons of a "gift", but the final amount will be much less. You are the only person who knows that.'

Ryan judged that it was not the time to question why the Libyans were not parting with all of their promised bounty. The conversation instead moved to a discussion on the characteristics of colonial rule in Africa, but Ryan was distracted. Given that the *Claudia* was only hours from being loaded, he would need to begin his own journey to the south-east of Ireland soon.

'Would you like to come down to the port and watch on later?' the man asked. Ryan declined the invitation, stood up and thanked the still nameless man for his time. There was no need for anything more to be said. As he side-stepped market traders on his walk back through the maze of the Medina, Ryan was already focused on what he needed to do next: return to Ireland and help organise the *Claudia*'s 'welcoming committee'.

* * *

As darkness fell in Tripoli, a Libyan Navy patrol boat guided the *Claudia* towards an isolated quayside in the port.[1] When the vessel was stationary, its German captain, Hans Ludwig Fleugel, went through his final checks on the Cypriot-registered freighter from the bridge. He had been hired by the ship's owner, Gunther Leinhauser, a German arms dealer, to sail the *Claudia* from Tunis, the capital of Tunisia, to Tripoli, where the arms shipment would be loaded before the ship started on the next leg of its journey, to the south-east of Ireland.

The captain's concentration was interrupted by the headlamps of three Libyan Army lorries illuminating the loading of cases of arms by uniformed members of the Libyan armed services. Joe Cahill was also watching, and holding tight to a suitcase of cash handed to him by a Libyan Army officer.

Hours later, under the north African afternoon sun, the *Claudia* and its crew, along with Cahill and McInerney, set sail for Ireland. The ship's cargo included 247 AKM rifles, 246 bayonets and scabbards, 243 revolvers, close on 100 anti-tank mines, 24,000 rounds of ammunition, 850 magazines, 500 grenades, 300kgs of gelignite and 48lbs of high explosives.[2] In all, five tons of material were on board the vessel, but the IRA's chief of staff had expected to be returning home with a 100-ton war chest. His enemies had expected the same.

A British Intelligence operation was tracking the *Claudia*. MI6 had had the vessel under surveillance for seven months after discovering that she was going to be involved in smuggling weapons to Ireland. On 23 March 1973, as the bow of the *Claudia* cut through the water of the Mediterranean, an urgent telegram sent by the British Foreign Secretary, Sir Alec Douglas-Home, was handed to Sir Arthur Galsworthy, the British Ambassador in Dublin:

> The *Claudia* left North Africa a few days ago carrying up to 100 tons of small arms and explosives reported to have been provided free by the Libyans for delivery to the IRA in the Republic. At least one senior member of the IRA is believed to be on board. The ship is due to rendezvous with two Irish fishing trawlers off the coast between Dungarvan and Waterford ...
>
> *Claudia* is to be located and kept under discreet surveillance by British maritime forces. The latter will not repeat any attempt to intercept or board on the high seas, nor take any action in the final stages which would infringe Irish sovereignty. The primary purpose of the surveillance operation is to establish beyond all reasonable doubt that *Claudia* is proceeding to

the rendezvous. We consider that interception of this arms shipment should be a matter for the Irish government ...

You should take urgent steps to inform [the Taoiseach] Mr Cosgrave of the above ...[3]

Galsworthy did exactly what he had been ordered to do.

Taoiseach Liam Cosgrave had only been in power for ten days when he learned the detail of the British Intelligence report, but in this new Taoiseach the IRA faced a formidable foe, both ideological and personal. Cosgrave's childhood underpinned his unyielding opposition to militant Irish republicanism. One of his earliest memories was standing in the burnt-out ruins of his family home in County Dublin, which had been destroyed by republicans during Ireland's Civil War.[4] Decades later, the Provisional IRA that emerged in 1969 was the single biggest threat to the legitimacy of the Irish state, and Cosgrave had already proved himself adept at halting arms shipments intended for use by northern republicans. As leader of the opposition in 1970, he provided the then Taoiseach, Jack Lynch, with information that implicated government ministers in the illegal importation of arms into the Republic, which were intended for use by Catholics in the North to defend themselves against rising violence. The scandal, known as the 'arms crisis', culminated in the dismissal of Ministers Neil Blaney and Charles Haughey, although in July 1970 charges of conspiring to import arms illegally were dropped against Blaney, while Haughey was acquitted of the charges in October of that year, following two trials.

It was now March 1973 and over eighty people had been killed since the beginning of that year alone as a result of the violence in Northern Ireland. A 100-ton IRA arms shipment on board a Cyprus-registered steamer had to be stopped from reaching its destination. The new Taoiseach wasted no time. Cosgrave summoned his Minister for Defence, Paddy Donegan, and a major security operation got underway with the sole objective of intercepting the *Claudia*.

Patrick Ryan had already made his way back to Tipperary. His return journey from Tripoli was consumed with one question: why was the arms consignment considerably less than what the Libyans had promised? His pursuit of the answer would have to wait. Ryan had been tasked with alerting the IRA's Munster Brigade Commander that an arms shipment was en route, and he had deployed his priestly attire in an effort to expedite his journey home. A Roman collar marked out a man of God in a crowd of any size, but in Ireland it literally opened doors. On his arrival at Dublin Airport the customs officer waved the priest through so he didn't have to wait in line. Ryan nodded solemnly in gratitude, but the irony was not lost on him – all going well, men wearing a different uniform just one hour's drive north would soon be in the crossfire of the guns he had returned to disperse. The customs officer had no notion of whom he had helped, and Ryan was all too aware that few people, if any, would suspect that a Catholic priest was consumed with the dispersal of instruments of bloodshed.

As he drove through the Tipperary countryside, Ryan's eyes were drawn towards the lush green valleys on either side of the road. Bruise-coloured clouds hung heavy overhead and he switched on the car's headlights in anticipation of a heavy rain shower. The scene was a world away from the dry heat of Tripoli, but the clock was ticking. The *Claudia* was only days away from reaching Irish waters.

Earlier that day, Ryan had met with Tom O'Sullivan. 'Paddy and myself ended up organising drivers and dumps at very short notice in Tipperary and down into Waterford.' Ryan's lack of confidence in Cahill had been further heightened on learning that the whole operation had come as a surprise to O'Sullivan. Given that his men would be vital in transporting and arranging dumps for the arms shipment, Ryan thought it reckless that O'Sullivan had been kept in the dark. There was no time to untangle what had happened, however, and Ryan already suspected the arms shipment was doomed to fail, having had a bad feeling about the mission since the Libyans had provided far less than what they had promised.

Despite the last-minute preparations, a plan for an operation to offload the arms was put in place. When the *Claudia* was inside Helvick Harbour off County Waterford, its arms would first be loaded onto a smaller boat at sea, which would then land the shipment at Helvick Pier. From there the arms would be moved onto trucks and driven to various IRA dumps where they could be safely stored. O'Sullivan dispatched half a dozen men from the IRA's Clonmel and Cashel units to Waterford but gave them strict instructions: 'I told the drivers to hang back until we were sure that the shipment was over the line.'

At sea, ominous signs of failure were in plain sight. Two days out from the Irish coast, the captain of the *Claudia* asked McInerney to accompany him to the bridge of the ship. Fleugel pointed to the periscope of a submarine and wanted to know if McInerney felt that they were being followed. 'I remember saying to him it probably was a Russian, as they were always active in that area,' recalled McInerney in an account he gave about his experience decades later.[5] Cahill was also seemingly unperturbed by the possibility that the shipment was being monitored by a submarine, once the captain surmised that it was unlikely to be the British Navy. 'We did not pay a lot of attention to it after that,' he recalled in his biography, 'and were quite confident we were going to make it to Ireland.'[6]

Yet, the *Claudia* was being tracked on its journey towards Ireland both under and over water. As the vessel edged closer to Irish territorial waters, the captain once again spotted the periscope of a submarine and alerted McInerney. 'We saw it again and he pointed out something on the radar screen, saying that they were ships and he felt that they were following us.' Overhead, an RAF Nimrod aircraft, using the reference 'Dandoline', the code name for the *Claudia*, confirmed a sighting of the ship on Ireland's 12-mile territorial limit.[7] Hans Ludwig Fleugel's assessment of the situation was correct: the *Claudia* was sailing into a trap.

On 27 March at 1830 hours, the Irish Navy ship the LÉ *Deirdre* made covert radar contact with the *Claudia* and from that point constantly shadowed the boat. At 1800 hours the next day, the *Claudia* came to a halt and remained stationary just outside Irish territorial waters. Only then did Fleugel decide to share a critical detail with McInerney. 'Before we went into Helvick Harbour, the captain of the ship informed me that Leinhauser told him to expect trouble in Irish waters but nothing would happen to him. This was exactly what occurred.'

As the *Claudia* sailed into Irish territorial waters, three vessels of the Irish Navy were secretly watching and waiting. At naval headquarters in Dublin, Minister for Defence Paddy Donegan followed the incoming reports of the operation as it unfolded. First, a motor launch was observed coming out from Helvick Head. Both the *Claudia* and the launch were under radar observation until the launch made contact with the IRA's boat. Their signals remained merged for some fifteen minutes, time enough for McInerney to disembark from the *Claudia* onto the launch in order to go ashore and check that the onshore transport logistics were in situ before the *Claudia*'s cargo was unloaded as close to shore as feasibly possible. Both vessels then turned and headed in the direction of the small harbour at Helvick Head, while being tracked at a distance by the Irish Navy ships.

When the motor launch and the *Claudia* were a mile from the harbour, the Irish Navy ships turned on their searchlights. There was no escape.

McInerney, who had taken the suitcase of cash given to Cahill in Libya onto the motor launch, hurriedly tied a rope around its handle and threw it overboard. Soon afterwards the *Claudia* was boarded by Irish naval personnel from the LÉ *Deirdre*. There was, according to a report from the British Embassy in Dublin, 'apparently complete surprise and consternation amongst those on the *Claudia* when the boarding party came alongside'.[8] Joe Cahill later recalled being oblivious to what had happened until he felt a gun at his head. 'I was told not to move. It was quite a shock. The crew and the captain said they did not even see them approaching the boat.'[9]

The remaining two Irish Navy minesweepers, the LÉ *Grainne* and LÉ *Fola* moved to intercept the motor launch, which was trying to get away. Trace bullets were fired across its bows. Then a boarding party from the *Grainne* gave chase in a high-speed dinghy, from which more warning shots were fired from pistols.[10] The launch was overtaken just 100 yards from shore, and McInerney and two other men were taken into custody.

The IRA had failed to land its arms shipment and now had two positions to fill: those of chief of staff and QMG. The *Claudia* was escorted to Haulbowline naval base in Cork Harbour, where it was searched, and soldiers from the local barracks unloaded its cargo into army trucks.

Miles from the shoreline, Patrick Ryan and Tom O'Sullivan were waiting in a lorry provided by an IRA sympathiser when word reached them that the *Claudia* had been intercepted. O'Sullivan was incensed. 'We had the men and we would have had the gear if it hadn't been compromised. I was sitting in the lorry and when we got the news, I had a fair idea who had shagged the whole thing up: Joe Cahill.'

The IRA had been caught in the act. At a press conference, Donegan said the successful operation had demonstrated that the

Republic was a law-and-order state. As for the *Claudia*, the minister said that no action would be taken against it or its crew: 'She'll get a boot up the transom and be told to get out of our waters fast.'[11]

However, at least potentially, not all had been lost for the IRA. When Ryan and O'Sullivan learned that the briefcase of cash had been thrown overboard, they knew the man they needed to call on for help to locate the missing loot. Pax Whelan was a former IRA OC during the War of Independence, but more crucially for the task at hand, he was a fisherman in County Waterford. Decades of trawling the seas off the south-east coast of Ireland had gifted Whelan with an innate knowledge of the currents that would be holding the suitcase hostage under the waves. His motivation for trying to salvage something of value from the IRA's failed operation was also personal – his son, Donal 'Duck' Whelan, had been arrested on board the launch boat that was intercepted while taking McInerney from the *Claudia* to Helvick Harbour's pier.

Pax Whelan, along with a number of local fishermen, studied tidal charts and weather forecasts to pinpoint the area to which the suitcase may have drifted. His advice to Ryan and others was explicit: the suitcase could be found, but time was of the essence. They needed to land the bag of cash before waves smashed it to pieces against the rocks.

Ryan was all too aware that salvaging anything of worth was now dependent on the skills of men of the sea. 'The fishermen were able to figure out where the suitcase might be located given the particular area of the sea it was thrown into, so, en masse, they went out.'

The local flotilla faced competition from the Irish state. On land, gardaí were conducting a wide search of the coastline in the hope that whatever was dumped overboard would be washed up on the shore. At the same time, at sea, Irish Navy divers were combing the seabed in ten-minute intervals over several hours in an effort to retrieve the suitcase from under the waves. Their combined efforts may have been rewarded had they paid closer attention to what was happening on board one of the fishing trawlers circling the same waters. When a local fisherman spied the piece of rope in the sea he reached in, carefully tied it to the boat and towed the suitcase into the port, right under the nose of the navy.

The IRA's then finance officer, Des Long, who was aware of the recovery efforts, made his way to Dungarvan. 'I got word about the suitcase, so I went down and was handed a soggy mess in a pillowcase. I brought it to Marcus Fogarty, the officer commanding of south Tipperary and said, "Marcus, I have a job for you, here's a pile of money for you to dry."'[12]

In a one-bedroom flat in the town of Cashel, Marcus Fogarty and Patrick Ryan got to work. The flat had been loaned to the IRA by a couple who had vacated the property without asking any questions. 'The money was saturated right through,' said Marcus Fogarty, 'but the Padre and myself were determined that not one note would be lost on our watch; we were days at it.'[13]

The production line began in the bathroom, where Ryan filled the bath with water. The first stage in cleansing the notes of seawater involved washing them one by one before pegging them onto a makeshift clothes line that ran the length of the living room. 'The money was full of seawater, so we decided we'd first better wash the money to try and remove the stench of the salt water.'

In the kitchen, Fogarty focused on the second stage, drying each note individually. 'It'd come off the clothes line and I'd get to work with a hairdryer until eventually we were taking turns using the dryer and then an iron to straighten the notes out once they were dry. The Padre and myself were money laundering and we didn't even know it.'

The three-day operation yielded $100,000 dollars and £16,000, a sum that Ryan had initially feared was lost forever to the sea. 'I made sure to give it over to the right person, who forwarded it to its destination in the North.'

In Marcus Fogarty, Ryan had made a friend for life. It was Fogarty who coined the moniker that would follow him for decades: the Padre. 'I started calling him that rather than saying Father Paddy. I suppose given what we were up to, the Padre was fairly neutral.'

By the time Fogarty and Ryan were tidying up the flat to hand it back to its tenants, the *Claudia* and its crew had long left Irish waters. Just twelve hours after they had been intercepted, the German captain and his crew, escorted by a pilot vessel, sailed out of Cork Harbour. As the *Claudia* pulled away, an Irish Navy commander called out to Hans Ludwig Fleugel: 'We don't want to see you back again.'[14]

The *Claudia* had not reached Hamburg, Germany's largest port, when its owner described the Irish security crackdown as a 'regrettable flop'. In his remarks, Gunther Leinhauser conceded he had done a deal with the IRA but appeared keen to distance himself from what had gone wrong. 'We had been contacted by the IRA for the shipment,' he said. 'The cargo was to be taken off the ship outside the three-mile zone and then this regrettable flop occurred. It was our first and only contract with the IRA.' Leinhauser added that he feared reprisals from Middle East contacts if he spoke too freely about the ship and claimed that the seizure left him short-changed – he had only received half his payment on the deal, on a 'half before, half afterwards basis'.[15]

The cargo, like Leinhauser's payment from the IRA, had come up short. Just like the IRA and British Intelligence, the German arms dealer had expected the *Claudia* to be carrying about 100 tons of arms and explosives. 'I don't know what happened to the other 95 tons. They could have been dropped overboard when the crew realised what was going to happen,' he said.

As the *Claudia* docked on a windswept quay in Hamburg, West German police confirmed that they had already launched an investigation into the ownership of the ship. Leinhauser insisted that, in this instance, a technicality meant he could not be accused of smuggling. 'The West German arms export laws only forbid the export of West German arms to areas of tension or war. None of the arms in this shipment were German.'[16]

It was not the first time that the arms dealer had come to the attention of the police and security agencies. In 1967 he received a suspended nine-month prison sentence for smuggling Czechoslovakian arms to Kurdish rebels in Iraq. 'I supported the Kurdish cause,' Leinhauser said. 'The deal with the Irish was more business.'

At the Special Criminal Court in Dublin on 21 May 1973, Joe Cahill was sentenced to three years for his role in the *Claudia* gunrunning operation. In a speech from the dock, he told the three judges: 'It has been my proud privilege and honour to serve as a soldier of the Irish Republican Army. If I am guilty of any crime, it is that I did not succeed in getting the contents of the *Claudia* into the hands of the freedom fighters of this country. And I believe that national treachery was committed off Helvick when the Free State forces conspired with our British enemies to deprive our freedom fighters of the weapons of war.'[17]

Denis McInerney received a two-year sentence and shouted to the judges: 'You can now go ahead and earn your thirty pieces of silver.' Gerard Murphy and Donal Whelan, who had gone out in the motor launch to rendezvous with the *Claudia*, were each given suspended sentences of two years. Another man, Sean Garvey, who was found aboard the *Claudia*, was sentenced to two years in prison.

In Tripoli, ahead of their ill-fated voyage, Cahill had shared a decision he had made with McInerney. 'Before we left Libya, Joe Cahill informed me that he intended to appoint Paddy Ryan, a priest from Tipperary, as our representative there when we returned home.' The *Claudia* episode marked Ryan's emergence as the IRA's man in Libya, but the failure of the mission motivated Ryan to make a critical decision concerning his security. 'After the *Claudia*, I decided then that I would spend all my time, as much as possible, out of Ireland. You see, McInerney and Cahill were gone, so effectively I was the only one that was left.'

SEVEN

THE SLEEPERS

A relentless drizzle of rain sheathed everything in its path including the seven escapees as one by one they slid down a steel hawser mooring the prison ship in Belfast Lough. Weeks of plotting had led to the daring moment just minutes earlier, when one of the prisoners used a fretsaw that had been smuggled on board to cut through a metal bar on the outside of a porthole. The blade worked better than the men could have hoped for; when pushed outwards, the bar snapped like a twig.

Peter Rogers was the second-last man to crawl out, and the socks he was wearing to protect his hands helped to propel his glide down the steel cable that overshot catch nets and barbed wire. The razor entanglements were set up to crush any prisoner's ambitions of escape, but there was a critical design flaw: the wardens had failed to spot the opportunity presented by a cable that ran out at an angle from the prison ship into the waters of the lough. By using a deck brush, the escapees had been able to reach out and pull that particular cable towards the porthole, catch onto it and slide down into the water, avoiding the security nets.

After Rogers carefully submerged his body into the lough, he counted five other pairs of discarded socks bobbing like apples on the surface of the water. To survive he needed to start swimming, and fast.

It was 17 January 1972 and Rogers, Tommy Gorman, Thomas 'Tucker' Kane, Martin Taylor, Seán Convery, Jim Bryson and Tommy Tolan were seven of some 150 detainees on board the prison floating in Belfast Lough. Originally a Royal Navy submarine depot ship, HMS *Maidstone* had been dispatched to Belfast in October 1969 as emergency accommodation for 2,000 British troops, but in 1971 she was recommissioned as Her Majesty's Prison *Maidstone* to help cope with overcrowding at Belfast city's Crumlin Road Gaol, where there was not enough room to hold the scores arrested as a result of the army's Operation Demetrius – internment without trial.

The devolved government in Northern Ireland had introduced internment to deal with escalating violence. Ministers, reluctantly backed by London, decided to use the Special Powers Act in an attempt to take those it believed responsible for the violence off the streets. Northern Ireland Prime Minister Brian Faulkner said that the aim was to smash the IRA. Just before dawn on 9 August 1971, troops raided hundreds of homes in republican areas in the hope of arresting and interning IRA leaders and activists, but the intelligence the army relied on was largely out of date and most key IRA members avoided the round-up. Within forty-eight hours, a third of those detained had been released.

Internment without trial inflamed an already volatile situation: instead of halting the violence, the policy marked a milestone in its escalation. The mass arrests sparked a terrifying wave of rioting, shooting and bombing, which engulfed Northern Ireland. Twenty-three people lost their lives in three days alone, including the ten people who died in the Ballymurphy Massacre in west Belfast.

Peter Rogers, like other IRA men, had managed to avoid being picked up in the first tranche of army arrests. Months later, his brigade commander ordered him to undertake a specific task. 'Myself and another IRA fella had been looking for targets and reporting to

Seamus Twomey. One evening the news came on and Paisley was kicking off over two separate IRA escapes that had happened within weeks of each other from Crumlin Road Gaol.'[1] Ian Paisley, the unionist MP and firebrand preacher, was incensed that the IRA was appearing to make a mockery of prison security – on 3 December 1971 three IRA men, using bed sheets roughly fashioned into a rope ladder, managed to scale the wall of Crumlin Road Gaol just weeks after another nine IRA members, dubbed the Crumlin Kangaroos, had fled after climbing rope ladders over the outside wall in the prison exercise yard.

After the second prison breakout, Belfast was brought to a standstill, with roadblocks set up on all the main exits from the city, but it was too late and the IRA men had already made it safely over the border to Dundalk. As Twomey watched a television news report about the escape, a particular remark caught the IRA commander's attention. Rogers recalled, 'This British Army Major came on and he went as far as to say that there was only one place that was secure and that was the *Maidstone*. So when the news was finished, Seamus Twomey turns around and says to us, "Make the *Maidstone* a priority target."'

Rogers had little time to carry out the order from the outside looking in. 'We were in the throes of what we could do when we were picked up and ended up on the ship as prisoners, so we had to work from the inside out.'

The assertion that the *Maidstone* was secure was not a boastful remark. With hundreds of troops billeted on board, regular patrols of its prison quarters by warders, an army patrol of the docks adjacent to the ship, and the hazards of low temperatures and tidal currents in Belfast Lough, the *Maidstone* was regarded by many as 'escape proof'. However, Rogers was one of a group of IRA men who were willing to test that theory. 'The ship was berthed against the quay wall and there was an army base on that side so you couldn't escape out in that direction – our only option was to get out on the other side and swim across the Musgrave Channel. It seemed like a crazy idea, but I was prepared to take the risk.'

For a few short weeks, the group focused on testing the ship's security infrastructure with forensic intensity. After stoking tensions between the local warders and those recruited from England who were better paid, the men managed to reduce what had been near-constant patrols of their living quarters. The lack of prying eyes allowed Rogers and a select few to study the security infrastructure in more detail. 'We needed to find out if there were sounding devices in the water and, as luck would have it, a supply ship pulled up one night alongside the *Maidstone* and the security lights from the dock cast our ship's silhouette onto the side of the supply ship, which is how, through a porthole, we could see the shadows of the soldiers patrolling the ship's top deck. We filled gallon cans with water and when the soldiers above came in line with the porthole we dropped the cans into the water.'

The splash only caused ripples, proving that the soldiers did not hear the cans drop into the lough, while the continuing silence afterwards confirmed the absence of underwater alarms. A visual lack of insulated cables reassured the men of an absence of electric wires welded to the ship, and a hungry seal feeding off waste food they threw from portholes proved to be a helpful portend of what was to come. 'If the seal could freely swim so close to the entanglements, then so could we.'

By mid-January 1972 Rogers and others were increasingly aware that time was against them. The transfer of fifty men from the ship to a new internment camp at Magilligan Army Camp in County Derry on 16 January, raised fears of a complete evacuation of the *Maidstone*. 'We were nearly three weeks on the ship and authorities had to decide within twenty-eight days whether to release, charge or intern you elsewhere, so a decision was imminent and could be made at any time, so we had to move very fast.'

On 17 January a Belfast sky full of heavy clouds and a calm lough created near-perfect conditions to activate the escape plan. It took eight minutes for the seven men to slide down the steel cable and into the water. Rogers, like the others, was prepared for a drastic change in body temperature. 'We'd stripped down to our underwear, but we didn't feel the cold because we'd slathered boot polish and butter on our bodies and, at the very last minute, our faces, which effectively waterproofed our skin.' There was no going back; the men could either swim for their lives or succumb to the current. Rogers steadied himself before he committed to a breaststroke across the channel. 'I wasn't a strong swimmer, but I could see the lads in front me and my confidence started to grow. As the current got stronger, my arms got weaker, so I turned over on my back and floated for a while and did the back paddle. What really got me going was what I thought was a ship coming up the middle of the channel that turned out to be a marker buoy. I feared I'd be spliced in two and by Jesus that spurred me on to shore.'

The seven men swam the near 400 yards across the Musgrave Channel and eventually reached the agreed rendezvous point on Queen's Island. However, their IRA transport had been and gone, forcing them to improvise. One of them, Tommy Gorman, found an empty bus and Rogers, who had been a bus driver with Belfast Corporation, took control of the double-decker. 'It was mayhem, we had a two-mile journey in front of us to get clear of the docks and I was flying along at full speed and all the while the lads were shouting to hurry up and then they started shouting, "Up the Provos", while waving at people waiting to be picked up by our bus.' The escapees made it out of the docks and across Belfast's Queen's bridge a few minutes before it was blocked by a military cordon after the alarm was raised. By the time the army put a cordon around the Markets area of the city, a republican stronghold to which they'd fled, the *Maidstone* escapees were long gone.

The customary IRA press conference followed days later in a Dublin hotel, where the so-called 'Magnificent Seven' were paraded before waiting journalists and photographers. The escapees were joined by the IRA's then chief of staff, Seán Mac Stíofáin, who was keen to highlight what the men had achieved. 'An escape is a great publicity coup and every escape is of great importance,' he said.[2] Asked why the seven men had been singled out for the escape attempt and what they would do now they were free, Mac Stíofáin replied that the men had been chosen by the escape committee on board the *Maidstone* on the 'basis of their future contribution to the republican movement and the IRA's Army Council would decide what they should do'.[3]

Peter Rogers immediately returned to IRA active service and by the summer of 1973 was based in the south-east of Ireland, working on a ferry that travelled between Rosslare, County Wexford, and Le Havre. His job as an assistant steward was merely a front for what the IRA had tasked him to do: assist IRA men and women who were travelling back and forward, as well as set up a guns and money-smuggling route. Rogers' shift patterns, along with the ferry schedule, gave him ample time to try to locate material in France that might prove useful to the IRA's armed campaign. 'I first went and got all the literature I could on remote controls that were used on model aeroplanes and I took that back to the General Headquarters [GHQ] staff in Dublin. At that stage, I was back dealing with Seamus Twomey again and another man, J.B. O'Hagan.'

Father Patrick Ryan had also made contact with Twomey, who was the IRA's new chief of staff. It was only months since the *Claudia* debacle, and Ryan was keen to follow through on Joe Cahill's suggestion that he should become the IRA's representative in Libya. There was just the matter of two specific conditions that the IRA needed to agree to before Ryan would commit to working for them. First, he would not join the IRA, and second, he would walk away if any money or material he acquired was misappropriated. His self-determined parameters went to the very core of what he wanted most in his life: control.

Ryan had little regard or sentimentality for his priestly vocation. His status as a Catholic priest may have afforded him the ease of doors opening within Irish society, but the novelty had long worn off. He feared he could be ordered to return to missionary work and resented the control his superiors had over him, as well as the political machinations and bureaucratic submissiveness it would take for him to progress within the Church's ranks to any position of power. His experience with Bishop Winters in East Africa had taught him that he was far more productive, and safer, when he acted alone.

For Ryan, there was also the matter of a very different ideology to be acted upon. Following the events of the summer of 1969, as he saw it, religion was a folly in the face of a very different dogma. 'Nationalism motivated me more than anything else; sure, what use was religion to me when dealing with a colonising power?'

His first trip to Libya had made him feel confident in his own abilities, and the fact that the operation – for which he had no re-sponsibility – had failed only added to his feeling that he would be of more use as a lone operator. He was determined to demonstrate to the IRA that a far superior system could be seamlessly set up, that it just needed to be carefully tended to and that he was the man to do this.

Ryan's meeting with Twomey took place in an IRA safe house in Whitehall, a residential suburb situated on the northside of Dublin city. The one-time Belfast commander was then living in Dublin and had taken over as chief of staff in the immediate aftermath of Cahill's arrest on board the *Claudia*. (Twomey would later have to vacate the position following his own arrest by gardaí in County Monaghan.) A priority for Twomey at that point was getting the Tipperary priest who had been singled out by his predecessor to formally begin working on behalf of the IRA. Also present at the meeting was Joe B. O'Hagan, who, like Twomey, was a founding member of the Provisional IRA.

The three men sat in a living room devoid of any natural light. Heavy velvet curtains blocked out the sun, making the starched white square of Ryan's clerical collar glow. A knock on the front door signalled the arrival of a fourth man: Peter Rogers. 'I was told to meet Seamus and J.B. in that house, and it was where I was first introduced to Father Paddy Ryan. J.B. said hello to me and ran upstairs to get me money and a list of items they wanted me to try and find in France, so I sat down and listened to the conversation between Seamus and this priest fella.'

Ryan spoke with the conviction of a priest giving a sermon he had crafted for days. He had practised his proposal aloud as he parked his car around a corner from the safe house. Before he turned off the ignition, he had watched two young women pushing prams. The scene reminded him of his time in Barking and, in particular, of the mothers who would ring the parish house, nervously pleading for baptismal dates for their newborns. Whatever lay ahead, Ryan was certain that he had no interest in ever being dispatched again to a parish to administer the Holy Sacraments.

Twomey did not interrupt as Ryan carefully outlined the conditions on which he would accept his IRA posting. 'I will give you a hand out, but I won't join the IRA and remember I am rendering my services for free, and they can be taken back any time, and equally you can accept my services and you can reject them at any time.'

The chief of staff was curious. Why would a man about to travel the world to collect money and weapons for the IRA, not want to join the organisation? Ryan did not miss a beat. 'I joined the Catholic Church, that's bad enough.'

Rogers sat still and waited to be spoken to. It was not the fact that a Catholic priest was offering his time and effort to the IRA's cause, contrary to the morality espoused in the Church's teachings, which struck him; rather it was that this particular priest spoke with a ruthless clarity of purpose. 'It didn't come as a surprise that Father Paddy was willing to help – I'd met many a priest within the movement that would help me – but, in this instance, Father Paddy was very clear on what he wouldn't do; he wasn't going to join, he was going to be his own man.'

Twomey took no time to reflect on what was being proposed and turned towards Rogers. 'Seamus Twomey said to me, "Peter, will you look after Fr Ryan as regards getting him civilian clothes and stuff."'

On their excursion to department stores in Dublin city, Rogers and Ryan were quite the odd pairing. Despite his education and travels in Africa, Ryan appeared to have no idea about how to dress as a so-called 'civilian' and the Belfast man was flabbergasted by some of Ryan's sartorial choices. 'By God, you would want to see the get-up that he was wanting to buy. He really hadn't a clue about how to dress normally, I mean he was picking out the likes of shirts you'd see in Hawaii or someplace and I was saying, "Jesus, Paddy, no, you can't buy that, you're going out to represent people, put that stuff away." Then, whenever we'd sit down in a restaurant, it was like a sermon whenever he was talking to you. He'd say, "Oh, my illustrious friend," and I told him, "Paddy, would you ever tone that down a wee bit." I mean, Jesus, Mary and Saint Joseph, everybody who heard him would know from the way he was talking that I was sitting there with a priest, and, to be fair, he did tone it down and we got on very well.'

In Rogers, Ryan recognised someone who was a valuable asset; a straight talker, but streetwise enough to know when to stop speaking, with an energetic eagerness to please but cunning enough to recognise when to dial it down and quietly ingratiate himself with those who were oblivious to his true intentions. In a bustling restaurant off O'Connell Street, Ryan had listened to Rogers explain how he had worked hard on the ferry to get promoted out of the catering quarters to a role that put him front of house and, therefore, in a more valuable position to carry out what he was actually there to do. Rogers also disclosed that he had already sized up a number of long-haul lorry drivers who signalled that they would be willing to help a friend at some stage down the line. The Belfast man now had a reason to call in those promises.

With a suitcase of smart civilian clothes, and furnished with false identification documents including a passport, driving licence and seaman's record book, Ryan was now on the brink of beginning his travels, in earnest, on behalf of the IRA. His clerical collar was *in absentia* as he took cover as a passenger in the back of an IRA-'friendly' lorry. 'I was lying low in a sleeping bunk so I'd get on board the ferry. Peter had it organised for me to go straight into a cabin while the ferry was sailing.' When the ferry docked in Le Havre, Ryan knew to remain in situ. 'I waited three hours and only left as the staff were going downtown, so no one clocked me. That system was all thanks to Peter.'

It was only after he had arrived in France that Ryan realised that he was without one vital document – proof of vaccinations for foreign travel. In Dublin, word got back to Seamus Twomey that Ryan was stuck in limbo at Le Havre and, once again, tasked Rogers with sorting out the problem. In Cork city, Rogers went to see a doctor who was willing to help the IRA get over the proof of vaccinations predicament.

'I was expecting to get the yellow book stamped and that would be it, but the doctor left the room and all of a sudden the nurse tells me to roll up my sleeves. I had to take the injections and I was as sick as a dog for days. When I went back to Le Havre, Paddy couldn't believe how far I'd gone. He said, "Peter, if I need something I'll not bypass you." I said, "Paddy, that's what I'm here for." I didn't see him again for many months; he was doing his own thing.'

EIGHT

OUR MAN IN TRIPOLI

France was in turmoil. As Patrick Ryan walked past a newspaper kiosk in Paris, he paused to scan the front pages of *Le Parisien* and *Le Monde*. The woman standing in the kiosk's little box looked at him and gloomily shrugged her shoulders; there was little respite from daily headlines of high unemployment and rising inflation during an ongoing energy crisis.

It was 1974, decades on from the time when a Nazi swastika flew above the Arc de Triomphe after German troops entered and occupied Paris, and yet, once again the City of Light was being plunged into darkness. A ban on illuminated advertising, lighting in shop windows and empty offices between 10 p.m. and 7 a.m., as well as the darkening of public monuments, were just some of the fuel-conservation measures in place to reduce energy consumption. 'The French economy is not isolated, nor can it be isolated,' the Finance Minister, Valéry Giscard d'Estaing, said. 'It is linked in thousands of ways first to the economies of our European partners and then to the entire planet.'[1]

The French minister was echoing the economic despair being felt across much of Europe and beyond. The political and economic foundations of the Western world had been overturned by a dramatic event in October 1973: the Arab oil embargo. Designed initially to

punish the US for its support of Israel during its war with a coalition
of Arab states led by Egypt and Syria, the oil embargo by the
Organisation of Arab Petroleum Exporting Countries (OAPEC) on
the US led to the quadrupling of oil prices. Although France was not
subject to the embargo, its economy was not immune to the global
recession that followed in the wake of the shortages.

With a newspaper under his arm, Ryan discreetly took a couple
of steps back from the painted white lines of a pedestrian crossing
to allow a man wearing a faded cardboard sign marked 'S.V.P. DE
L'ESSENCE' (petrol please) wearily cycle past without having to
brake. The cyclist's homemade plea for fuel seemed light-hearted in
comparison to reports Ryan had read about fights breaking out amid
long queues at some petrol stations as tempers reached boiling point
over the shortages. Ryan purposefully touched the inside breast pocket
of his heavy wool coat for the envelope he had collected earlier that
day from the Libyan Embassy in the city. The visa it contained was
his gateway to Tripoli, and his timing, as he saw it, was serendipitous
– his return to Libya coincided with a transformation of the power
and influence Gaddafi could wield on the back of his country's black
gold.

When Libya became independent in 1951, it was considered by
many to be one of the poorest countries in the world and depended
on foreign aid for its survival. All that changed in 1959 with the
discovery of significant oil reserves in the Sirte Basin. In late 1961
Libya made its initial entry into the international petroleum market.
Less than eight years later, the country occupied a position of
international importance as one of the world's major oil-producing
nations.[2]

Location and a major geopolitical edge gifted the north African
country profit-making advantages over other major oil producers.
It took about ten days for an oil tanker to reach England from

the Arabian Gulf via the Suez Canal, compared with just six days from Libya, a market advantage that only accelerated with Egypt's unexpected closure of the Suez Canal for eight years from 1967. Libya dramatically went from being one of the poorest nations in the world to a very rich one based on average per-capita gross domestic product. But ordinary Libyans felt that little of the country's new wealth from the oil boom was filtering down, and so Gaddafi's coup in 1969 had been met with popular support.

Only months after taking power, Gaddafi demanded a higher price for Libyan oil and a majority share of the revenues. When the oil companies responded with what he considered an insulting offer, he announced, 'people who have lived without oil for 5,000 years can live without it again for a few years in order to attain their legitimate rights'.[3] The gambit succeeded and Gaddafi became the first Arab leader to stand up to the oil companies and win a better deal for his country, causing the Shah in Iran and the King of Saudi Arabia to follow suit. In October 1973 governments in the West woke up to the reality of the extent of their vulnerability to oil-producing countries, as the oil embargo signalled a seismic shift in global politics and economic power. The era of low-priced oil was over and the crisis marked a dramatic shift in international relations.

While the IRA's *Claudia* arms operation in March 1973 had failed, this did not discourage Gaddafi from publicly reiterating his support for the IRA. In an interview published in *Le Figaro* in April, the Libyan leader admitted that his government had given aid to the Irish organisation. Gaddafi was asked: 'You are said to have financed, and to be continuing to finance, the Irish guerrilla army against the English. Was there something during your stay in England that led to this decision?' His reply was, 'No, you can't say that it was my stay in England which provoked my hatred against the English. There is a history of English dealings with the Arabs which goes back for decades, even before my birth. So the reason for our support to the Irish guerrillas is justified. It is a little country which has taken up arms to defend its rights and its freedom. We have given it our support.'[4]

At a press conference in Paris in November that same year, Gaddafi said that Libya intended to continue aiding the IRA because they were representatives 'of a little people fighting for their liberty against a great State'.[5] His vocal support for the IRA did not go unnoticed. At Westminster in January 1974, Lord Balniel, the Minister of State for Foreign and Commonwealth Affairs, told the House of Commons that 'strong protests' had been made to the Libyan government 'on a number of occasions about Colonel Qadhafi's support for the IRA. We have made it clear that Her Majesty's Government regard this as a blatant interference in the internal affairs of the United Kingdom … A close and constant watch is being kept on the supplies which are made available to the IRA.'[6]

As he left Paris in 1974, Ryan felt more at ease about what lay ahead on this trip, given that this time he was travelling alone on behalf of the IRA. It was only his second trip to Tripoli and, despite Gaddafi's public support, in the wake of the *Claudia* debacle, the extent to which the Libyan regime remained committed to providing material help to the IRA was unclear. So re-establishing a form of diplomatic contact was among the tasks Ryan had been asked to see through. At forty-four years of age, the Padre was beginning a new phase in his life, one in which he was determined to be solely responsible for the choices he would make.

It was two decades on from his first mailboat trip across the Irish Sea, and as he joined the queue at the departure gate for Tripoli at Le Bourget Airport, Ryan noticed the long line of businessmen standing in front of him who were leaving France to finalise contracts and cash in on opportunities in Libya. The two countries had signed an agreement in principle for a long-term programme of Libyan economic development. In short, France would get oil in return for aid in a variety of industrial projects; the official communiqué published with the agreement included ships, telephone installations, agricultural development and financial and banking services as areas for future specific deals.[7]

Libya was a country in economic and social flux. Increasing state control over the oil sector had seen gross domestic product rise three-fold, to $13.7 billion. Gaddafi's RCC, which governed the country, had the economic ability to dramatically improve living standards. Education had been made compulsory up to the age of sixteen and, in an attempt to address a shortage of technologically trained manpower, the government encouraged the growth of engineering, agriculture and medicine in the universities. A shortage of trained teachers was made up by importing them from other Arab countries, and lucrative contracts attracted dozens of young teaching graduates from Britain and Ireland on 'Teaching English as a Foreign Language' (TEFL) sabbaticals.

In his hotel in Tripoli, Ryan waited for his Libyan intelligence contact to signal that a meeting would be forthcoming. There was no way of knowing when the message would come and Ryan knew he had to be patient – contact would eventually be made. Over breakfast every morning, he observed the other hotel residents with curiosity. He surmised that many had travelled to take advantage of the skilled labour shortages. 'The Libyans had their own people, but not too many, as they were only beginning to get on their feet, so they had a lot of foreign labour, professionals like engineers and teachers.' As he drank his coffee, Ryan noticed in particular how few of the foreign hotel guests made eye contact with each other; it was like they had to steel themselves for another long day of negotiations in order to close whatever deal had brought them to the city.

The days may have been longer for some of the guests on account of a ban on the sale of alcohol. Before the revolution in 1969, foreign workers could find recreation in nightclubs or gambling dens, but Gaddafi banned alcohol in all its forms from the first days of coming to power. He also closed bars, nightclubs and casinos. On Saturdays and Sundays the hotel breakfast area was noticeably quieter, and Ryan assumed that many guests had cashed in some of their oil dollars and crossed the border to Tunisia for a weekend of drinking and partying.

In Tripoli Ryan met all manner of people on the make from the oil-rich Libyan regime, including former US military helicopter pilots. 'They had been hired to train Libyan army pilots and it was striking how those who had fought in Vietnam were all damaged in some intangible way by what they went through. They only ever wanted an ear to listen to them, but they told me everything that was going on and we would discuss philosophy and religion. Whatever they believed in or not, they never met an atheist in a foxhole in Vietnam.' The individuals linked to the United States' Central Intelligence Agency (CIA), who were behind the supply of some of these former US military men to train Gaddafi's army, would emerge from the shadows at a later point.

During his days of hanging around while waiting for meetings, Ryan did what always proved productive for ruminating over plans – he walked and walked. Being a *flaneur*, and wandering the streets of Tripoli with no particular destination, was how he first came across the Ahmed Pasha al-Qaramanli mosque in the heart of the Old City. He was unsure of the etiquette he was required to adhere to, so he followed the lead of the other men who had arrived ahead of midday prayer. An older man helpfully gestured towards the area to leave his shoes and Ryan duly complied but skipped ablution before he entered the prayer hall. The absence of any seats or pews momentarily took him aback. He had known not to expect any, but the vastness of the relatively empty space stood in sharp contrast to the richly decorated blue and yellow floral tiles that covered the walls, along with white marble columns and geometric stuccowork displayed on the arches and domes. He had read about the mihrab, the point nearest to Mecca in each mosque, and stayed watching from the back of the prayer hall out of respect and curiosity.

When Ryan arrived back in the hotel, the receptionist gestured to him and handed him a note stating only a time and location for the following day. The sparseness of the message spoke volumes – if he had been under observation he had passed the test and, as he waited in the assigned teahouse the next afternoon, he instinctively knew that there would be no mention of the *Claudia* by his Libyan intelligence contact. 'There was no chatter about what had gone wrong and I didn't raise it, partly because we got more supplies after that and some of these supplies came on smaller boats, totally unannounced belonging to certain, if you like, private people, and these got quietly through the net. Gaddafi was committed to providing assistance, so why would I bring up the mess that was the *Claudia*?'

Ryan noted how his intelligence contact spoke English with a lyrical cadence, in rhythm with the gestures of his right arm. The man's style of almost conducting his spoken thoughts explained why he only began to converse in earnest after he had placed his teacup back on its saucer, when his right arm was free to gesticulate his thoughts in order to emphasise the point he was building up to: how Ryan would access the support Gaddafi was willing to make available to the IRA. 'We agreed a system whereby the officials I'd liaise with in Tripoli would give me a certain time period to call and collect packages from the Libyan Embassy in Rome or from their Embassy in Paris.'

Whether it was considered gauche or plainly unnecessary, neither Ryan or his intelligence contact explicitly spoke about the one thing that lured almost every outsider to Libya in an effort to make, borrow or steal it, and the thing he would be collecting in those packages from the embassies: cash. 'We never once mentioned money, we spoke about everything else under the sun except money and that's how it was from that trip onwards.'

In the Libyan capital Ryan was also introduced to the man whose patronage the IRA was eager to retain: Gaddafi. 'I was dealing with the Colonel in Libya a lot of the time. I'm loath to talk about our discussions – he was more informed about the IRA than they might ever have thought likely, but our discussions were of matters far beyond Ireland or Britain, and in terms of money from Libya, I took what I got. Over all the years I was involved, there was more than one million pounds involved; far more millions.'

Patrick Ryan was playing the long game and his endeavours on behalf of the IRA were bolstered by an early ambition to cultivate his contacts within the Libyan regime who could prove useful in recommending other potential opportunities for him to pursue in Europe. Returning to Libya necessitated careful security considerations and when he travelled to Tripoli later that year, he was somewhat taken aback to learn that he was not the only Irish man on IRA business in the country. In the hotel lobby, he spotted a small man of a slight build with lank brown hair almost to his shoulder. On hearing the man's accent, he immediately recognised it as Irish. 'There were various people who turned up in Tripoli while I was out there, for what or by whose directive, I was never too sure, but they weren't doing me, or what I was at, any good, and one of those was a man named Eddie.'

Eddie O'Donnell, a schoolteacher from County Monaghan, had first travelled to Libya in 1972 to teach mathematics at Tripoli College. He was back in Ireland when he was approached by a member of the IRA Army Council and asked to instead act as an 'ambassador' for the IRA.[8] In 1974 Shane Paul O'Doherty, an IRA bomber from Derry, was introduced to O'Donnell. 'My stock with the leadership was high on the back of a letter-bomb campaign I'd carried out in London and that's how I met Eddie O'Donnell. He was hanging around with senior IRA men, telling stories about his meetings with Gaddafi and how interested Gaddafi was in the IRA.'[9]

Tom O'Sullivan, the Munster OC, was unimpressed when he met O'Donnell at an IRA meeting in Dublin. 'Some of the Belfast crew had so many different agendas you wouldn't know what they were up to, but O'Donnell didn't strike me as a man that should be sent to Libya. Don't get me wrong, Paddy [Ryan] could be hard enough to handle at times, he was very set in his ways, but he was very well got with the Libyans and had a level of access at the very top.'

Eddie O'Donnell's travels to Tripoli were not clandestine, nor was he too modest to go on the record about his connection to the Libyan leader, albeit not about his IRA role. 'Teacher from Monaghan who is Libya's Irish middleman', said the front-page headline of an *Irish Times* report about him in April 1975. In the interview, O'Donnell claimed that he had met the Libyan leader when he took part in a rally outside Gaddafi's home. The gathering was in response to the shooting down by Israeli fighter jets of a Libyan Arab Airlines plane that had flown off course into prohibited air space over the Sinai Peninsula in 1973: of the 113 people on board, there were just five survivors. O'Donnell said that during the rally he carried a placard which, 'to the best of his memory', stated, 'Ireland mourns for you', and when Gaddafi saw the placard, he asked to meet the Irishman, who went on to become an 'educational adviser in the Libyan government'.[10]

'Colonel Khaddafi's interest in Ireland began at the time of his own revolution,' said O'Donnell. 'There were many Irish nurses and teachers here at the time. There was also the history of Ireland: most Arab states are pro-Irish because of their common history of colonialism. If Cornwall was occupied by the French or Yorkshire by the Danes, Colonel Khaddafi would give support to the British. He says that himself, but he took a stand against what he called "unrightful interference" in Ireland's affairs.[11] However, O'Donnell was less forthcoming about Libyan arms shipments to the IRA: 'There has never been any firm evidence of this.'

Patrick Ryan's surprise at meeting the Monaghan man quickly turned to suspicion when he spoke to O'Donnell. 'He told me that he was a teacher and that he was on a mission to establish peace between the loyalists and the IRA.'

The Monaghan man's peace mission backfired in 1974. That November, he secured an 'invitation' for the Ulster Defence Association (UDA), the largest loyalist paramilitary group in Northern Ireland, to travel to Tripoli at the same time as a delegation from Sinn Féin, the republican movement's political wing, was also there. Reports that the talks had been peace negotiations between the IRA and the UDA were described as 'marvellous pieces of invention' by a Dublin businessman, who claimed that the talks had concerned financial matters and the development of Ireland's offshore oil and gas resources.[12]

The episode, however, proved to be a publicity coup for the UDA, after its representatives said they had used the trip to press for a reversal of the Libyan policy of supplying arms to the IRA. 'The Libyan Government appeared to be under the impression that the IRA were Freedom Fighters,' said Glenn Barr, a leading UDA representative on the visit. 'We were able to show them the other side of the coin.' Newspaper reports of a *tête-à-tête* between Ulster loyalists and Irish republicans in Tripoli prompted the IRA to issue a statement denying that negotiations of any sort had taken place: 'We wish to state that no representatives of the IRA Provisionals had any discussions with members of the UDA in Libya.'[13]

Whatever Eddie O'Donnell was up to in Libya, Patrick Ryan thought little of the man he regarded as a mischievous interloper. 'My assessment of him was that he was representing an outfit that was trying to torpedo the connection that we had with the Libyans.' O'Donnell had become a nuisance that Ryan could do without. 'The Libyans wanted to take him out and shoot him, so I said, "Don't, leave him to me, but if you are holding him, will you put him someplace where there is no glass in the windows and let the mosquitos get at him for a few nights. That way he won't be in any hurry to return." I also told my Libyan contact, "I'll get word back that when Eddie goes home, his passport is to be taken off him so he won't be able to travel back here again."'

Such was Ryan's annoyance over O'Donnell, a man he deemed a liability to the IRA, that he deliberately returned to Ireland to meet with Seamus Twomey. Twomey was on the run from the law when the two men met. His tenure as IRA chief of staff had ended after he was arrested by gardaí in September 1973, in a remote farmhouse in County Monaghan, and brought under heavy guard to Dublin's Special Criminal Court, where he was charged with membership of the IRA. He was only able to meet Ryan face to face because, a short time into his three-year prison sentence, a hijacked helicopter airlifted him and two other IRA men out of Mountjoy Prison in Dublin. Ryan left the meeting confident that O'Donnell's days of showing up in Tripoli were behind him. 'I made it my business to go to him [Twomey] and explicitly told him to take the passport off Eddie. I said, "Don't allow him back," so Twomey agreed that he wouldn't let him travel to Libya again.'

Then, in the autumn of 1975, when Ryan was once again in Tripoli and enjoying a coffee in a hotel, 'I was looking out the window and I could not believe my eyes. He was back again, Eddie O'Donnell. The man I had gone to Ireland to complain about and to be told that his passport was to be taken away from him.'

Ryan was incredulous. 'I don't know how in hell he managed to travel over. The Libyans were also incensed, they again wanted to take him out to the desert and shoot him. I said, "Don't, it's not going to help; listen, give him some more time with the mosquitoes and they will have a feast on him" and that's what they did, before the Libyan police collected him and put him on a plane for Rome. He never returned.'

Back in Europe himself after that trip, Ryan was busy shuttling between the Libyan embassies in Paris and Rome, collecting money. 'I had three options: directly from the Embassy in Paris, directly from the Embassy in Rome, or arrange to be handed a suitcase on the street from my contacts in either city.' In Rome there was the added bonus of exceptional gelato: 'The man I used to meet in Rome would always have a suitcase in one hand, two fine, big ice creams in the other, and them both melting in the heat.'

Ryan soon realised that, in getting around the European mainland, he needed to be more self-sufficient than he had first planned for, so he set his mind on obtaining his own transport: a camper van. Booking into hotels had proved tedious and left a door open to unhelpful conjecture. 'If I stayed at hotel that was decent, I could have been accused of living the high life; too low and you'd be accused of having another less-decent type of taste, so I came to the conclusion that a camper van was the best option. I bought a second-hand van in Switzerland, and it paid for itself within a year. Not only did I save money, but I also had 24-hour freedom to come and go as I pleased.'

The camper van allowed Ryan to stay relatively under the radar for however long he needed. 'There were many places where you could pull in where you could stop for an hour or stop a month, but the bottom line was that nobody would bother me.'

The hearty aroma of a freshly cooked chicken casserole proved to be an attractive lure for some parked in the same lay-by, specifically long-distance Irish lorry drivers who relished the opportunity to be served a feed of chicken and potatoes by a seemingly eccentric Irish man driving his camper van around Europe. 'After a while they knew full well what I was about and not to be asking any questions of me. They were helpful in tipping me off about various customs checks and the likes. They would get a fine chicken dinner with spuds, and I'd get some gossip from back home; it was a mutually beneficial arrangement.'

But Ryan was cultivating these contacts for more than just gossip. 'For a long time there was very little captured after the *Claudia* and we were able to get some material lifted in southern Europe. I had lined up some obliging lorry drivers, so business just continued.' Ryan's resourcefulness would soon be put to the test.

NINE

ON THE MOVE

It was 16 June 1975. As they walked out of the Holy Rosary Church in Belfast, the young children, two boys and two girls, clasped the side handles of a white coffin so tiny it looked lighter than the school bags their small hands usually carried. The body the child's coffin contained was that of three-year-old Michelle O'Connor, killed when a loyalist booby-trap bomb exploded shortly after she got into her father's car in a mixed area of the city. The *Irish Times* coverage of the funeral included a photograph of the three-years-old's distraught mother, Nora O'Connor, kneeling over the graveside of her toddler at Milltown Cemetery in Belfast. Her husband, John, had survived the attack but was seriously injured in hospital.

The horror that led to four schoolchildren carrying the coffin of a toddler had been unleashed three days earlier. John O'Connor was following his normal routine of taking his only child to nursery school along with her friend, who, that morning, insisted on staying home. 'Michelle was standing by his side holding his hand. I told him my little girl did not want to go to school today. He laughed and said he understood,' the other girl's father later recounted. 'Then he turned, walked over to the car and seconds later I heard the huge explosion.'[1]

The man went on to describe how he bolted towards the burning car where John was staggering around, badly injured. 'He was crying for his daughter so I went to the car to see if I would find her but all I could find was bits of her dress.'[2] The mutilated body of little Michelle was found underneath another car. No reason could be established for the attack other than sectarianism.

An indiscriminate bomb attack that killed a child, though still shocking, was not all that unusual as the violence of the Troubles took a grip on Northern Ireland. Among the newspaper headlines the day after Michelle's death concerning the relentless blood-letting and political situation in Northern Ireland was a brief two-paragraph report with the headline: 'Cahill said to be in Libya'.[3] Time spent in prison had not dissuaded Joe Cahill from returning to the country whose regime had promised the IRA a bountiful supply of weapons and money.

In January 1975 the IRA's former chief of staff left Portlaoise jail on health grounds after serving twenty months of a three-year sentence for his part in the *Claudia* arms operation. On his release, he immediately set about re-establishing contact with members of the IRA's leadership, including fellow Belfast man Seamus Twomey, who was still living on the run after his helicopter escape from Mountjoy.

Cahill's return visit to Tripoli, accompanied by Twomey, had been arranged by the very person he had recommended take charge of the Libyan effort, Father Patrick Ryan, who by then had established himself as the main channel of contact between Gaddafi and the IRA. 'I brought out Cahill and Twomey because I knew that if I took them out to see Gaddafi, they would see Gaddafi, so I brought them out on that understanding.'

In 1975 the IRA was just one of several paramilitary groups that Gaddafi was giving material support to in the form of weapons, training and finance. These included the Red Army Faction, also known as the Baader-Meinhof gang, in West Germany, the Red Brigades in Italy and ETA in Spain. To avoid the risk of Cahill and, in particular, Twomey being recognised by any interested parties in Tripoli, on their arrival both men, along with Ryan, were driven to a private villa outside the city. The only demand made on the three-man group was to be patient, a character trait that came easily to Ryan. 'We were there for over six weeks and occasionally you would get a visit to see how things were going.'

Every knock on the door prompted the expectation that a meeting with Gaddafi had been scheduled for that day, but disappointment quickly crushed any excitement. It would soon become apparent that their hosts were merely checking on whether their guests had enough food to see them through another bout of waiting. Ryan began to notice that the Belfast men's tolerance of what was going on was hovering close to zero. 'I know that Cahill and Twomey were missing a few creature comforts. The food, for a start, was basic and there was so little moisture in the air that if you had a nice fresh loaf, it would be it as hard as a brick the next day. But, ultimately, as the weeks were going by they were totally frustrated with the waiting around.'

The morning when two jeeps instead of one parked outside the house caused further bafflement. Ryan did not recognise the intelligence officers who had been tasked to pick them up. 'They took us on some kind of a sightseeing tour and I'll always remember that they lined up Cahill and Twomey a number of times, taking their pictures when we were out walking around the desert. There was a sizable amount of rocks and Twomey went over and announced, "Come on, I want my picture over here." He was standing on top of this big lump of rock and he fell off it, cut his face and then had to go to hospital for stitches. That was about as much excitement as happened.'

Every week that went by proved more challenging for Cahill and Twomey, who had travelled to Libya for the explicit purpose of meeting their ideologically driven and cash-rich benefactor. Their frustration at the obvious snub was on the brink of spilling over into anger at how they were being treated.

'After more than seven weeks one of Gaddafi's intelligence officers pulled me aside. "Patrick," he said, "take those two gentlemen home and come back yourself and we will talk." They didn't get to see Gaddafi, he wouldn't see them, and Cahill and Twomey were so annoyed. As for the ultimate reason why they were sent home, my conjecture was that the Libyans knew things about them that I didn't know.'

Previous to this trip, Ryan had been able to bring whomever he wished to Libya, without having to first run the person's name past Gaddafi's henchmen. 'You see, I was always trying to put in somebody else. It was sensible that there was somebody left in situ in case I got arrested or wiped off the scene. The first IRA man I brought out was a chap from Donegal who was a level-headed fellow, but after a couple of months he said that he couldn't handle the locals, so I took out a chap from Carrick-on-Suir in south Tipperary, Eamon Doherty. He was a fine fellow, highly intelligent and a great soldier, who had spent some early years in the SAS. I took him out and asked him to take over, but he said that he hadn't the patience, so I continued on myself.'

Whatever observations the Libyan regime had made during the Cahill and Twomey visit, Ryan's system for taking individuals out to Tripoli was changed thereafter. 'The arrangement I had was that I could bring out who I liked, it was never a problem, but the Libyans changed the rules for me after that trip – if I ever wanted to bring anyone out again, I had to consult them, give them the person's name and get that to the Embassy first for approval.'

Changes would also need to be made when Ryan next returned to Ireland. On the Rosslare to Le Havre ferry crossing, Peter Rogers' system had been compromised. Ryan was no longer a complete unknown – he had become a person of interest to some within the gardaí.

This new-found status had been some time in the making. Early on, Ryan had used couriers he trusted, like fellow Tipperary man Marcus Fogarty, who had spent days in a flat in Cashel with Ryan drying out the loot from the *Claudia*. Fogarty recalled, 'I'd gone out to the Continent on two occasions to collect money from the Padre. I met him in Paris and when I got back, I stopped in Dublin to give the bundle to Joe Cahill. My next trip to meet the Padre was to Schipol Airport in Amsterdam, and again, I brought it back and gave it to Cahill, but it was unsustainable for me to keep doing that, so he started using other couriers, and then Peter Rogers.'[4]

After Ryan first left for France, it did not take Rogers long to observe an upsurge of incoming material bound for the IRA. The Le Havre to Rosslare route became the main route Ryan was using, via couriers, to channel bundles of cash back to the IRA's GHQ in Dublin. 'Once Paddy was away off, things started to happen fairly soon. Volunteers were coming aboard to go to France, coming back, and some of them were leaving bags of weapons with me. Then there were others coming back with money saying to me, "Peter, how do we go about getting this money off?"'[5]

The IRA couriers waited in a hotel close to Rosslare port. They were young men and women, most often on their own, who appeared to be in need of sustenance from the hotel buffet even though they had just stepped off the ferry. The rendezvous point was on Peter Rogers' recommendation. 'I'd tell them to go get something to eat there and when the coast was clear, I'd come down and give them the money.'

All was going well, until some money went missing. It was only when Rogers spotted Ryan in his camper van in Le Havre that he was made aware of a problem that necessitated radical change. 'The van was a mighty little thing. You'd want to have seen how he'd kitted it out, but there we were, the two of us sitting in the van with its little curtains closed, and he says, "Peter, there's a bump in the road."'

An IRA man from west Belfast, closely connected to the IRA leadership in the city, claimed he had been robbed. In the camper van, Rogers listened to Ryan explain what would happen next. 'As far as Father Paddy was concerned, there'd be no more money given to any of the couriers. He had a verbal message for me to pass back to GHQ and it was that any money coming into Ireland was going to go through me.'

Within the IRA, Seamus Twomey had acquired the nickname 'Thumper' for his habit of banging the table with his fists when angry. When Rogers fed Ryan's message back to GHQ, Twomey's short temper came to the fore. 'When I told him, he flew into a temper. "Who the fuck does Ryan think he is?" he says. But what was Twomey going to do? Ryan was collecting a fortune for the IRA. I know that for a fact because I was sent money transfers to get changed in Dublin from contacts I'd been given. I would say there was about a quarter of a million pounds in each one and I did it at least eight times. And the thing is, I hadn't a bob, I'd be heading to give suitcases literally full of money to Twomey and it was all I could do to pay for the taxi to bring it to him.'

This new system was going according to plan until Ryan's courier felt the hand of the law on his shoulder. Rogers was arrested in Wexford and questioned by Special Branch officers, a dedicated unit within the gardaí focused on threats to state security, of which the IRA was the main one. 'They start questioning me about gunrunning. One of them seemed to have plenty of information on it, but it wasn't coming from me, and then they changed tack and, by Jesus, didn't they go away off and come back with two photographs, one of

Eamonn O'Doherty and one of Father Paddy. When they released me, the boat was already away off in France, so I went up to Dublin and met up with Eamonn for a debriefing. The next thing he turned round, and he said to me, "Peter, you weren't the only one that was arrested, people have been arrested in Dundalk, Tipperary, Wexford," and these were people we'd been working with.'

The IRA's Rosslare to Le Havre gunrunning and money route appeared to be compromised. Rogers made it a priority to warn Patrick Ryan to lie low and the opportunity to do so occurred when Ryan was about to board the ferry in France to return home for a meeting with an IRA contact. In Le Havre, Ryan noticed that Rogers was on edge. 'I could see that there were more French police around than usual. Things were tight but Rogers told me what lorry to jump into to get on the boat.'

The lorry, transporting vegetables for delivery to a market in Dublin, was a decoy. On board the boat, Rogers and Ryan prepared a plan of action for when the ferry reached Rosslare. As the ship edged closer to its berth, Rogers was focused on the quay wall: 'It took the best part of twenty minutes to manoeuvre around. Eventually I could see the wall and there they were, a line of different gardaí than usual, Branch men. So straight away, I went to get Paddy and said, "It's on."'

Ryan changed into a dirty boiler suit and smeared some oil on his face as Rogers barked at him with a Belfast-accented fury to hurry the hell up. 'I roughed up his hair up a bit, stashed his luggage away and the two of us rushed down to the car deck. I said to Paddy, "You stand there until I shout down to you; I'll only shout whenever I get up on the quay level with whoever is there."'

Ryan stood beside two milk churns.

As soon as the boat was docked, Rogers starting shouting orders to his deckhand. '"Jesus Christ, look what they give you for a helper!

Would you for frig sake come on, to hell with you!" The Branch started laughing at that, but up he comes, my helper, struggling along with these two milk churns.'

Patrick Ryan walked past the detectives who had been tasked with bringing him in for questioning. 'They didn't recognise me. All it took to fool the Branch was a bit of grease on my face. I jumped into a waiting car and was spirited away.'

The lorry driver who had made a deliberate show of giving Ryan a lift onto the ferry in Le Havre became the focus of garda attention. Rogers watched on from a distance. 'They searched his cab, then started taking out the vegetables from the back, but the loading bay got too full, so they had to put everything back in. Off he went to deliver the goods and he later told me that the Branch never let him out of their sight. They were standing at the back of his truck waiting until the last pallet came off at the food market in Dublin and, lo and behold, no Paddy Ryan. So, they went out to the driver and asked him, "Where's that fella you gave the lift to?" He said, "I don't know of giving anybody a lift." "You did," they said, "you gave a fella a lift in France." The driver played a blinder. "Oh him, that was an odd one, he asked me for a helper's ticket and sure you'd do it for anybody, I was looking forward to sitting down having a chat, but we got onto the boat and he disappeared. Jesus he was an odd one." At that stage the Branch knew that their eye had been wiped.'

Ryan had evaded arrest, but his days of returning to Ireland relatively carefree had come to an end. On the times he did need to come back, there was one person's home he trusted – that of Marcus Fogarty in Cashel. 'We would have known that the Padre was heading back out on his travels because he nearly always left from my home, but he played his cards very close to his chest. He would have confided more to my wife, but he was what I would consider an ideal ambassador: he had no baggage. The fact that he was a priest was no matter, he was one of us.'

In 1979 Peter Rogers packed in his work on the Rosslare to Le Havre ferry. He had married, and, with a child on the way, he decided another job with more sociable hours would better suit his new family. He did not, however, walk away from the IRA. On 13 October 1980 he was driving a van with a hidden bag of guns and explosives bound for the car ferry to Britain. 'There was a team in England waiting on the gear. It was coming up to the first hunger strike in 1980 and the leadership wanted to send Margaret Thatcher a message.' As Rogers drove his blue Ford Transit in the direction of Rosslare, a garda patrol investigating bank robberies signalled at him to pull over at Ballyconnick Quarry in Wexford.

An initial search of the van by Detective Garda Seamus Quaid and Detective Garda Donal Lyttleton, who was on first-name terms with Rogers, yielded nothing. Rogers was on the brink of continuing his journey. 'We were standing talking when Detective Quaid turned round and said to me, "What's the carrying capacity of that van?" I said, "About two ton" and they walked back, opened the doors again and the next thing – whoosh – the marzipan smell of the explosives, which had built up like a cloud, hit us all in the face.'

When both detectives climbed back into the van and started asking Rogers to come clean on what was in the bags hidden behind sacks of potatoes, the IRA man had a decision to make. 'I produced the gun that I had on me all the time. I cocked it and I said, "What's in the bag is for the Irish Republican Army against the British, now get the fuck out of the van." The two of them came out together, so I fired a shot in the air, pointed the gun back at them and said, "Do what you're fucking told."

'With that Donal Lyttleton, who knew me from working on the ferry, said, "Peter don't. Whatever you're doing, whatever you're carrying it's not worth it." I lashed out at him and when he fell, didn't he started scurrying along the ground towards the back of the van. I thought, Jesus, he's trying to get his gun out. Seamus Quaid jumped into the darkness of the quarry and immediately a shot rang out. I just turned and fired right away towards the shot and all I heard was "Ahh."'

Rogers' shot had struck and killed Detective Garda Quaid, a forty-two-year-old father of four. When word eventually reached Patrick Ryan, he was not surprised at the outcome. 'I told Peter that he should never be carrying a weapon, because my assessment of him was that he'd use it. I said that to him, but he had this fixed idea that no matter who came along, they weren't going to get him if they had a weapon.'

In Wexford, all shops, factories and offices closed on the day of Quaid's funeral as a mark of respect to the man who had worked twenty-two years in the community. In the midst of all the formal ceremony of a state funeral, his only son, Eamonn, placed his father's garda cap on the tricolour-draped coffin during the Offertory of the Mass. Detective Garda Lyttleton, his colleague and friend who was with him in his last hour of duty, broke down and wept. In all some 5,000 mourners, including more than 2,500 gardaí from every rank and division in Ireland, made the last journey with Detective Garda Quaid through heavy rain to Crosstown Cemetery.

In October 1980 Peter Rogers was convicted of the capital murder of Quaid, a crime which then carried the death penalty.[6] A week before he was due to hang, his sentence was commuted to a forty-year prison term (he was released in 1998 under the terms of the Belfast Agreement). 'I regret it and I was sorry and remain so. It was of no benefit to anybody, none whatsoever.'

TEN

SWISS TIMERS

The young sisters drew their last breath as they slept. Nine-year-old Bernadette and three-year-old Carol McCool were in the upstairs bedroom of their home in the largely Catholic housing estate of Creggan in Derry in June 1970, when an explosion in the kitchen propelled a fireball through the house. A suffocating mix of hot gas and toxic fumes stilled the two children in their slumber. Their mother, Josie, and three siblings only managed to escape the blaze because they were in the downstairs sitting room; their torment began seconds later.

A thundering crackle and hiss of flames roared in fury over the screams of fifteen-year-old John McCool, who desperately pleaded with those whose arms were gripped around him to let go; he wanted to run back into the burning house to try to save his sisters. Neighbours eventually had to sit on the teenager to hold him down.[1]

Thick black smoke bellowed and swirled into the midsummer night sky as fire crews arrived to an unfolding scene of horror. In the kitchen they found the bodies of two men: the children's father, Thomas McCool, and Joseph Coyle. A third man, Thomas Carlin, was found badly burned in a neighbouring garden and later died from his injuries.

The passing of minutes was a cruel measure of the brutal ferocity of the blaze that turned the McCool family home into a smouldering, blackened ruin. An eyewitness said the house at Dunree Gardens was 'gutted within three minutes of the start of the fire'.[2] Earlier that evening, Bernadette had taken a pair of green tartan bows from her hair and placed them on top of the family's television before she ran upstairs to bed.[3] Just hours later, firemen carefully carried her lifeless body down the steps of the scorched staircase. Carol, the baby of the family, died in hospital the following day.

Shock and grief numbed the tight-knit community of the Creggan on a night when a visceral rage had already spilled over in nearby streets. Built on a windswept hill high above Derry, the housing estate overlooked the Bogside, another Catholic area of the city, from where, for hours that night, the distinct, pepper-like smell of tear gas drifted across the city.

A wave of rioting had broken out following the arrest of the civil rights activist Bernadette Devlin. The twenty-one-year-old, who had been elected in April to the House of Commons for Mid-Ulster, had failed in her bid for leave to appeal to the House of Lords against a six-month prison sentence for her part in rioting during what became known as the Battle of the Bogside in 1969. 'I was involved with people in defending their area. They were justified in defending themselves and I believe I was justified in assisting their defence,' she told a press conference before her detention that day. 'If the same circumstances rose again I would have no problems helping them again.'[4] Devlin planned to address a meeting of her supporters in Derry that evening before handing herself in to the police, but was detained at a roadblock four miles outside the city. When word of her arrest reached the waiting crowds in the Bogside, the reaction was quick and furious.

As some of the assembled crowd hurled stones and petrol bombs at the police and army in the Bogside, Bernadette McCool and her baby sister were falling asleep in their beds, oblivious to what was to come. The inferno that claimed their young lives was initially assumed to be an accidental house fire, but after their father, Thomas, was given an IRA military funeral, the real cause of the inferno was revealed. An IRA bomb being prepared in the kitchen had accidentally exploded.

Thomas McCool, Joe Coyle and Thomas Carlin were three of Derry's most senior IRA men. The inquest into their deaths was told that firemen found 'what appeared to be the remnants of a wooden crate containing bases of two pint milk bottles and five large mineral bottles'.[5] A tin containing sodium chlorate and a white cloth gauze were also recovered, along with 'a brown paper bag containing one-and-three-quarter pounds of sodium and a plastic funnel'.[6] The device the three men were working on around the kitchen table was intended to take the lives of, or at the very least maim, others, but instead they became the first members of the IRA to be killed by their own bomb during the Troubles.

The premature explosion was indicative of one of the early challenges the IRA faced; how to keep its bomb-makers, and those who planted their creations, alive in the face of crude and unreliable bombmaking techniques.

A basic bomb required no more than some sticks of gelignite taped together with a detonator and length of fuse inserted into one of them, which an IRA volunteer would ignite at the chosen location. Time-delay mechanisms began to be used where a longer delay was necessary to allow the person planting the bomb to safely get away. One simple timing device involved using a wooden clothes peg with drawing pins pushed through the end as contacts. Soldering wire would be wrapped around the other end of the peg to keep the contacts apart, and the spring would gradually overcome the wire until the pins met and the circuit was completed.[7] However, the bomb-makers could not always gauge the strength of wood or the spring of the clothes peg, which made the timing of the device haphazard at best.

Just months after the explosion in the Creggan, another IRA man was killed by his own bomb when the drawing pins met in the device before the bomb had been set in place.[8] Michael Kane died instantly when the device he was planting at an electricity transformer in south Belfast exploded prematurely. A second IRA man who was seriously injured was discovered after the police followed a trail of his blood to a nearby house.

IRA bomb-makers soon began to modify alarm clocks as time-delay mechanisms in a number of ways. A drawing pin attached to a wire could be pushed through the plastic lens and the other wire would be attached to the body of a clock. The bomb-maker would then remove one of the hands, according to the time delay required. Eventually the other hand would make contact with the pin, setting off the timer, and the bomb would explode. The process, however, was not foolproof; if a layer of paint or lacquer had not been scraped off the clock hand or body when attaching a wire, it could prevent the bomb from detonating, while standards of soldering were often poor, which accounted for the premature detonation of many early improvised explosive devices (IEDs).

The risk of death or injury to bomb-makers and those planting the devices did not quell the violent intensity of IRA bomb attacks. By the end of 1970 the IRA had planted 153 bombs and the following year that number increased to more than 1,000. In 1972 the IRA was responsible for 1,300 explosions.[9] Hundreds had been killed by these bombs, including civilians. In April 1972 Martin McGuinness, the IRA commander in Derry at the time, revealed a casual disregard for human life that characterised the IRA's campaign. When asked during an interview if it was inevitable some civilians would be hurt in bomb attacks, he replied: 'That is quite right, you know, we have always given ample warning, and anybody that was hurt was hurt through their own fault. Being too nosey, sticking around the place where the bomb was after they were told to get clear. It is only been [*sic*] through their own fault they have been hurt.'[10]

As the 1970s unfolded, Northern Ireland became synonymous with violence. Deaths and injuries were being reported in the world's newspapers on a near daily basis, and the IRA was still losing some of its own personnel in accidental explosions, known in Belfast as 'own goals'.

In 1975 Patrick Ryan was thousands of miles away, but the safety of IRA bomb-makers and those who planted the devices, rather than that of the intended targets or possible civilian casualties, was at the forefront of his mind. 'I used to think of them on dark frosty nights, perished cold and wearing gloves while trying to get a bomb under a lorry or a car. They'd be wearing thick gloves but working with something as delicate as a watch to set off the bomb; the wonder was that more of them weren't being blown up.'

Driving across the French border on his way to Geneva in Switzerland, Ryan felt a chill as his camper van grew noticeably colder. He reached down for the pair of black leather gloves he kept tucked under the driver's seat before rolling down his window a couple of inches to help clear the condensation that was creeping up the inside of the windscreen. The *autoroute* was eerily quiet and he grew concerned that the *Bise*, a cold, dry wind that sweeps across the Swiss plateau and funnels down Lake Geneva towards the city, might herald snowdrifts for the final stage of his journey. He put on his gloves and gripped the steering wheel a little tighter as he reminded himself to check the forecast before he left Geneva.

Ryan didn't intend to hang around the city for too long. His plan was to get back on the *autoroute* soon after safely depositing the large sum of cash he had packed neatly into the brown leather satchel hidden under the mustard-coloured seat in the back of the van. He always looked forward to doing business with Swiss bankers and in particular, one he calls Monsieur Bouée. 'We got on exceptionally well, as I did with a lot of people I came across at the time. I don't know if that was down to my outlook or that I was a crooked villain who was fooling everyone, which I had no intention of doing.'

In Switzerland, Ryan had the perfect location to keep the IRA's money from Gaddafi on deposit before forwarding it on. The country's centuries-old tradition of banking secrecy was enshrined in Swiss law, via the Banking Act of 1934, which made it a crime for anyone to share clients' banking information, particularly with foreign authorities. Ryan learned from Monsieur Bouée that Swiss bankers were required to guard secrecy like lawyers or priests: numbered bank accounts meant that a depositor's true identity was only known to a select group of bank employees, and in order to withdraw cash or make a wire transfer, the account holder was required to provide a codeword. 'When I turned up in his bank, he always invited me into his office where we'd talk over coffee and a pastry. He used to say to me, "Patrick, we have not conquered any country, but we have an empire."'

In Geneva, Ryan parked on Square Pradier and closed the camper van curtains before carefully locking it up. He wasn't particularly anxious that the van might be broken into or stolen; it was the ritual of checking that everything was tidy and in its correct place that he relished. Taking the route past the Basilica Notre-Dame, the city's main Catholic church, on his short walk to the bank, he noticed a tall, blonde woman wearing a long belted brown suede coat and leather boots walking up the steps towards the church. From a distance she appeared to be a double of Monsieur Bouée's wife, whom he had first met when she called in to the bank ahead of going for lunch with her husband. Ryan had politely declined an invitation to join them, so the couple instead insisted on making plans to bring him horse riding in the hills above Lake Geneva when the weather improved in the spring.

The air had turned noticeably crisper, so Ryan pulled his satchel into his chest and increased his speed. Then the window of a shop specialising in Swiss watches and clocks caught his eye. 'I stopped in my tracks straight away. I noticed these small timers in the very right-hand corner of the display and I just had a hunch that I could make a difference with them.'

That day Ryan decided to decline the near obligatory coffee and pastry with Monsieur Bouée. His mind was racing with the sense that he had inadvertently stumbled across something potentially more valuable than the tens of thousands of US dollar notes he had deposited into his Swiss bank account.

A bell above the door jingled as Ryan pushed it open, the sound like a tuning fork for the cacophony of ticking clocks that adorned every wall space. The more valuable clocks were kept under lock and key inside glass cabinets. A row of cuckoo clocks appeared gauche and out of place amongst the more intricate clock faces, all vying for the attention of a buyer.

The grey-haired man behind a glass counter must have heard that he had company, but, nonetheless, he remained focused on methodically placing gold and silver pocket watches into a blue-velvet-lined tray. His apparent lack of interest irked Ryan, who waited for him to look up before enquiring about the cost of the small timers in the window display. The query caused the man to laugh so much that he momentarily turned his back on his potential customer in order to compose himself.

Ryan soon found out why his question had garnered such amusement. He had asked about the price of the cheapest items in the shop: Memo Park timers. 'They were small, round mechanical timers used by the locals to remind them when their parking meter was about to run out. It was ingenious really, you come into town and you park your car for an hour and if you had one of those in your pocket, you could set it so that at the end of the hour it rang a little bell to remind you that you had to get back to your car because your money had run out. I had a hunch about what I was going to do with them.'

Ryan assumed that the man's overstated mirth was an effect, a mockery of his naivety about the monetary value of Swiss timepieces, but he smiled at the thought that the joke was on the shopkeeper, who had no idea that what he was about to sell the tourist standing in front of him had the potential to ensure the punctual explosion of bombs hidden under cars or buses, tables in packed restaurants, even little shops such as his own – literally anything the IRA deemed worthy of blowing up.

Ryan left the shop with five of the small pocket timers and returned to his camper van, where he placed each one on the small foldout table. Much like the winter in Tipperary when he figured out how to get piped running water up a hill to his mother's home, he was certain that there was a way to use these to develop the IRA's timer technology. 'I had been pondering the problem; you see, the IRA's explosive devices, like any bomb, needed some electricity to trigger them. So, let's say that the bomb used batteries, which of course provided electricity, but the electricity had to be got to a part of the bomb known as the detonator that would trigger the explosive charge, you see. The IRA bomb-makers were using watches as timers and various things, but they were unreliable, and if the person who had put the bomb together had made a mistake, well, there was no visual way of knowing it. The last thing the person planting the bomb had to do was to throw a switch, but if it was wrong, well, they were gone. If there were any mistakes at all and the circuit completed, they came out from under the car in bits and pieces.'

Ryan first heated the leftovers of a beef stew on his gas stove and then, using a small screw, carefully opened up one of the Memo Park timers. 'I did a bit of thinking that evening in Geneva. I was sure that if I slightly re-engineered the mechanism, I could turn out a device that was foolproof. If it worked, it would be foolproof against any IRA man, even the lads going in under the cars, no matter what the weather was like.'

Ryan re-engineered the timer by attaching a metal arm to the dial of the Memo Park so that when it rotated, it completed an electrical circuit rather than activating the buzzer. 'When the Memo Park was wound up it would slowly tick back in the space of an hour to where it started. So, just where it started, if we had a little brass pin standing up that was one side of the circuit to the detonator, then the other one coming around could be the one that carried the live current. But until those two met you just couldn't damage yourself. I also inserted a further precaution by using the valve of a bicycle wheel as a little sleeve over the pin that was carrying the electric current live. When the bomb-makers were quite content that the device was mechanically correct, the last thing they were to do was remove the little safety tube.'

Ryan's re-engineering produced the perfect bomb timer to be utilised in IEDs.

The next morning the shopkeeper looked up from reading his newspaper as the door's bell jingled. When Ryan stated that he wished to buy his entire stock of Memo Parks, the man blithely shrugged his shoulders before he left the counter and returned with a box containing almost 400 of the little round timers. There was no jeopardy involved in the purchase; it was perfectly legal to buy any quantity of Memo Parks and the absence of serial numbers made them nearly impossible to trace to a particular city or shop in Switzerland.

Ryan was eager to leave Geneva for Le Havre in order to get the box of timers, along with his template of a suggested redesigned timer and power unit, back to the IRA's bomb-makers. As he walked towards his camper van he thought of Newton's Third Law of Motion, which he first learned in the Christian Brothers' school in Thurles. 'For every action there is an equal and opposite reaction, and the ingenuity of the Memo Park timer was that it could save a life, as well as take life. I modified it and then sent it home. All they had to do was to copy it.'

Ryan's modification radically transformed the proficiency of IRA bomb-makers – it was now easier to train these bomb-makers and consequently safer for IRA bombers to plant devices. The IRA's engineering department went on to develop time power unit (TPU) kits consisting of an adapted Memo Park built into a small plywood box, which contained the power source (usually batteries) and all the necessary wiring. The addition of Ryan's Memo Parks meant that even nervous bombers were handling easy-to-operate devices. The bomber simply wound up the Memo Park to the required timing, attached the explosive and placed the bomb. The TPU kit could be incorporated into a variety of devices, including car bombs, mortar firing systems and landmines, either as a firing switch to initiate the bomb or as an arming switch to arm the electric circuit in preparation for firing.

Also known as a 'safe to arm' switch, the TPU created a time gap between a bomb being armed and exploding. In turn, the IRA's engineering department adapted the technology into long-delay electronic timers, which could be used to detonate bombs at a predetermined time, ranging from a few hours to several days or even months after being set. The ability to delay an explosion to exactly the time a bomber wanted it to occur went on to have a devastating effect.

Memo Park timers became a hallmark of IRA bombs and were used in scores of IRA bombs and attacks in Northern Ireland and Britain, including the 1979 Warrenpoint ambush that killed eighteen soldiers (the British Army's worst loss of life in a single incident in Northern Ireland), the February 1985 mortar attack on Newry's Corry Square Barracks that killed nine RUC officers (more than in any other single attack since 1969),[11] and the Canary Wharf bomb in February 1996 that killed two civilians and marked the end of the IRA's 1994 ceasefire.[12]

Reports of IRA atrocities rarely failed to remind Ryan that the smallest of adjustments could bring about calamitous results. 'It was like most ingenious things: very, very simple when you get to the bottom of them, and the timers were so successful the redesign went worldwide and many resistance movements began to use the same technique. The Memo Parks were the little timers that made all the difference.'

ELEVEN

BENIDORM

Patrick Ryan swam only in the first hour after sunrise, when the morning sun teased soft rays of light across Benidorm's crescent-shaped Poniente Beach, making the Mediterranean Sea look like navy velvet buffered against a golden curl of fine sand. Fierce sunlight during the day would gradually bleach the sea to varying shades of cerulean blue, but Ryan preferred the morning's darker hue. The early hour also nearly guaranteed that he would be alone in the water and free to chart a steady course without being hindered by other swimmers blocking his path.

Ryan's early morning swimming ritual was augmented by a run along the shoreline, where he would sometimes nod to acknowledge other joggers, who, like him, were trying to get ahead of the hot temperatures that would make running on the beach foolhardy, if not impossible, later in the day. 'After I came out of the water, I would jog for the same length of my swim before walking back to my flat and washing the sand off my feet before breakfast.'

Situated on eastern Spain's Costa Blanca coastline, by 1975 Benidorm had long been transformed from a small fishing village into a vertical city on the sea by a mayor who envisioned a future in tourism. Pedro Zaragoza Orts, the mayor of Benidorm from 1951 to 1967, dramatically changed the skyline of Benidorm by dispensing with building height restrictions. The move heralded a boom in the construction of skyscraper hotels designed to cram in as many northern European tourists as possible. He was also willing to petition the National Catholic regime in defence of a by-law he had put in place permitting the wearing of a sartorial icon of female liberty: the bikini. When threatened with excommunication by the Catholic Church for allowing sunbathers to wear two-piece swimsuits, Zaragoza made a direct appeal to the Spanish dictator, General Francisco Franco. 'I set off for Madrid on my Vespa at 6 a.m.,' he later reminisced. 'It took me eight hours. I changed my shirt but I went in to the General with my trousers spattered with motor oil. He backed me and the bikini stayed.'[1]

Patrick Ryan first arrived in Madrid on 20 November 1975, the day of Franco's death. 'I remember the airport was paved with the military and there was a very strange atmosphere. Everyone appeared to be on the edge and after a couple of days in the city, I made my way to the south of the country.'

Soon after his arrival in Spain, Ryan decided on Benidorm as the location for his European base. He still used his camper van to shuttle between different cities in Europe, but more often left it locked in parking spots he knew were secure close to Paris or Brussels, choosing to use public transport for his travels to and from southern Spain. 'The van worked a treat, but I needed to switch things up. I picked Benidorm because it was a very crowded place with tourists of all kind, including a high sprinkling of Brits, and the population changed nearly every week or so, and therefore I wouldn't be noticed too easily.'

His assessment had some merit – by the time Ryan's chapter in Benidorm got underway in earnest, the turnover of visitors to the Spanish coastal resort had surpassed the ambition of its transformational mayor. After the opening of Alicante Airport in 1967 and the rise of the package holiday, the number of visitors to Benidorm began to rapidly increase. In 1977 alone, the resort reportedly welcomed some 12 million visitors.

Such was Ryan's commitment to the holiday resort that he purchased a studio flat in one of Benidorm's high-rise towers. 'I decided that I'd invest in a bedsit for the princely sum of 6,000 pesetas. It was very basic, but it meant that no one could say I was wasting money staying in hotels. The only criticism I got when I was handling millions of pounds was that I should have dressed myself a bit better, but I had no interest in these things. The bedsit meant that, for the first time in Europe, I had an address from where I could come and go as much as I needed to.'

From his modest home, Ryan only had to stroll a short distance to reach Poniente Beach, one of Benidorm's longest, measuring more than three kilometres in length. 'I was only a few minutes' walk from the beach and every morning around 5 a.m., when there were very few people up, I would go down and swim about 100 yards into the water before swimming parallel to the shore for well over two kilometres at a time, and every second day or so, I swam wearing a snorkel.'

Anyone who may have been watching the lone swimmer maintain a steady pace, his arms slicing through the Mediterranean brine as he effortlessly turned and made his way back to his starting point, may have admired his stroke, but they could hardly have imagined what inspired such early-morning commitment. Patrick Ryan was yet again applying himself in the pursuit of a particular goal: the blowing up of a boat in Monte Carlo. At Poniente Beach, Ryan was engaged in a vigorous exercise regime to improve his odds: the stronger a swimmer he could become, the better the likelihood that he could carry out an act that could result in the lifeless bodies of others bobbing in the Mediterranean Sea.

The idea had presented itself as a proposition worth pursuing while he was staying at the Monaco home of a retired diplomat from an Eastern Bloc country. In Monte Carlo, Ryan took an interest in the *Brave Goose of Essex*, a 115-foot superyacht that was then one of the largest yachts in the world.[2] Its British owner, Sir Donald Gosling, had served in the Royal Navy during the Second World War and went on to make his fortune in the business of multistorey car parks. 'Sir Donald was very well connected but he wasn't the target. My ambition was more about sending a signal. If the IRA was seen to be blowing up such boats, it could have closed off a part of the Mediterranean to British-registered boats.'

For Ryan's ambition to be feasible, he needed to be as strong and proficient a swimmer as he could be. It would not be enough to be fast – he needed the strength of a lifeguard making his way towards a person in distress. Only in Ryan's case, he would be swimming out to the *Brave Goose* while it was moored in Monte Carlo in order to attach a bomb to the underside of the much-coveted vessel.

In the end, his plan had to be abandoned because of a separate IRA operation. 'I learned that weapons were coming into Monte Carlo for the IRA, not from Libya I might add, but I didn't want to do anything that would wreck that operation.'

Having a base in a corner of Europe, but not in Paris, was timely. Ryan was beginning to receive what he interpreted as warnings from those who were aware he was operating within their jurisdiction. 'A couple of times I came back to my hotel room in Paris only to find a couple of bullets left in the ashtray. It was, I later found out, a message from some within the French security service letting me know that I was being monitored. The IRA were not blowing up Paris, so they were never really going to bother me.'

The IRA may not have carried out attacks in the French capital, but individuals who were part of its overseas active service units used the city, for a time, as a hub – IRA members like 'Voyage Man', who said, 'The 'RA in its wisdom decided to set up bases on the Continent

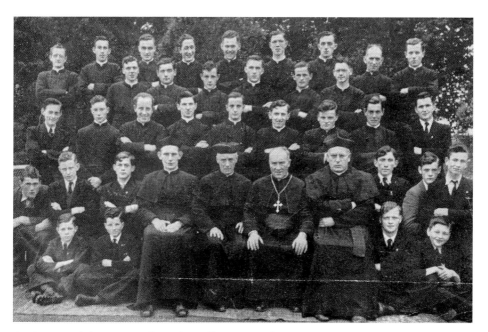

An image of those attending the Pallottine Fathers' Seminary in the 1950s. Patrick Ryan can be seen fourth from left in the second row from the top. Bishop Patrick Winters is seated third from the left in the front row.

The Pallottine Fathers' Seminary hurling team in the 1950s. Patrick Ryan is standing at the right staring directly into the camera with his arms crossed.

Patrick Ryan and Sinn Féin President Gerry Adams march to the British Embassy in Dublin on 19 August 1989 as part of a demonstration to demand a complete British withdrawal from the north of Ireland. © Eamonn Farrell/RollingNews.ie

Patrick Ryan campaigning outside a church as part of his effort to win a seat in the Munster constituency of the 1989 European Parliament election.
© 'Holy Terror', *This Week*, Thames Television, June 1989

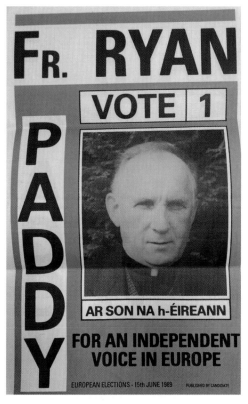

Two of the posters used by Patrick Ryan during his 1989 European Parliament
election campaign. © Author's collection

Patrick Ryan in an
interview with the
author for a BBC
series on the Troubles.
© *Spotlight on the
Troubles: A Secret
History*, BBC, September
2019

Patrick Ryan outside what remains of his family home in Turraheen,
County Tipperary. © Author's collection

at different levels. I first heard about Paddy from the Dog, who always referred to him as "this effing priest Fr Paddy". You see, the Dog would have hated priests full stop; whether they were good, bad or indifferent, he didn't like the cloth.'[3] 'The Dog' was Brian Keenan.

At a meeting in a discreet location in Paris, 'Voyage Man' picked up on the palpable tension between Keenan and Ryan. 'Keenan introduced me to him [Ryan]. We had no particular business together, but my initial reaction was that Paddy was worth his weight in gold. That said, I could sense that there was friction. I gathered that because Paddy was, as the Dog put it, an "effing priest", he wasn't very biddable.'

The antipathy was not exclusively one-way. Ryan detested Keenan. 'I hated the sight of him. He used to be roaming around Europe for a while and I always tried to stop him; my assessment of him was that he should not have been let loose on society. That said, Brian was the only one at that level [senior IRA and QMG for a time] who would ever go out with the lads chasing the Brits at night on patrol. He would undergo the same dangers and risks as them and that has to be acknowledged, but he was a peculiar character.'

'Voyage Man' liaised with Brian Keenan until the latter's arrest in Northern Ireland in March 1979 put him behind bars. 'The Dog got locked up blaming Martin McGuinness and came out [in 1993] blaming Martin McGuinness. He was probably right, because the Dog wasn't stupid; he might have been impetuous and a psychopath, but his analysis of the situation was always quite good, he had a very good military brain.' Keenan was arrested when the RUC stopped two cars travelling north on the main road from Dublin to Belfast and was extradited to England to face charges relating to the IRA's Balcombe Street Gang's 1975 campaign. His capture was considered a blow to the IRA, particularly because he was carrying an address book listing his contacts, including Palestinian activists in the UK.

Keenan's detention was of no consequence to Patrick Ryan, who was still enjoying life in Benidorm. When engaging in casual conversations with people he met in the Spanish resort, Ryan identified himself as a tourist or a resident, having no cause to invent an elaborate backstory due to the growing popularity of the resort. Crucially, there was another aspect to the influx of tourists to Benidorm that would prove unintentionally beneficial for Ryan's network of contacts: lost passports.

With the rise in the late 1970s of tailored package holidays from British tour companies, the resort was flooded with Club 18–30 tourists eager to indulge in what had become the party capital of Spain's Costa Blanca coastline. The high numbers of young raucous British visitors to Benidorm were of consequence to Ryan. 'Some of them had an interesting habit when drunk of running races along the roofs of the cars in the early hours of morning or pulling up plants and just being a nuisance.'

Ryan turned his attention to those whose job it was to assist British citizens in the aftermath of such drunken incidents or other types of holiday mishaps: the staff of the British Consulate. 'If a certain branch of the Spanish police came across the drunks running across the cars, it was straight into the clink for those who were caught, so the consul staff were called in and I made it my business to watch who was turning up to help get the young lads out of trouble.'

Once he had identified a target within the Consulate, Ryan could take his time staking out different bars or restaurants in order to establish the daily patterns of the person he needed to befriend. 'I made it my business to run into certain people. I'd learn where the Brit would be having his coffee in the morning and where he'd be living and taking a walk from – it was all just part of the information I was watching out for as I strolled around.'

The bureaucratic frustrations of some diplomatic staff working long hours in a resort overrun with partying tourists was a frequent complaint Ryan pretended to be interested in as he ingratiated himself with the people he knew had access to a glut of lost passports. 'A lot of the time there were ferocious rivalries within those offices and the thing is that if you respect people they will talk away. It wasn't just the Brits in Benidorm – I found that to be the case in other embassies as well, a lot of rows between themselves. Many have a worry and want the ear of someone to listen to them in a world where nobody wants to listen. But in Benidorm, the upshot was that I was able to get some of those passports nice and handy. I had no artistry – you would want a course in book-binding to carry any weight if you wanted to start manipulating them – but I knew some people who were anxious to get their hands on them.' For those wishing to travel under an assumed identity to avoid scrutiny, the value of access to such a resource could not be denied. Ryan was once again proving his worth as an IRA asset.

TWELVE

CHRISTINE

She always slept soundly at night. No matter how many heavy wheeled trucks trundled past, she was dead to the world. Even during the early hours before sunrise when the temperature felt like it was near freezing in the camper van and Patrick Ryan could see his own breath as he exhaled, Christine never awoke complaining of the cold. Her restful slumber, she said, was because she felt safe with him.

Ryan was keen that she check into the hotel nearest to whatever city they had parked close to. For a start, a hotel bed would almost certainly be more comfortable, allowing her to sleep for longer. Money was not the issue – he had the cash to cover the bill for a room – but Christine always insisted that she would much rather stay in the van with him than be on her own. It was all part, she said, of their glorious travels together, touring around parts of Europe while on an adventure.

The so-called adventure was a game in which one of the players was the pawn.

It had started in East London, a welcome distraction to break up the tediousness of his role as a priest. Ryan had resented having to take up the posting near Dagenham but had no choice other than to bide his time until he could return to Tanganyika. (He never refers to that country by any other name, despite the territory being renamed the United Republic of Tanzania in 1964 after it merged with the island of Zanzibar, another newly independent nation.)

Like his beloved corner of East Africa, Ryan was intent on gaining autonomy. He never planned on staying any length of time in England and looked forward to returning to his missionary work as soon as he had raised enough money to buy his own plane, which would enable him to continue, independent of Bishop Winters.

Change manifested itself swiftly in the northern hemisphere. Only a couple of weeks after his arrival in East London, Ryan's African tan faded. His pallor, he observed, was beginning to match the tone of his surroundings: grey. Then in his late thirties, Ryan began to notice the same two young women who were always eager to help around the St Thomas More church after Mass on Sundays. There was not that much for them to do aside from picking up pamphlets or checking the pews for forgotten purses or spectacles, tasks that the altar boys should have been doing. But the pair would politely shoo the boys away if any of them insisted on helping.

Ryan welcomed the women's eagerness. Their help was underlined by a sense of frivolity when compared to the cloying subservience of others. There was little that he could do, only acknowledge what they were doing and thank them for taking such an interest in the church. 'Christine was about five years younger than me. She was a Protestant and used to come to Mass with a friend of hers. The two of them were around the church and they would stay and help, that was how we came to know each other.' He came close to telling them to go and embrace the freedom they had, before remembering that he was supposed to be enthusiastic about those who wished to stay longer in a house of God.

Eventually, one of the women began to peel away with the rest of the congregation after Father Ryan's blessing to the faithful. The wistful lament 'Lord in your mercy, hear our prayer' signalled that the Mass was coming to a close and at times prompted some of the faithful to excitedly shuffle, like horses before a race, ahead of a rush to the door.

As he left the altar, Ryan also felt like running away, but one person continued to stay on: Christine. 'There was talk that the friend might have started doing a line with some fellow. I don't know for sure, but Christine, who was single and lived on her own, was hanging around more and more.'

To test her resolve while waiting for what had become their near weekly chat after Mass, Ryan increasingly took more minutes than necessary to change out of his vestments in the sacristy. Christine never failed the mock trial of loyalty she wasn't even aware she was being subjected to; Ryan would walk triumphantly back into the sanctuary of the church and see her sitting alone in a pew. Her forlorn expression would transform into a smile on seeing him.

It was only when Ryan broke the news that he was leaving London to return home that Christine gave up her secret. She began to cry. Her tears were not prompted by concern for Mrs Ryan in her sickbed in Tipperary. To avoid a scene, Ryan started to pray aloud, stemming any further escalation of emotion, but there was no denying what had become obvious. 'I would say she was in love with me, yes. I gave it no thought, but I kept in touch with her because you see, you never know when you might need to call in a favour.' That day would come.

Within a few short years, Ryan's clerical collar only saw the light on days when he needed a ruse. His priestly vocation had become a costume. Yet there were some for whom a first impression is lasting, those who first met Patrick Ryan as an intercessor between man and God – people like Christine. He remembered that she rarely looked bored during his homily on a Sunday and, as they sat side by side in a pew afterwards talking about everything and nothing, she appeared to have faith in his every word.

Ryan knew from experience that the power of belief could make men and women agree to do all sorts of things. He began to send Christine postcards from Paris: the Champs-Élysées with the Arc de Triomphe in the background; the cathedral of Notre-Dame. Snapshots of a world outside her own. Whatever the scene, the picture-postcard sky was saturated blue and more vivid than the one she woke up under in Barking. His gesture was a little reminder that even though circumstances had taken him down a different path, she was never far from his thoughts.

Christine's fortitude was about to be tested again, this time as a money mule. 'When I got over to the Continent, I had no idea that all this cash was going to come into play and to that end I contacted her.' The phone call went better than the scripted version he had mentally prepared. She had heard idle chatter that Ryan had left the Pallottine Order but never questioned why; she only wanted to know when she could see him again. Such was Christine's enthusiasm, she insisted that she could get to France on her own volition, and it only took one crossing of the English Channel for her to become part of his network of helpers. 'She used to come over and collect some of the money from me in Calais and take it back to send on to my contacts in Ireland.'

There was just the small matter of a cover story to explain the bundles of cash in her suitcase should she ever be pulled in and questioned by an industrious customs officer. For such an unlikely event, Ryan came up with a fable that reeled her in. 'You see, for a long time she didn't know what the money was really for. I told her it was for a nice house I would build on my brother's land at home in the years to come, and sure maybe the two of us could end up living there. That was my line. Belief can be a powerful persuader.'

Christine's trips on the ferry went uninterrupted. 'No one in their right mind would have stopped her on the Dover ferry. She was a good-looking woman, slim with dark hair and a touch of the innocent about her. I had something else in mind that she would ultimately be helpful for, but that's how it started.'

When she could get to France, Christine's visits extended to a week or two at a time, keeping Ryan company on the road. 'I never once lay down in the bed with her in the camper van. I could have been tempted, but, no, that never happened. She was level-headed and I was no fool.'

From his base in Benidorm Ryan could easily travel to France or Switzerland or any corner of Europe he wished. There was one location, however, where he had unfinished business of a type: London.

'By the mid-1970s I had the Libyan side of things nailed down, so much so, that if I could have gotten someone to take my place it would nearly have run itself. That would then leave me free to go to London, get into the building sites as cover to organise attacks in London.' Christine, he surmised, could be far more useful to him in London than she was sleeping over in his camper van on the Continent.

'At one stage she had been ferrying a lot of money for me. She was very loyal, very solid, but I figured that in the long-term if I got to London, the heavy missions I had in mind for her wouldn't be easy at all. Ah, it got to the stage that she knew about the IRA business and what I was about, and if she was caught I had a feeling that she wouldn't talk, but you can never be sure of a person.'

The time had come to dangle Christine in front of British Intelligence.

'I was in Spain and I gave her a ring suspecting there was a chance that the Brits would be listening on the line. You see I'd started to hear a strange click a couple of times before, so on this occasion, I spun a story for the ears that were tuning in. On the call I said that I wanted to transact a bit of business with her and that I would meet her in Zurich. I knew that the Brits would tip off the Swiss secret service and the moment I collected her from the airport there they were, a couple of plain-clothes lads, and they followed us the whole time.'

It was the summer of 1976 when Christine left London for Switzerland. She was oblivious to the extra company in the background, who were watching as she browsed the stalls of the Rosenhof Markt, went grocery shopping and admired the stained-glass windows of the Grossmünster church. However, Ryan sensed the shadows of the watchers at every turn. 'I had no interest in sightseeing. I wanted to take the money out of my bank accounts, but, with these Swiss lads sitting on us, I left it alone in case they'd grab it.'

At the end of their week-long tour of Zurich and its environs, Ryan waved goodbye to Christine at the airport, knowing what lay ahead for her when the plane landed back in London. 'I knew that the moment she set foot in England she'd be pulled in by the Branch and I would see how she turned out.'

Ryan drove away from Zurich Airport to cross the Swiss lowlands en route to Geneva, confident in his prediction that Christine would be stopped by the Metropolitan Police on her return to London. 'I knew she would be arrested, but as it turned out I faced the same hassle in Geneva. I was picked up with some of those famous timers on me.' However, with the absence of an offence having been committed on Swiss soil, the Swiss had to release Ryan from custody. The only question was where.

'They had to expel me, so they notified the French, but the French wouldn't let me near the place. So I opted then to take a plane, at Swiss expense, to Sweden. I was only up to mischief because when the plane landed in Belgium, which I knew it would for a stopover,

I discontinued my journey there. I had to send a chap I knew in Luxembourg to Geneva to retrieve my van.'

In custody in England, Christine, it seems, kept her secrets. 'She was rock solid, she'd have got through anything. She used the old story I had originally sold to her about the house in Ireland I was going to build for the both of us, that's what I heard. You see, a good woman is as good as a hundred men at anything. Far more focused and intelligent. If she's on the wrong road, she's very good at that too, but I was lucky that Christine was level-headed.'

Despite Christine passing his test, Ryan decided that the nights of sharing a camper van with her were over, along with any nebulous plans to use her for future operations. 'She was a great woman, but I could not contact her anymore after that. It was going to get tougher and too dangerous, and I felt, on balance, it was best to leave it because I wasn't going to stop.'

Patrick Ryan had no intention of retreating from his mission: crossing borders in the pursuit of money and material for the IRA. And he still had a network of other money mules to bring bundles of cash to Ireland on his behalf.

* * *

Christine was merely a play, but the game he'd involved her in exposed one invaluable fact to Ryan. 'It was only a lot of hassle really but here's the thing – I flushed out that the Brits were on to me. I'd have to be more careful.'

In March 1977 Patrick Ryan was again detained during his European travels. The details of his arrest in Luxembourg were outlined in a diplomatic cable marked 'Immediate Urgent Confidential' to the Department of Foreign Affairs in Dublin. 'It would seem', the cable outlined, when accessed a decade after the event, 'that Ryan's photograph had earlier been circulated to police stations in the Grand Duchy and a young Luxembourg lady employed in a city café recognised Ryan after having seen his photo a few minutes previously in the police station when she was reporting a lost identity card. She reported his presence to the police and they took him into custody within minutes.'[1]

A judge, the cable added, remembered having 'disposed of' the Ryan case without 'any formal judicial proceedings' and 'allowed Ryan to depart for Spain' at a time when 'the Belgians refused Ryan entry and Ryan himself refused to return to Ireland and showed distinct unwillingness to be sent to Britain'. Despite being wanted enough to have his photo reportedly on show in Luxembourg police stations, Ryan was not charged with any offences and instead was 'gently removed, care being taken to consult his own wishes, eventually bowing to his preferences in the matter of his ultimate destination'. The authorities in Luxembourg arranged a flight for him to Barcelona and Ryan was once again free to continue his work for the IRA.

THIRTEEN

'A MAJOR CALAMITY'

White and violet crocuses swayed softly in the garden of the British Ambassador's residence in The Hague on the morning of 22 March 1979. The sky was an angry shade of grey, but the soil, where the vivid-hued harbingers of spring nestled, was thawing out. Winter had lost its icy grip and given way to the hopefulness of a warmer season.

It was 9 a.m. and the Ambassador's car, a Rolls-Royce Silver Shadow, was parked in a narrow archway facing towards the street at the front of the residence indicating he was almost ready to leave. Sir Richard Sykes was two years into his posting as Britain's Ambassador to the Netherlands. The route to his office in The Hague was short; the half-mile drive took only four minutes through the city's 700-year-old winding streets. That Thursday morning, however, the diplomatic papers and briefings on his desk would have to wait. His first appointment was in Voorschoten, where he was scheduled to chair a meeting about a forthcoming official opening of a new British School in the Netherlands (BSN).[1]

Set up in 1931, the BSN was temporarily disbanded after Hitler's army invaded the Netherlands in 1940. Its founder, Gwen Brunton-Jones, along with her husband and son, spent the next five years in internment camps in Germany.[2] But by 1979 Europe was decades-free of the fascism that resulted in the deaths of millions, and some of those who had fought on the front line against Hitler's armed forces were engaged in an expressly different form of duty: diplomacy.

The British Ambassador to the Netherlands was a decorated hero of the Second World War. As a younger man, Sykes had taken part in the Normandy landings, for which he had been awarded the British Military Cross and the French Croix de Guerre, and the liberation of the Netherlands. A series of roles in the Foreign Office took him to many countries, and in his last posting before going to The Hague, he was one of its most senior officials, in charge of security and Irish affairs. It was an experience in which he learned about the IRA's ruthlessness when it came to selecting assassination targets.

The murder of one Foreign Office colleague and close friend had demonstrated the IRA's commitment to following through on such plans. On a bright summer morning, 21 July 1976, a stately black Jaguar Daimler drove down the tree-lined avenue of Glencairn House, the British Ambassador's residence in south County Dublin. Christopher Ewart-Biggs had been Ambassador to Ireland for precisely twelve days. Prior to his new posting, he had been a senior liaison officer between the Foreign Office and MI6. However, the fifty-four-year-old diplomat had been hand-picked by Prime Minister James Callaghan for the delicate Dublin assignment and given the specific task of improving Britain's relations with Ireland after years of tension because of Northern Ireland.

On receiving word of his ambassadorial appointment, Ewart-Biggs wrote in his diary: 'It sounds interesting at least; possibly dangerous ... I have never followed the Irish affair. My resolution will be to avoid agitation, internal and external.'[3]

That July morning, the Ambassador was on his way to his first formal meeting with the Irish Minister for Foreign Affairs, Dr

Garret FitzGerald. Travelling with him in the car were Judith Cooke, private secretary to the Northern Ireland Office (NIO) in Belfast, Brian Cubbon, permanent under-secretary at the NIO, and Brian O'Driscoll, the Ambassador's official driver. The car had been fitted with armour plating and the Ambassador met with senior gardaí officers just days beforehand to discuss his security. Writing in his diary, Ewart-Biggs said, 'They are not very reassuring ... They do not seem to have given much thought to the scenario of attack. They thought for some reason that an attack on the car was unlikely – "it hasn't happened yet". I ask them to keep us informed about any changes in their assessment of the risk.'[4]

Before he left Glencairn House, Ewart-Biggs spent some time with his youngest daughter, Kate, who was then eight years old. 'I spent the morning with him, choosing his tie, having breakfast with him,' she recalled many years later. 'I remember going downstairs with him and sort of not wanting him to go.'[5]

As the Ambassador's car exited the heavily guarded grounds, the driver turned right; a short distance later, a massive bomb, which was hidden in a drain crossing under the road, was triggered by command wire. The car took the full force of the enormous blast, somersaulting in the air before landing on the passenger side in the deep crater. Cooke and the Ambassador were killed instantly, while Cubbon and O'Driscoll were seriously injured, but survived the attack.

The assassination of Ambassador Ewart-Biggs prompted widespread condemnation and expressions of shock and revulsion. 'This atrocity fills all decent Irish people with a sense of shame,' said Taoiseach Liam Cosgrave, who called an emergency session of the Irish Cabinet. In London, Prime Minister Callaghan told a sombre House of Commons that the killing of Ewart-Biggs was 'illustrative of the fact that hundreds of innocent men and women have been slaughtered on the altar of Ireland'. There were murmurs of sympathy in the Commons chamber when he said, 'It was only a few weeks ago that I saw him and he told me how much he was looking forward to this post. He was my own choice for Ireland. I thought his qualities and talents would be suited there.'

The IRA claimed responsibility for the bombing. 'We make no apology for it,' an unnamed IRA leader was quoted as saying in a newspaper interview. 'He was sent here to co-ordinate British intelligence activities, and he was assassinated because of that.'[6]

Richard Sykes had been close friends with Ewart-Biggs, as well as being one of the most senior officials at the Foreign Office with special responsibilities for security. He was dispatched to Dublin to work with the Irish authorities in investigating the assassination and 'report back urgently on the situation' on the explicit instruction of the Prime Minister.[7] His report on what had occurred made several recommendations for the increased protection of British diplomats abroad, including around ambassadors' residences.

The timing of the report concerning the security of British targets abroad was prescient. During August 1978 IRA bombs were planted at various British Army barracks in West Germany; neither MI5 nor the rest of the British Intelligence community gained any advance warning of the bombing campaign.[8] The British military and their families were warned to be on alert where they were stationed and where they went for a break. The IRA had identified a potential weak link and was expanding its armed campaign on the Continent.

An IRA spokesman later outlined the strategy behind these attacks. 'Overseas attacks have a prestige value and internationalise the war in Ireland. The British government has been successful in suppressing news about the struggle in the North ... But we have kept Ireland in the world headlines, our struggle is kept in the news and sooner or later an expression of discontentment probably from the English people rather than from the army will snowball and the

British government's ability and will to stay, which we are sapping, will completely snap.'[9]

In early 1979 some British officials in Brussels were put on high alert. Late in the afternoon of 25 January Roy Jenkins, the first British President of the European Commission, had a visit from the head of his protection service, accompanied by a British security officer 'in great agitation and secrecy'. 'British sources' had informed them that 'there was a serious IRA plot to assassinate in the fairly new future, a senior British representative' in Brussels. They had narrowed the list of possible targets to Jenkins, the diplomats Christopher Tugendhat and Crispin Tickell, and 'two generals'.[10]

British Intelligence had obtained remarkable detail about the assassination plot. Jenkins was told that the IRA had 'set up some sort of watching or firing post quite some time previously, outside the house of the person who was the target and that they had reported that his habits are somewhat irregular'. Jenkins recorded in his diary, 'not true of mine' – he was a regular morning runner. The intelligence detail also indicated that the house in Brussels under surveillance was near a school, 'which posed certain dangers of shooting the children by accident'. They had been told that the assassination 'was likely to be made in the course of the next few weeks'.[11]

The intelligence continued to be disseminated. On 19 February an MI5 report on the assassination threat in Brussels was being discussed in Downing Street.[12] Yet in The Hague, four weeks later, there were no Dutch policemen on duty on the morning of 22 March when Richard Sykes left his residence shortly before 9 a.m. and stepped into his Rolls Royce. As his nineteen-year-old footman, Karel Straub, closed the car door, two assassins emerged from the back of the courtyard. One fired a revolver through the rear side window of the car, hitting Sykes four times: once in the head, twice in the chest and once in the right arm.[13] The second gunman shot Straub twice at close range. Both gunmen escaped on foot into a maze of alleys and side-streets.

The Embassy chauffeur immediately drove off at speed with Sykes slumped in the back seat, transporting the Ambassador to Westeinde Hospital, a few hundred yards away. Straub was brought there by ambulance. The two men died within minutes of each other.[14]

Many in The Hague were taken aback by the apparent lack of security measures to protect the Ambassador and his staff. Straub's parents said their son had told them of repeated bomb threats against the residence, but Sykes had no bodyguard, the car was not equipped with bulletproof windows[15] and his residence was unguarded.[16] The British chargé d'affaires in The Hague, Mr Roger Harvey, said there had been no reason to take special precautions. 'Nothing at all would suggest that Sir Richard made enemies of anyone. He was one of the most beloved members of the diplomatic service anywhere.'[17]

At the BSN, where people had been awaiting Sykes' arrival, news of his assassination was met with shock and devastation. Mike Weston, who was then head of the German department, said, 'I remember that day and how horrified and deeply shocked we all were. Sir Richard was a man with real presence and charisma, and he was very supportive of the school, but above all else, he was a good man.'[18]

* * *

The blood spilled outside the Ambassador's residence in The Hague had not been cleaned off the cobbles when another IRA operation on the European continent got underway. An assassination plan had been put in motion on the back of a key piece of intelligence from a person well positioned to identify so-called 'high value' targets on behalf of the IRA: Patrick Ryan.

On the day Ambassador Sykes was killed, Ryan was in Brussels where, just like The Hague, the hopefulness of springtime was outwardly taking shape in the Belgium capital. Dozens of magnolia trees had burst into pink and white star-shaped blossoms in parts of the city. As the day unfolded, details of the shooting dead that morning of a British diplomat in The Hague had slowly begun to filter through on Belgian radio news bulletins. At the same time, fax machines impatiently spat out hurried reports in consulates across the city.

By the afternoon the IRA had still not claimed responsibility for the gun attack, though British officials began to brief journalists that Sykes had been a likely target because he had directed the investigation of the bombing which had killed Christopher Ewart-Biggs.[19] As phones rang almost constantly into the afternoon in security agencies, police and newspaper offices in London and The Hague, one man in Brussels was in quiet meditation.

At Lucie Ninane's home in the Ixelles neighbourhood, Patrick Ryan was taking time to brew his mid-afternoon coffee with a moka pot. He enjoyed the ceremonial filling of the bottom chamber with water and the funnel with ground coffee before tightly screwing the pot's top on and placing it on the stove, then listening for the hissing and gurgling sound that indicated his coffee was done. Each step of the process was equally important and had a bearing on the end result. The same principle applied to a detail he had picked up that he knew would be of particular interest to the IRA. 'I was blessed really, because Lucie Ninane had some very interesting friends with all sorts of connections and homes in important addresses across the city.'

Maurice Beerblock, a left-wing activist largely based in Paris, first introduced Ryan to Ninane.[20] 'My first contact with Maurice was in Paris. He said that I should move to Brussels and, when I did, he

took me straight to her house. They were the very best of friends.'
Beerblock, however, was not just the man who introduced Ryan to
Ninane; he was also the link man between the Padre and IRA active
service units on the European mainland. 'Maurice stayed with Lucie
Ninane when he was in Brussels and he was my man on the ground.
I did not exist as far as the IRA gunmen in Europe were concerned,
they never saw me and had no need to. I was in contact with Maurice,
who would pass my information on.'

For years, Ryan and Maurice convened in Ninane's home, replete
with its paintings, artefacts and books on European art and history,
to discuss areas of potential interest for IRA active service units in
Europe – namely, targets for assassination. 'Maurice had a head for
planning and we would come up with ideas that might be helpful for
the people on the front. He would go off and have a chat with them,
but he would never say it was coming from me or that he was talking
to me or anything like that.'

All the time Ryan remained a shadow in the background, increasingly mindful that IRA operatives were likely to have been compromised by British security and intelligence agencies. 'The IRA hit team
never saw me, that was the whole point of using Maurice as the intermediary, because I was convinced that if I made any direct contact
with the IRA, especially in Belfast or Dublin – well, I thought I may
as well be talking directly to the Brits.'

The two mens' host, Lucie Ninane, was incredibly well connected.
A curator at the Royal Museum of Ancient Art in Brussels, where she
had worked for more than thirty years, she was renowned for her
guardianship of a museum dedicated to European painters from the
fifteenth to the eighteenth centuries. The art historian, who graduated
from the University of Ghent in 1928, also taught at the University
of Liège. Such was the force of her personality that a documentary
film about her was entitled *La souris péremptoire* (the peremptory

mouse), a metaphor for her obstinate character in spite of her petite stature.

Then in her late seventies, Ninane's social circle went far beyond the city's artistic and cultural scene. She was a woman who had been unafraid to act in the face of Nazi fascism. During the German occupation of Belgium during the Second World War, she had been part of an underground network of the Belgian Resistance, who rescued Jewish people from the Nazis' 'Final Solution' – the daily transportation of Jews to Auschwitz-Birkenau concentration camp.

At her home in Brussels, where Ryan often stayed when he was in the city, Ninane sometimes recounted her efforts against the Nazis during the war. 'She had saved many Jews and had a great sense of justice for all people. I'd say if there was a resistance any place, she would have been part of it. She was tiny in stature but such a sharp mind and a powerhouse of energy. We became great friends.'

Tom O'Sullivan, the first IRA man to work with Ryan, also travelled to Brussels. 'I went out working on the Continent myself for a time and used to meet Paddy. We'd make an arrangement and the camper van would be there, and that's how I knew he had arrived. In Brussels I was introduced to Lucie Ninane, who was the coolest little thing you ever met, a very wise woman. Maurice was a shrewd character, clued in to a lot of security matters.'

Among Ninane's dinner-party guests was another Irishman who was attuned to many of Patrick Ryan's viewpoints: Richard Behal. As head of Sinn Féin's foreign affairs bureau from the mid-1970s to 1982, Behal was at that point largely based in Belgium, a country in which he had sought and won political refugee status in 1967. He had been on the run in Ireland after escaping from Limerick Prison, where he was awaiting a retrial in connection with an attack on a British naval ship, HMS *Brave Border*, in Waterford in 1965. A member of the IRA since the 1950s, Behal had also been involved in disturbing the visit of Princess Margaret and the Earl of Snowdon to Abbeyleix Castle in January 1965, an occasion that was greeted by the explosion of an electricity transformer at the edge of the estate.

Behal, like Ryan, admired his host for her acts of patriotism during the Second World War. 'Lucie Ninane would talk about the Nazi officers coming into the museum where she would bring them around and show them the art. They assumed she was a collaborator, but she was only playing them to pick up intelligence for the Belgian resistance. She was a wonderful woman; I'd say she was one of God's chosen and she took Fr Paddy to her heart as well. He was always in good humour, he was polite, but you always knew that there was a lot behind the smile.'[21]

Ninane introduced her friend Ryan to an eclectic mix of professionals and contacts who moved at all levels within Brussels' political and social circles. For Ryan, every introduction was a potential opportunity to exploit further down the line. 'A particular friend of hers who lived in the wealthy suburb of Uccle used to invite me to her home for lunch and one fine day she said, "Do you know who is living nearby?" That is how I came to know that a British diplomat was living in a house towards the end of the cul-de-sac.'

A small seed grew into cruel intent. Ryan's rationale behind his choice of target was ruthless. 'Wars usually evolve with one poor man's son killing another poor man's son, and yet it's the villains of all these wars who have their chests lined with medals and I always believed that you start at the top of the line, if you can.' He made it his business to take up the invitations for lunch in Uccle more often, with the clear motive of carrying out reconnaissance on the potential target. The information he could glean from being in such close proximity to the home of a British diplomat could be used by an IRA active service unit to kill the man. 'The woman who told me who lived near her never really knew why it was such an important little nugget. She didn't have a clue what she had revealed, but when you hear information like that, you just pick it up and say nothing.'

Ryan began to take sketches of the area, as well as noting the registrations of the cars coming and going from the different houses. 'I knew how it would be put to use and my intermediary passed on the information to the IRA so that the hit team on the Continent got the detail.'

What had been shared as a seemingly throwaway remark by a friend of Lucie Ninane's was the catalyst for a targeted IRA operation, and Ryan's meticulous record-keeping and information was acted on. 'I later found out that they carefully observed the place, particularly at night, and they used to see the Brit around his garden.'

The British diplomat under IRA surveillance was Paul Holmer, the Deputy British Ambassador to the North Atlantic Treaty Organisation (NATO). Formed in 1949 to counter the threat of post-war communist expansion as the Soviet Union sought to extend its influence in Europe, the first NATO headquarters was in London, where it remained for two years before relocating to Paris and then, in 1967, to Brussels.

Nine hours after the British Ambassador to the Netherlands had been shot dead in The Hague, another IRA operation, this one aimed at assassinating Holmer in Brussels, got underway. At 6.15 p.m. two IRA gunmen approached a car close to his home and fired eight bullets in three bursts from a distance of a few yards. The sole occupant of the car was struck in the head and arms by several of the bullets and died later in hospital.

The IRA had demonstrated its ability to carry out two shootings in two European cities on the same day. However, this time they had assassinated the wrong man. André Michaux, a senior official of the Central Bank in Brussels, who happened to live on the same street as Holmer, was dead. Ryan learned of the shooting victim's identity the following day, while listening to a Belgian radio news bulletin. 'It went horribly wrong. The banker must have been turning his car. You see, they lived on the same cul-de-sac and the road outside their houses was very narrow, so much so that if a car was parked close to the entrance of the banker's house, he was sort of blocked in, he couldn't turn towards the main road. Instead, he had to go down towards the cul-de-sac, turn his car at the big wide entrance of the Ambassador's house and comfortably drive back up, towards the main road.'

In his car, Michaux was oblivious to the men hiding in the shadows waiting to shoot a British diplomat in the name of the IRA, based on a tip-off from Ryan. 'When the IRA men made their move, they did so because they saw a car at the Ambassador's gate and put bullets in the man's head. But it was the wrong man. They shot the banker and it was a major calamity.'

As the Dutch government searched for the killers of Sir Richard Sykes, extra police officers were assigned to the country's borders and security at the airport was tighter than usual, with patrolmen carrying rifles in main concourses. Given the fatal gun attack on André Michaux, the Belgian government now had cause to follow suit.

The next morning, in Brussels, Roy Jenkins had to forego his usual morning run on 'security grounds because of news the previous day of the assassination of Richard Sykes'. 'Still more threatening news [for us],' he added in his 23 March diary entry, referring to the shooting dead of a Belgian, 'probably' in mistaken circumstances, tied up 'with the intelligence we had received about possible threats six weeks before, but had typically forgotten about in the meantime'. The President of the European Commission travelled to his offices that morning 'with screaming police cars, motorcycle escorts, and a guard of about fourteen policemen' as the Belgian police were 'thronging rue de Praetère'. The increased security measures were based, as Jenkins saw it, 'on the good old principle of shutting the stable door'.[22]

Despite having a place to stay in Brussels, Patrick Ryan was all too aware of the risk of being picked up, given his previous detention in other European cities; he needed to get to a safe house. 'I had to move away from Ninane's home so that I wouldn't draw any heat on her. The military were starting to surround the city and I was told to go on foot to a certain street in Brussels and when I came to a particular number there would be a gateway, to push it open and follow the steps up to a door, push that open and go straight up the stairs and across a landing to a bedroom and it was there that I took refuge.'

A thick layer of dust on the bed frame and small table beside it indicated that the bedroom in the safe house had apparently not been used for some time. Ryan made the room his home for the next couple of weeks. 'Things were hot, so I had no choice. There was a toilet next to the room, and my contact left water and some food outside the door for me on a few occasions, but I couldn't stay there indefinitely, I had to move to the next phase of the plan. An acquaintance of mine arranged for an ambulance to come and collect me.'

If any passers-by had stopped to enquire what accident had befallen the man being taken away by ambulance, they would have been told a farcical tale of an alcoholic in a coma who needed urgent medical attention in hospital. There may have been an exasperated, knowing look exchanged before the ambulance doors were closed, but, as it happened, no one enquired and the ploy to extract Ryan from Brussels went off without fanfare.

For Ryan, his next safe house was a property where, given his religious vocation, he felt superficially at least, more at home. 'I was dropped off at a monastery. It had been organised beforehand, so the monks were expecting me. We never spoke about the business I was in or why I needed somewhere to lie low, but they couldn't have been more hospitable.'

Ever willing to embrace whatever environment he needed to in order to survive, Ryan adjusted his habits to suit his new hosts. 'I got up at the same time as them in the early hours of the morning to say prayers, devoured mountains of black coffee, not in a cup I would have been used to, it was kind of in a bowl you catch with both hands, and I'd have it with blackish rye bread. I went along with it all for the next six weeks and then I hit the road.'

By the summer Ryan was on a brief sojourn in Ireland. On 27 August 1979 he was just miles from the small fishing village of Mullaghmore in north County Sligo, close to the border with Northern Ireland. It was a gloriously sunny morning and from Mullaghmore Harbour, a 29-foot green-and-white boat, the *Shadow V*, sailed a quarter mile off the coast to go lobster fishing. The boat belonged to Lord Louis Mountbatten, a cousin of Queen Elizabeth II, an uncle of Prince Philip, former chief of the British defence staff and the last Viceroy of India. He and his family were on holiday, gathered as usual at Classiebawn Castle, which Mountbatten's wife, Countess Edwina, had inherited in 1939.[23] On board was a party of seven: Mountbatten; his daughter Patricia; her husband, Lord Brabourne; her husband's mother, the eighty-three-year-old dowager Lady Brabourne; the Brabournes' twin fourteen-year-old sons, Timothy and Nicholas Knatchbull, who were godsons of Prince Charles; and fifteen-year-old Paul Maxwell, who had landed his dream summer job working as a boat boy on the *Shadow V*.

Suddenly there was a massive bang. Watching from afar, terrorists had just detonated the radio-controlled IRA bomb that had been planted on the *Shadow V*. The fact that there were children on the boat had no influence on their murderous intent.

A column of water rose high into the air as fragments of the boat, along with the shattered bodies, exploded upwards. Lord Mountbatten's legs were blown off and he drowned. His grandson

Nicholas and Paul Maxwell were both killed instantly. Lady Doreen Brabourne was critically wounded and died the next day. The other passengers survived.

John Maxwell was reading his newspaper in the sunspot at the back of his family's holiday cottage in Mullaghmore. 'It was a God almighty explosion, and I knew from the direction of the explosion that that would be where the boat was – they took the same boat trip each day.'[24] He rushed to Mullaghmore Harbour where he found the body of his beloved son on the boat which had brought him ashore.

Gerry Moriarty, one of the first journalists on the scene, witnessed a father's visceral grief for his son. 'As the boat berthed beneath the harbour wall, John Maxwell looked down on the dead body of his child and cried repeatedly: "Look what you've done to him, look what you've done to him. I'm an Irishman, he's an Irishman, is this the sort of Ireland you want?" It's a phrase that bore deep down into my own consciousness and the few others of us who looked on helplessly that day.'[25]

The IRA had struck at the heart of the British establishment. At Buckingham Palace, a spokesman said that Queen Elizabeth, who received the news at Balmoral Castle in Scotland, was 'deeply shocked' at the loss of the cousin whom she and the rest of the Royal Family called 'Uncle Dickie'.

News of the bombing quickly filtered through on news reports. In the car, Patrick Ryan turned up the radio dial. 'I was driving some twenty miles away from where the boat was blown up. I had nothing to do with it, but it came on the news. I remember saying to the passenger, a Belgian lawyer who had travelled to Ireland to see me about a particular matter, "We are close to that spot." I knew that a net would be thrown about the place and fast, so we folded our tent, metaphorically speaking, and made our way further south.'

The IRA was not yet done for the day. Prime Minister Margaret Thatcher had already been informed of the assassination of Lord Mountbatten and was working on official correspondence at Chequers when a member of her staff broke the news to her.[26] Within hours of the *Shadow V* bomb, a British Army convoy had been ambushed at Narrow Water, near Warrenpoint in County Down. The IRA set off two remote-controlled 800-pound bombs, strategically timed to cause maximum carnage. The first, planted under hay on a flatbed lorry beside a road, killed six soldiers in a convoy truck. Twenty minutes later the second was detonated, killing twelve more soldiers, some of whom had been sent in as reinforcements following the first explosion. The attack was biggest single loss the British Army had suffered in an IRA incident in Northern Ireland.

As he made his way further south that day, Patrick Ryan resolved to return to the Continent as soon as he could. 'The purpose of my trip close to north Sligo that day in August, a potential target that I was interested in having a look at, had to be aborted, and anyway, I was only on a flying visit home.' His next visit to Ireland would prove to be one of his most significant in terms of the life he had chosen.

FOURTEEN

LION OF THE DESERT

Patrick Ryan parked up and walked determinedly towards Dublin Airport's homage to the power of the Catholic Church in Ireland: the Church of Our Lady Queen of Heaven. Built in 1964, the church's simple modernist architectural features belied its implicit message that the Catholic Church would have a presence in every part of Irish society, even within the grounds of an airport, the very manifestation of a modern country.

In the years before the church was built, an airport hangar would be transformed into a place of worship every Sunday. Pilots and air hostesses in their pristine uniforms would stand alongside mechanics in their overalls, solemnly bowing their heads as a priest said Mass under the giant wings of aircraft. In Catholic Ireland, even the flying machines of the national airline were blessed. From its founding in 1936, into the 1970s, the annual blessing of the fleet ceremony took place on the runway of Dublin Airport. The choreography of the ceremony was meticulous in its execution. Pilots would park Aer Lingus planes in a semi-circle, noses facing a makeshift altar, while a priest went from one to the other, dousing the planes with holy water.

Science and aeronautical engineering heralded safety advancements in air travel, but, to and from Ireland, passengers of Aer Lingus, the national airline, were also flying via two wings and a prayer. Those who sought divine intervention could take comfort from a prayer included in the safety instructions folder for every traveller: 'Oh God, who has made all creatures for Thy own Glory, and has destined all the things of this world for the service of mankind, bless, we pray Thee, this machine built for air travel, that it may serve – without loss or danger – for spreading even more widely the praise and glory of Thy name, and for the quicker dispatch of the world's affairs and may foster in the hearts of those who travel in it, a yearning for the things above through Christ our Lord.'[1]

The overhead roar of an aircraft engine accelerating after lift-off tilted Ryan's focus upwards; he recognised the distinctive rich-green roof and tail of an Aer Lingus plane with a large white shamrock on its fin. He was not able to make out the name of the aircraft, but each was unique and holy. Aer Lingus planes bore the names of Irish missionary saints of Ireland, including Pádraig, Breandán, Brigid, Cillian and Columbán. Ryan squinted his eyes as the aircraft's wheels tucked neatly into its white undercarriage; seconds later, the plane moved beyond his field of vision.

Decades on from when he had first left Ireland, Ryan was just a couple of hundred metres from the terminal in Dublin Airport where another generation of young Irish people was saying tear-filled goodbyes. It was early autumn 1981 and, given the growing dole queues in the Republic, Ryan surmised that Ireland's national flag carrier was almost certainly shuttling young men and women to London in search of opportunity. Those who were less well-heeled would still have to take a ferry across the Irish Sea, but whatever mode of transport they chose to take it was, as Ryan saw it, a sacrifice worth making in search of the dignity of work.

As he walked into the church's atrium, he was immediately struck by the near-silence of the space and paused to look at the copper sculpture, 'Madonna Fountain', in the centre of the landscaping. The copper had largely oxidised to a blue-green patina and the arms of the Madonna were open wide and held aloft, her hands and face pointing towards the sky.

The stillness of the atrium was the antithesis of a summer of death and destruction. Tens of thousands of mourners had marched in grief and fury behind tricolour-draped coffins; death marches that occurred alongside a surge in sectarian killings in Northern Ireland. Ninety miles north from where Ryan was standing, ten men of the same generation that was leaving Dublin Airport in hopeful droves had wilfully starved themselves to death on a point of principle.

The 1981 hunger strike marked an escalation of a five-year protest by republican prisoners in Her Majesty's Prison Maze at Long Kesh, ten miles south-west of Belfast. Up to 1975 political prisoners in Northern Ireland had been given 'Special Category' status, which allowed them, among other things, to wear their own clothes. However, following internment the British government announced that those convicted of terrorist offences after 1 March 1976 would be treated as ordinary prisoners and be subject to ordinary prison rules.

By 1981 increasing demands for the reinstatement of Special Category status by republican inmates were met by a prime minister who never wavered. 'Crime is crime is crime,' Mrs Thatcher declared. 'It is not political. It is crime. There can be no question of political status.'[2]

The stand-off became a contest of wills, with the IRA hunger strikers prepared to carry their demands to the grave. Bobby Sands, OC of IRA prisoners in the Maze, refused food on 1 March 1981. Five days later came a totally unexpected event. A snap by-election was announced for the Westminster constituency of Fermanagh/South Tyrone and, after much internal argument, the republican leadership decided to nominate Sands as a candidate. Forty days into his hunger strike, Sands was elected MP for Fermanagh/South Tyrone, narrowly defeating the unionist candidate. His election transformed politics in Northern Ireland; at the next Sinn Féin Ard-Fheis (annual party conference), Danny Morrison famously gave voice to 'the Armalite and ballot box' strategy, in which elections were contested by Sinn Féin alongside the IRA campaign.

The death of Sands, the first of the hunger strikers to die, occurred in the early hours of 5 May. As the news spread through Catholic areas of Belfast before the sun rose that morning, crowds were summoned onto the streets by a fury of whistles and a raging clang of metal dustbin lids being relentlessly banged off the ground. Burning barricades quickly shrouded the city in acrid smoke and the grief-laden murmur of women's voices reciting the prayers of the Rosary at street corners in some parts of the city was soon drowned out by the angry thud and spatter of petrol bombs hitting police and army targets.

During question time in the House of Commons that afternoon, Thatcher served notice that, despite the death of Sands, her stance on the hunger strikers would not change. 'We are on the side of protecting law-abiding and innocent citizens, and we shall continue in our efforts to stamp out terrorism. Mr. Sands was a convicted criminal,' Mrs Thatcher said. 'He chose to take his own life. It was a choice that his organisation did not allow to many of their victims.'[3]

Over the next three months, nine further men – six IRA and three Irish National Liberation Army (INLA) – died on hunger strike. The events attracted the attention of Colonel Muammar Gaddafi, who urged the head of the United Nations to intervene. In a letter addressed to Dr Kurt Waldheim, the then United Nations secretary general, the Libyan leader described the prisoners' deaths as 'courageous'. 'These men should be granted a political status in view of the fact that they are indeed fighting for a just and sacred cause, the freedom of their nation, which is one of the world's smallest, but which still has its place under the sun, free as God created it.' British authorities, in response, urged the United Nations not to circulate the letter. Irish civil servants in the United Nations and the Anglo-Irish section of the Taoiseach's office insisted there should be no reply.[4]

At the church in Dublin Airport, Patrick Ryan did not have time to admire the architecture or even contemplate how, in death, the hunger strikers had been elevated to Irish republican martyrdom. He needed to get a move on. The instructions for the rendezvous had been clear – his meeting with the IRA's chief of staff would take place inside.

A faint smell of incense permeated the church's brick-lined interior. As he sat in the pew at the very back of the church and waited, Ryan thought about how it was well over a decade since he had poured bright grains of incense onto red-hot charcoal in a thurible, blessed it and then swung the metal censer suspended from chains, sending clouds of fragrant smoke wafting through the air as part of a symbol of the prayer of the faithful rising to heaven. The altar's timber-lined backdrop accentuated the darkness, reprieved in parts by shafts of light filtered through two bands of stained glass running the length of the right- and left-hand sides of the church.

A gentle whoosh from a draft of fresh air, and the movement of shadows, alerted Ryan to the fact that he was no longer alone. A slim and smartly dressed man carefully genuflected before sitting in the pew directly in front of him. At almost the same time Ryan noticed a second man, who purposefully lowered his right knee to touch the ground before sitting down right beside him. The straight-backed man directly in front of him was a stranger, but Ryan did not need to turn his head to confirm the identity of the man to his left. The coarse, wavy hair and slightly stooped posture gave him up – it was the chief of staff. 'I could tell from the corner of my eye that it was Martin McGuinness.'

McGuinness had been a trainee butcher in Derry in 1970 when he abandoned his apprenticeship to join the IRA. He rose quickly through its ranks, gaining international notoriety as celebrities visited his home in the Bogside and headlines proclaimed: 'The boy who rules Free Derry' and 'Derry's blue-eyed boy'.[5] He was a man of many faces; by 1977 he had become the first northern commander of the IRA, after a successful move against the old southern-based leadership; the following year he took over as IRA chief of staff, only standing down from the role as chairman of the IRA's Army Council after signalling his intention to stand for a seat in the 1982 Assembly election.

Ryan's previous meeting with McGuinness, in a safe house close to the border, had taken place a year beforehand, with just the two of them present. 'I was back in Ireland with a good sum of money and I met McGuinness on my own and he said, "Paddy you are the only one who is really helping at present." I was always wary of him, irrespective of his compliments, but I remembered his remarks because they were a mighty contrast to what would unfold at a later point.'

It was now late summer 1981 and Ryan had returned to Dublin because the Libyan regime had tasked him with a particular job. 'Gaddafi was putting together a new unit of special forces, but they were deficient in electronics and needed training before they went on the job. I sent minimal word back and expected that there might have been progress, and that is how it came about that I was introduced to Éamon McGuire. I first met him in the very place where I learned McGuinness used to meet him – the Church of Our Lady Queen of Heaven in Dublin Airport.'

A meeting place within the grounds of the airport suited McGuire who, in 1981, was working as an aviation engineer with Aer Lingus;

equally the church was a discreet location for the IRA's chief of staff to meet with one of the IRA's most valuable assets. On the face of it McGuire had a respectable job, working full-time for the Irish national carrier, but he also had a secret life – one where he put his technical expertise at the disposal of the IRA and in his spare time bought equipment and designed bombs, landmines and rockets, as well as technology to shoot down British Army helicopters in south Armagh.

In the church, Ryan got straight to the point. 'There wasn't much talk between the three of us that day and there was no need to linger. I told McGuire what the Libyans were looking for and a date was arranged for the two of us to meet at my usual meeting spot in Paris a couple of weeks later.'

McGuire grew up a farmer's son in the border county of Monaghan and first learned about mechanics and aviation in the Curragh military camp as an Irish Air Corps apprentice in the 1950s. At the outbreak of the Troubles in 1969, he was working for Gulf Aviation in Bahrain, where he tested equipment in the desert. 'In order to produce some equipment for the war effort at home, I purchased components from around the world and built devices. Out on an isolated part of the desert I tested them out for operating distance, reliability, effectiveness and resistance to electronic countermeasures until I had what I was looking for. With seven weeks' leave per year, I was able to return to Ireland at intervals to check the devices in the battlefield, and if satisfactory, put them into service. When I returned to the Persian Gulf, radio reports allowed me to follow their effectiveness. In time, as skills were developed, they became more successful and helped to force the British army off the ground and into the air.'[6]

McGuire was the man put forward by McGuinness to be brought to Libya by Patrick Ryan in order to share his electronics expertise with the Gaddafi regime. He had chosen the right man for the job. McGuire went on to be described by the CIA as the IRA's chief technical officer. 'The Americans would claim that I killed more than anyone else. I would accept that,' he said.[7]

In Paris, the city was beginning to re-awaken. *La rentrée* marked the end of the weeks-long summer sabbaticals for locals, who returned to their city refreshed and renewed after their country and coastal getaways. As he made his way to the meeting point, Ryan observed the smart new attire of children and many adults alike: crisp school uniforms, fashionable scarf knots and suits worn with blindingly white shirts heralded the start of the city's school and work year.

As had been arranged, Ryan waited for McGuire under the Eiffel Tower, but the aviation engineer was a no-show. 'I had no way of contacting him, but I estimated that, well, he is a right-thinking man, he'll know that the same time tomorrow is an option and will rightly assume that I will return to wait for him and, sure enough, my hunch was correct.'

McGuire's own security measures in Ireland had delayed his departure. Instead of driving directly from his home in Dublin to Rosslare for the ferry to France, he went on an extended anti-surveillance loop around a number of counties in an effort to lose any possible Garda Special Branch detectives who may have been following him. His arrival in Paris twenty-four hours late was of no concern to Ryan, who returned to the exact same location the following day. 'He turned up and I was there to meet him. I had already arranged the flights to Tripoli and it proved to be one of the most important trips to Libya that I made.'

Ryan had already tipped off the Libyan Embassy about his esteemed companion, and a flight had been arranged for them both to Tripoli the following day. There was one matter, however, that needed attention prior to the flight: the concealment of electronic contraband from curious customs officers at the airport in Paris.

'McGuire brought pieces of miniature electronics that he needed as part of his training camp. They were very tiny little chips and pieces for electronic boards, small enough to hold in the palm of a hand, but we couldn't take the risk of them being seized, so I bought a steam iron the day before we flew to Tripoli. I opened it up and made a hole in the water tank, filled it with the tiny electronic pieces and sealed it up again, put it in my luggage and it went through alright, not a problem.'

The Libyans took extra care to keep McGuire off any foreign intelligence radar in Tripoli. On arrival he was discreetly taken down the maintenance steps of the plane and driven by Libyan intelligence officers to a separate hotel from Ryan. In Libya, the two men largely stayed apart. 'McGuire was extremely security-conscious and worked on the basis that he could have been under surveillance at any time. The very fact that he took his security so seriously endeared him to our hosts, and on top of that he was also a well-travelled man and had some words of Arabic, which gave him an authenticity when he interacted with the officials who were looking after us.'

Ryan was left in no doubt that it was McGuire's technical abilities that made the most significant impression on the Libyan regime. 'You see, McGuire was exceptionally skilled at what he did, and equally so at showing others how to copy those skills. A car would pick him up every morning from his hotel to take him to the training camp outside of the city and it wasn't just Libyans he was training in how to build electronic devices, detonate devices by radio signals and other such advancements in the world of electronics, it was guys from various parts of the Middle East, and he carried out his training methodically every day for nearly two weeks. The Libyans were very impressed, of course they were, they could see how skilled he was, and what he did on that trip helped to spread modern guerrilla warfare to the Arab world. My Libyan contact later described him to me as the first real soldier they ever had from the IRA.'

On his final evening, Éamon McGuire joined Ryan for dinner at the home of a senior intelligence official on the outskirts of Tripoli. 'The Libyans would have liked for Éamon to stay longer, but of course he had a job to return to and his profession was the perfect front for his ambitions in refining the IRA's technical capabilities. After our meal we were brought to another room in the house where our host had set up a showing of the film *Lion of the Desert* and it absolutely transfixed us.' Released in 1981, the Libyan regime had funded the production, an epic historical war film about the Libyan resistance against Italian imperialism in the early years of the twentieth century. The two-and-three-quarter-hour film told the story of Sidi Omar al-Mukhtar (Omar Mukhtar) who led a twenty-year guerrilla resistance movement against Italian rule in the province of Cyrenaica in eastern Libya until he was captured in 1931. The resistance against Italian colonisation ended on 16 September 1931 with al-Mukhtar's public execution by hanging in front of 20,000 of his followers, turning him into a martyr and national hero. *Lion of the Desert* starred Anthony Quinn as al-Mukhtar, Rod Steiger as Mussolini, and Oliver Reed as Italian General Rodolfo Graziani, who won renown and notoriety for his command of the Italian forces in Libya.

Not only did Gaddafi bankroll the $35 million film, but his regime also provided thousands of military personnel to be used as extras for on-location shooting in the North African desert. The final scene of the film depicted al-Mukhtar's forces on horseback charging in slow motion with their rifles held aloft. As the film credits rolled, McGuire turned to Ryan for his assistance on a particular matter.

'He said to me, "Paddy, we [the IRA] don't have one microswitch, our last supply line from California is dried up, I don't have one, could you do anything?" He had the name of the company in England that made them, but they were on lockdown to civilians so to speak. I said off-hand, "I haven't a clue but", I said, "I won't be caught for the want of trying, leave it with me."'

FIFTEEN

SWITCH AND SWITCH

In Tripoli, Patrick Ryan sat alone in a corner of the hotel from where he could observe the comings and goings at the reception desk. An impatient queue had formed of American citizens who were heeding advice and checking out. In effect, they had no choice: a decree had been issued by the White House days earlier when, on 11 December 1981, President Ronald Reagan's administration appealed to US citizens to leave Libya immediately and invalidated American passports for travel to that country.

Patrick Ryan had chosen to stay on in Tripoli after Éamon McGuire returned to his day job in Dublin. One of the reasons was for Ryan to try to source the microswitches needed to control the detonation of bombs. However, particularly after the American decision to pull their people out of the country, he needed a plausible cover story to explain what business he had in Libya. A political decision made a decade earlier in Dublin – Ireland's membership of the EEC – gave Ryan the perfect excuse.

When Ireland joined the EEC on 1 January 1973, the country's beef sector was amongst the first to profit. As oil wealth grew across the Middle East and North Africa, so too did the demand for cattle and beef, and livestock exports to non-EEC countries were generously supported by EEC subsidies. The Libyan market grew spectacularly and presented Ryan with a credible cover story. 'It worked out very well for me because I was able to say that I was in Libya representing the interests of Irish beef processors, that I was their man on the ground.'

The coffee Ryan had been drinking had gone cold, but he was too consumed with watching what was unfolding to care. The previous evening, as he had been sitting alone, he had tuned into a conversation where two Americans were discussing the additional payments they had been offered by their employer, an oil company, to stay on in Libya. The next morning, Ryan recognised the man who had spoken the loudest about the lure of a $100-a-day bonus; he was waiting in line to return his room key and settle any outstanding room-service bills.

In his first decade of power, Gaddafi delivered on his foreign policy strategy of providing material support, especially funds and arms, to any group prepared to use terrorist tactics anywhere in the world. Libyan oil money supported at least fifteen different terrorist groups and schooled Palestinian, Irish, German and Italian terrorists in secret desert training camps. Training that the IRA should have taken more advantage of, according to Ryan. 'Libya made several training offers but, contrary to popular opinion, the IRA made very little use of those offers except in particular circumstances, but the Libyans were supporting any kind of a rebellion against a coloniser. We weren't the only people.' The Gaddafi regime also offered a safe haven to Palestinians and others after terrorist attacks in Europe. At the end of the decade, on 29 December 1979, the US government designated Libya a 'state sponsor of terrorism' under the Export Administration Act.[1]

Early into his administration, US President Ronald Reagan demonstrated his intention to take a hard-line approach to Gaddafi, whose regime he regarded as a puppet of the Soviet Union. Four months after his inauguration in January 1981, Reagan ordered the closing of the Libyan diplomatic mission in Washington and gave all Libyan diplomats five working days to get out of the country because of what the US State Department described as 'Libyan provocations and misconduct, including support for international terrorism.'[2] The US State Department added that it was also advising American citizens not to travel to or to live in Libya.

That summer the Reagan administration demonstrated its unwillingness to allow even an appearance of letting Colonel Muammar Gaddafi 'set the rules'.[3] In August the President ordered US Navy ships to conduct exercises inside Gaddafi's self-proclaimed 'line of death', a base line across the mouth of the Gulf of Sidra in the Mediterranean Sea, the area south of which Libya claimed as its territorial waters. The Libyan Air Force responded by deploying a high number of interceptors and fighter-bombers.

On 20 August, in compliance with US presidential orders that any aircraft harassing US forces was to be pursued 'all the way into the hangar',[4] American pilots shot down two Soviet-built Libyan aircraft they deemed to be a threat. Reagan defended the action and vowed to continue the policy of prompt retaliation to make American power 'impressive to the enemies of freedom'.[5] In a handwritten diary entry he added: 'A few days after the incident over the gulf, security people obtained secret information indicating that Gaddafi had advised some of his associates that he intended to have me assassinated. So, it was back into my iron vest whenever I was out in public.'[6]

As tensions escalated, in December 1981 the Reagan administration appealed to the estimated 2,000 Americans working in Libya, most of them in the oil industry, to come home. 'Because of the danger the Libyan regime poses to American citizens, the President calls upon all Americans to leave Libya as soon as possible,' said acting Secretary of State William Clark. 'The United States recognises the gravity of these steps but believes that Libyan actions oblige us to take them. Indeed, it would be irresponsible of the United States government to do less.'[7]

In Dublin the Irish government, along with its EEC partners, came under pressure from the Reagan administration to impose a trade embargo on Libya. At stake was Ireland's financially profitable growing beef trade with Libya. 'We will not tolerate dictation from any Government – except our own – about where the products of our country's biggest industry, agriculture, are marketed around the world,' said a defiant spokesperson for the Irish Farmers' Association.[8]

US diplomatic efforts aimed at achieving a trade embargo against Libya received a cool reaction in many European capitals. A CIA intelligence memorandum titled 'West European Policy Toward Libya' noted: 'While US–Libyan relations had deteriorated, West European governments had sought to maintain – and in some cases improve – their ties with Tripoli.' The classified briefing document added that, in the absence of 'clear signs' that Gaddafi was becoming increasingly aggressive, 'Western Europe will probably continue to react negatively to US pressure for a harder political or economic line against Libya.'[9]

For Patrick Ryan, the largely ineffectual diplomatic wrangling by the US with Western European governments in support of a Libyan trade embargo meant that his cover story of being a representative for the Irish beef industry in Tripoli was still in play. 'Of course, the real purpose of my visits was to extract more aid and talk to the Libyans, plotting and planning what we might do. You see, it wasn't a one-sided effort on my part. The Libyans highly appreciated the help I could give, because as a white man it was sometimes easier for me to go into certain situations in Europe, so I obliged ... I saw myself as a runner, a type of fixer, and we always got on very well. In Tripoli, they would put me up in a hotel and I worked very quietly, and seeing that I was over on specific missions, it was even more important for me to operate that way.'

In December 1981 the Reagan administration's efforts to curb American involvement in Libya prompted a dramatic exodus by many of the 2,000 US citizens in Libya. Britain, however, was still some years away from advising its citizens to do the same, a fortunate happenstance for Patrick Ryan. While meeting some of his Libyan contacts for a coffee one evening, a person of interest was pointed out. 'This English fellow was coming in and out of the hotel, and it was the Libyans who first alerted me to this character when they said, "We are keeping an eye on that fellow." They knew him because he worked as an engineer in one of their military stores and I thought to myself, "Isn't that interesting," but in that world, you don't ask questions, you wait.'

He decided to cultivate the Englishman, whom he suspected could be of assistance in sourcing the switches that the IRA had run short of. 'An opportunity presented itself. The trick is to be patient because, you see, every person wants something badly, and if you can wait and slowly find out what that something is and then provide it, you are a winner, in any walk of life.'

Ryan began to closely observe the stoutly built, dark-haired man who always appeared to be interested in the company he was keeping. 'I got a hunch about him. I knew certainly that he was curious about my business because over a number of visits he eventually made his way into the company I was keeping, as I knew he would, because he wanted to get into the inner circle, that's what it was all about.'

A curious remark made by one of Ryan's Libyan contacts further piqued his interest in the stranger. 'One evening I was sitting with two of my Libyan contacts and as this same Englishman walked past, one of the Libyans nudged me with his elbow and said, "MI6". That is exactly what happened and that is exactly what I was told. Of course, I had no way of knowing if he was MI6 or not, but it was an interesting remark, so I watched and waited.'

In the English stranger, Ryan recognised a person eager to ingratiate himself. 'One day we were talking and he said, casually, that he was working in the electronics department of the stores. I didn't pursue it because you don't show any interest, you see.'

The first stage of Ryan's exercise in manipulation was establishing a motive: what did the Englishman want so badly that he would be blind to the likelihood of being compromised in some way in order to achieve his goal? Trying to establish the essence of a person's motivation was not an overwhelming challenge to a one-time priest who was trained in and had some experience of the art of coaxing penitents into confessing their moral failures and shortcomings during Catholic Confession. *Bless me Father, for I have sinned.*

Ryan had formed an opinion during his few short years of sitting on the priest's side of the division in a confessional box that people only whispered their transgressions because they wanted to be formally released from the guilt or shame of sin. The trade-off was genius in its simplicity – confess and you will receive the grace to carry on. *I absolve you from your sins in the name of the Father, the Son and the Holy Spirit.*

Sitting in dark confessional boxes, Ryan had sharpened his listening skills for what was unsaid. *And? Is that all?* On occasion he could sense from the tone of a person's voice who was battling with their conscience to stop themselves from confessing to a sin aloud, and who was merely making up all manner of failures to fill the silence.

In the hotel in Tripoli, as in almost every interaction Ryan had, the same set of principles applied: what did the person want to achieve, what was the trade-off? 'I got sensitive to what this lad wanted, it became very clear to me that he was craving to be recognised at a higher level. From my reading of the situation, I could see that he was craving to get a handshake from the Colonel and it was obvious that, correctly or otherwise, he figured that I was the stepping stone, but, instead, I used him to get what I wanted.'

The Englishman later spoke, albeit anonymously, about his dealings with Ryan in Tripoli. He claimed he had taken Ryan's background story at face value. 'He said he was a meat exporter, he was in Libya to sell meat to the Libyans. He was meeting with Libyan officials, going out with them in cars. A colonel in the police used to pick him up and take him out, assumedly to meet Gaddafi.'[10]

As American workers queued to leave Tripoli, the Libyan leader went on a public-relations offensive. In television interviews for British and American broadcasters, Gaddafi spoke at times in English, reiterating that American workers were under no threat in his country. He dismissed statements made by the US government and others that he supported European terrorist groups, including the IRA, with weapons and training as 'just propaganda, allegations without evidence'. This denial was at odds with an assertion he had made only months earlier, when he restated his support for the IRA during an interview for Italian television.

The Libyan leader's contradictory public statements about his support for the IRA were of no consequence to Ryan, who was more than willing to be of use to the Libyan regime; a type of payment in kind for Gaddafi's patronage of the IRA. 'On one occasion I spent some time in Malta collecting information about an electricity substation, but, yes, if they wanted information or details about a particular location and were not in a position to send some of their own men, I would often oblige.'

The suggestion that some IRA members should make themselves available to work for the Libyan regime was rebuffed by those to whom Ryan suggested it within the republican movement. 'I took back several requests for IRA people to work for them and I'd be politely told to fuck off and keep bringing back the money, but I always believed that if I was to have any long-term success with the Libyans, the relationship had to be mutually beneficial and that is why I volunteered to work for them.'

In a Libyan desert training camp, Ryan was taught how to use a sub-machine gun. 'It was target practice for purposes in Europe. You see, machine guns are good for bit of diversionary noise, handy to draw attention so that someone else can go about what they really want to do further down the road. The plan, as intended, never materialised, but I wasn't a stranger to the old subs and my attitude went beyond talking, if needed. I was prepared to take the same risks for the Libyans as they would for me.'

Every time he left Tripoli, Patrick Ryan was never in any doubt that money would be made available to him to collect via Libyan embassies in Paris or Rome.

In late 1981 Ryan was preoccupied with following up on his plan to task the Englishman to source the sought-after switches. 'I took my time before I brought up an utterly fictitious story, but I figured that if he believed there was any chance at all that I would introduce him to Gaddafi, he would dance to my tune.'

One evening after the Englishman had spun himself out from talking, Ryan brought up the supposed favour that could potentially garner a big reward. 'I said, "The Colonel is getting some teams together for an important job, but there is some issue with the security of radios and for some reason or another he cannot source the material that they need from the traditional sources – is there any chance you can help?"'

Ryan's request was straightforward but preposterous; nevertheless, he was certain in his conviction that the Englishman would not question the veracity of what he was being asked to do. 'It was as simple as that. He never questioned why a so-called beef industry representative was making such a request. He hardly blinked, he just said, "Give me a week and I'll be back to you."'

As promised, one week later the Englishman handed Ryan a folder of literature about electronics. 'The documents stated the places where all kinds of military weapons and gear were being manufactured, the countries in which the rules were very strict, as well as the countries where there were no restrictions, and he then says, and his distinct words to me were, "Paddy, anything you want, I'll get it."'

Ryan then upped the ante. 'I mentioned two types of radio switches along with the manufacturer in England and he agreed to source them for me. I gave him cash and we agreed a date to meet in Paris for the handover. It was as simple as that.'

The Englishman followed through on his promise to source the electronic switches and left for London to gather the material. In January 1982 he purchased two types of micro switches – FX401 and FX101 – from Consumer Microcircuits Ltd (CMC) in Essex, and later outlined some of the details in an anonymous interview for a television documentary: 'He [Ryan] said he'd been looking into a problem we'd been talking about in Libya about the security of Gaddafi's radios. I took them straight from CMC to London airport.'[11]

The Englishman's apparent haste to get to the airport did not deter him from taking care to conceal the switches before he boarded a flight to Paris. 'I took them over in a cigarette packet with me to Paris. The switches were no bigger than my fingernail … they were only in plastic bags when they were given to me, so I put them in there for safety. I flew to Paris and met Father Ryan in a coffee shop next to the Gare du Nord hotel and handed them over to him and he paid me the balance, my airfare, my expenses, plus he paid the hotel bill and I handed the receipt to Ryan.'[12]

The tiny switches were of huge significance to the IRA and Patrick Ryan. 'Éamon McGuire, the man who developed the IRA's bombing technology, told me in Libya that the IRA had not one microswitch left, which meant that they had run out of detonators – that is how important the purchase of those microswitches was to the IRA and it was an Englishman who did it for me.'

Ryan smiled to himself as he walked away from the coffee shop in Paris with the precious switches in his pocket – he had achieved his singular aim. 'I was only interested in what he could do for me. His bill was only a few hundred, I gave him his money and he gave me the receipt from the company in England, which I tore up immediately. I sent the switches back home so the IRA was able to put them to work. That is the story as it happened. The Libyans knew nothing about it, no one knew anything about it, only myself and the Englishman until, of course, the IRA bombs went off.'

SIXTEEN

HYDE PARK

The little girl pressed her nose against the nursery window. She wanted to see her beloved father. The clip-clop sound of horses' hooves in the courtyard outside signalled there was a chance she could catch a glimpse of him or, better still, that he would look towards the nursery and see her waving him off.

It was a warm summer's morning in mid-July 1982 and a heavy scent of hay and horses wafted from Hyde Park Barracks in central London, the home of the Queen's Household Cavalry Mounted Regiment, as well as many of the soldiers' families, who lived in a specially built residential tower block, the Married Quarters.

Four-year-old Sarah Jane Young excitedly scanned the men on horseback and caught sight of her cavalryman father, Lance Corporal Jeffrey Young. He was one of a sixteen-man squadron of the Blues and Royals preparing to leave the barracks to follow a tradition going back 300 years: the Changing of the Guard.

At precisely, 10.28 a.m. on 20 July 1982, the New Guard would leave Hyde Park Barracks, proceed past Buckingham Palace, down the Mall and into Horse Guards Parade to line up alongside the Old Guard. The spectacle was a major draw for tourists, who would gather to marvel at the meticulous timing and choreography of the Changing of the Mounted Guard, after which the Old Guard travelled back towards Buckingham Palace, up Constitution Hill, and into Hyde Park Barracks.

Sarah Jane looked on as her father calmed his 'Cavalry black', a majestic Irish gelding whose hooves, like the other Cavalry horses, had been branded with an army number on the back and a squadron number and regimental initials on the front. Many of the Household Cavalry horses had been sourced in Ireland by the Army Purchasing Commission. An Irish Draught cross named Sefton was among the horses lining up to leave the barracks that morning. Born in County Waterford, he was taken by his owner in 1967 to Pallas Stud in County Tipperary to be inspected by the Army Purchasing Commission as a potential mount for the Household Cavalry. The black horse was immediately accepted and his owner was paid the then standard £275. The new recruit was shipped via a ferry from Dublin along with other horses destined for the Household Cavalry. At the remount depot he was named Sefton after Lord Sefton, a former Household Cavalry officer, and when he 'passed out' in June 1968, Sefton had his regimental number, 5/816, marked on his hind hooves.[1]

The clock counted down to 10.28 a.m.; it was time for the Blues and Royal squadron to leave. Sarah Jane stayed at the window of her nursery to wave her father off. 'I remember they looked so smart in their uniforms and when they got to the gates, Dad turned to look up and smile at me before he left.'[2]

The Guard trotted under the shiny green foliage on South Carriage Drive in military splendour, their tack jangling and the metal of their red-plumed helmets glinting in the sunlight. Lieutenant Denis Daly was the troop commander that morning. The twenty-three-year-old had been married less than four weeks earlier in the Guards Chapel, inside Wellington Barracks, where a regimental brass band played the wedding march. His mother, Valerie, had a friend visiting from Australia and was proudly waiting at Horse Guards Parade for her eldest son to come marching round the corner at precisely 11 a.m.[3]

Simon Utley was also one of the troopers. At eighteen years old, it was his first ever Changing of the Guard duty. 'I was excited because it was my first time in the Household Cavalry. I remember I was talking to the guy to my left about what I would be doing later because of the position I was in.'[4] The troop formation included mounted policemen at the front and rear and the senior men three abreast in the centre.[5] Every moment was perfectly timed and purposefully so; the strict execution of the procession was maintained so that the Guard would arrive at the arch of Horse Guards Parade at exactly 11 a.m.

As the procession made its way down South Carriage Drive, the Guard passed parked cars to its left. Among them was a blue Morris Marina, registration number LMD 657P. The car had been purchased the week beforehand at the British Car Auctions in Enfield by a man with an Irish accent.[6] The Morris Marina was parked against the direction of travel; a deliberate tactic to maximise the carnage about to unfold.

A remote-controlled bomb consisting of approximately 25lbs of Frangex, a commercial high explosive, had been placed inside the boot of the car. Those intent on murder had factored in another brutal measure that would guarantee maximum casualties: nail shrapnel. A later report noted how a 'large quantity of four- and six-inch nails had been placed between the skin of the car boot and the charge as additional shrapnel'.[7]

And that was not all. The bomb makers had methodically factored in how the position of the nails would affect their direction of travel. The nails were packed on the side of the car nearest to the passing soldiers and horses, and deliberately 'placed in such a way as to be directed towards the troop. The nails would have been distributed at the speed of a bullet being fired, if not more. Their only purpose was to increase the likelihood of causing death or serious injury.'[8]

As onlookers admired the majestic sight and sound of the mounted troop of Household Cavalry trotting in the July sunshine, another person, with a line of sight to the car, was watching on with homicidal intent and precision execution. The bomb was set up to be detonated by remote control rather than command wire; an adaptation that allowed the bomb to be exploded at just the right time and place to devastate a section of the parade.

A woman pushing a baby in a pram in the blast field of the blue Morris Marina did not deter the IRA trigger person, who was standing on the edge of the park, from pushing the talk button on a CB radio handset, sending an electrical pulse that triggered the explosion at 10.40 a.m., precisely as the centre of the troop passed the Morris Marina. Debris and flesh, human and equine, scattered around Hyde Park.

Two soldiers were killed instantly: Lieutenant Denis Daly and nineteen-year-old Trooper Simon Tipper, who had also been married for less than a month. Several dozen people, soldiers and civilians, were injured. The woman who had been pushing her baby son in a pram close to the parked car was struck in the leg by an unknown object and passed out, but her baby was unhurt.

The mayhem caused the Cavalry black that Simon Utley was riding to bolt from the blast scene. 'The bomb went off. It was a noise that I can't describe, but it was a painful noise because it took my eardrum out. Then I was aware of the heat and at that point my horse just took off into Hyde Park. I couldn't stop it, it just galloped off with me on it. It took me a fair way into the park before I managed to stop it. I took off my uniform, I had a nail in the back of my cuirass, my breastplate.'[9]

Richard Raynsford, a retired troop leader of the Household Cavalry, was riding a motorbike through Hyde Park to his insurance job when he stopped to help. He raced up the pavement to the blast zone, pulling a trooper away from the wreckage, and borrowed a policeman's pistol to put down three stricken horses. In all, seven horses, brutally gashed by the flying metal and nails, were killed or had to be put down.

Sefton and the remaining horses sustained horrific injuries. Sefton's were the most serious; his jugular vein had been severed, he had a wounded left eye and thirty-four other wounds on his body. And yet when the bomb exploded and tore his flesh, he kept his composure. His rider, Trooper Michael Pedersen, later said that Sefton responded so competently that, when the bomb went off, there was no chance of his being thrown. After dismounting, Pedersen, who was still in full state kit and in severe shock, could do little to help his horse.

In Hyde Park Barracks, Regimental Commander Andrew Parker Bowles heard the explosion. 'It was similar to those in Northern Ireland, especially in the early 1970s, and seemed a long way off,' he later wrote. 'It didn't occur to me that the QLG was the target until a junior NCO came down from the tower block from where he had seen the bomb go off shouting "the bastards have got the Guard".'[10]

The children in the barracks nursery also heard the explosion, including Sarah Jane. 'I felt the building shake. From the window, I saw soldiers rushing out of the barracks to see what was happening.'[11] The barracks emptied of soldiers running down the South Carriage Road, as Parker Bowles later wrote, 'some in sweatshirts and trousers, braces hanging, some in boots and breeches, and the farriers, their long leather aprons flapping'.[12]

Major Noel Carding, a veterinary officer, was among those who ran to the bomb site. Another soldier, on orders, took off his shirt and used it to apply pressure to Sefton's severe neck wound. Major

Carding led Sefton into the first horsebox to arrive on the scene. 'Sefton was the worst injured and I knew that we had to get him back to the barracks if there was to be any chance of saving him.'

The human casualties and injured were quickly removed from the scene, but the lifeless, mangled bodies of the Cavalry black horses lay on the road for some time before they were covered with blankets. Long-range camera lenses captured, in brutal detail, the aftermath, with the shattered remains of the car bomb surrounded by dead horses.

Sefton was taken to the forge rather than the stables, as it was closer, where Carding began an emergency operation, becoming the first of the British Army's veterinary officers to operate on war-like wounds to a cavalry horse in more than half a century. He also directed the care of the other wounded horses before civilian vets arrived to assist. Between them, Carding, the civilian vets, farriers and troopers managed to save all of the horses who were brought back to barracks from the scene of the explosion.[13]

But on that summer's day in London, the IRA was not yet done. In nearby Regent's Park, a bomb was hidden under the bandstand, with a long-delay timer set to the date and time of a free public concert by the band of the 1st Battalion, Royal Green Jackets. The device exploded as thirty military bandsmen were on the stand performing music from *Oliver!* to a crowd of 120, many of them tourists and office workers eating lunch under sunny skies. Six of the bandsmen were killed instantly, a seventh later died of his injuries.

'I was just sitting in a deckchair looking at the band when everything seemed to come up from the bottom of the bandstand and blow right in the air – the bodies, the instruments, everything,' said Ronald Benjamin, who was in Regent's Park.[14]

From the nursery window, Sarah Jane Young witnessed an un-folding scene of horror, including soldiers returning to the barracks covered with blood and embedded with nails. 'I felt frightened, and then Lulu, my nursery teacher, took me away from the window and put me in a different room. I remember telling my mum afterwards, "Daddy should be coming now," but he never did.'[15]

The following day Sarah Jane's father, Lance Corporal Jeffrey Young, died in hospital, a week before his twentieth birthday. Squadron Quartermaster Corporal Roy Bright, aged thirty-six, who had been carrying the regimental standard for the Blues and Royals, clung to life for two more days before dying in Westminster Hospital with his wife at his bedside. His widow donated his kidneys, saving the lives of two strangers.

On the evening of the bombings, the Cavalry Guards' colonel-in-chief, HM The Queen, rang Andrew Parker Bowles to express her sadness and to enquire into the condition of the wounded soldiers. 'I talked away about the condition of the horses and Her Majesty reminded me that we can buy more horses but can't buy soldiers.'[16]

In the aftermath, the search for forensic clues yielded a significant find lodged in the grass of Hyde Park: a fragment of a circuit board, which pointed to the use of a particular type of switching device – an FX401.[17]

SEVENTEEN

THE DUCKS OF THE GREEN

A tranquil calm was slowly returning to St Stephen's Green in the autumn of 1982. The lunch hour was over, forcing a flurry of office workers and college students who had sought respite from the bustle of Dublin city centre to reluctantly return to their offices or library desks. The shoulders of some had become heavy with the dread of the afternoon that lay ahead; they would have to shuffle through papers while counting down the clock, or tortuously attempt to make a lucid argument in a treatise on an academic point of principle.

As he entered the park from the Grafton Street entrance, Patrick Ryan walked under the Fusiliers' Arch. The war memorial was built to commemorate non-commissioned officers and men of the Royal Dublin Fusiliers who were killed fighting for the British on a distant African battlefield in the Second Boer War of 1899–1902. At the opening of the monument in 1907, the Earl of Meath described the purpose of the memorial: 'Situated in the centre of the Irish capital this memorial, recording the gallant deeds of brave men, will be an ever-present reminder to coming generations of the citizens of Dublin of the obligations of loyalty, of faithfulness, to duty and honour which Ireland demands of all her sons.'[1] The unveiling of the arch, however, coincided with a burgeoning Irish nationalist movement who resented its colonial iconography and labelled the structure 'Traitor's Gate'.

Ryan did not stop to look up at the names of the 212 fallen officers and men inscribed on the underside of the grey granite monument, nor did he pause to view the bullet holes left like pock-marked scars on the arch in crossfire between the Irish Citizen Army (ICA) and British troops during the 1916 Easter Rising.

A few hundred metres into the park, Ryan noticed that the relentless noise of cars and double-decker buses shuttling between stops outside had dimmed. The audible calmness allowed him to overhear the pleasantries exchanged between two smartly dressed elderly gentlemen, one of whom was also trying to cajole a stubborn Jack Russell terrier to heel.

Named after the Church of St Stephen, the chapel of a leper hospital in medieval Dublin, what had been a marshy common used for the grazing of livestock and public executions up to the mid-1600s was eventually enclosed and transformed into a park following the construction of magnificent Georgian townhouses around its perimeter in the late 1700s. The park was then accessible only to wealthy residents of the nearby area who held a key, but it opened to the public in 1880 after the politician and philanthropist Sir Arthur Edward Guinness of the brewing dynasty, later to become Lord Ardilaun, purchased, landscaped and donated St Stephen's Green to the people of Dublin.

Dappled light and shadows appeared to marble sections of the pathway that Ryan strolled along in the direction of the park's duck pond. He was alone on the path aside from a scurry of squirrels nervously darting between mossy tree trunks and carefully tended flower beds.

At the pond, two young children squealed in delight as they tore at stale slices of bread to throw at nonchalant swans and hungry

ducks. The woman standing behind them had placed a hand on each
of the children's rain jackets in order to prevent them from following
the trajectory of the bread into the shallow water. She turned her
head to smile at Ryan as he walked past; it was as if she needed
reassurance that the stranger had not been annoyed by the children's
boisterous shrieks.

The ducks of the Green had a heritage in prompting the
unexpected; during the week-long Easter Rising of 1916, heavy
gunfire around the park between the opposing sides of the ICA and
the British forces was stopped every day to allow them to be fed.
The *Times History of the War* recorded that St Stephen's Green 'was
well stocked with waterfowl, and the keeper, who remained inside
all the time, reported that his charges were well looked after and fed
by him, and were very little perturbed by the bullets flying over their
heads'.[2]

Patrick Ryan took his time while walking a loop of the park
before returning like the long arm of a clock to where he had started,
only now he was alone at the duck pond. The two children and their
mother had moved on and a kit of grey and greasy-looking pigeons
greedily picked at the detritus of the breadcrumbs they had left
behind. The pigeons' cooing grew louder before they suddenly took
off, beating the tips of their dirty-looking wings together to make a
sharp slapping sound that could almost be mistaken for a round of
applause.

Ryan had not followed the path back to the pond to feed the
ducks; he was standing at the agreed rendezvous point to meet with
Martin McGuinness and another IRA man. He had no expectations
of what the appointment would be about, but he knew not to ask
too many questions of the republican movement's military and
strategic thinker when he arrived, and he did not trust his word
even when it was freely volunteered.

When Ryan and Martin McGuinness had met previously, they were usually alone, with each driving to a safe house situated along the border. Ryan would arrive at these meetings to hand over Libyan cash but would leave with little insight about what Gaddafi's oil dollars were being used for specifically. 'Libyan intelligence was able to tell me more about what was going on in the IRA than McGuinness ever did.' Ryan had not formed much of an impression of McGuinness from these earlier meetings, only that he was not to be trusted.

The two men's sure-footed arrival coincided with the heavy plop of a seagull landing on the calm pond water. The splash startled a raft of ducks into a furious paddle, their beaks jutting forward resentfully as they jostled each other. The aggressive interruption was a harbinger of what was about to unfold.

'There wasn't even a "Good afternoon, Paddy," no sort of a greeting whatsoever from either of them. McGuinness just straight away began to lay into me.'

McGuinness's fractious greeting was caused by the shockwaves from an incident that had occurred some weeks earlier in the French capital. When the IRA bomb in Hyde Park had detonated, Ryan had been in Paris and paid little attention to reports of the carnage. It would be some years before he would learn for certain that the switches he had tasked the curious Englishman to obtain on his behalf had been used in the bomb.

Ryan had been focused on a different task and was expecting a visitor to the city who went by the pseudonym of 'Duty Man'. The directive he had been given was unambiguous – the IRA leadership specifically wanted Duty Man to be taken out to Tripoli. 'A date had been set ahead of his arrival in Paris and the meeting point had not changed: the Eiffel Tower. He turned up, as I expected he would do, on his own.'

Duty Man, who met Ryan under the city's iconic wrought-iron lattice tower, was not an individual he had previously been introduced to in Ireland, nor a character about whom he had picked up reports. However, his lack of knowledge about his newly arrived visitor was not a situation that gave Ryan cause for concern, as a new generation of decision-makers was coming to prominence in the IRA and promoting its own men and women. Yet, irrespective of Duty Man's long-held role within the republican movement and the high regard afforded to him by some of the leadership of the IRA, Ryan had no way of expediting his travel documents from the Libyan Embassy in Paris. A de facto screening system set up by his Libyan intelligence contacts still had to be complied with.

Since the ill-fated trip by Joe Cahill and Seamus Twomey to Libya some years earlier, Libya's intelligence apparatus had seemingly become far more selective about who was given a document to visit their country, and a semi-formal system had been put in place. Ryan was now required to hand in the name of the intended visitor to his contacts at the Embassy and await further instructions. 'At that point, the Libyans were somewhat more circumspect, so I did my part of the deal and in this instance an answer came back: "A couple of us will be over in Paris on such and such an evening, we will meet and have dinner in a hotel." That was the protocol I was asked to follow.'

Paris had also changed. Over the course of the early 1980s, a wave of terrorist bombings and assassinations by various Middle East factions had set the city on edge. In 1982 alone, an American military attaché was shot dead in January as he was walking to his car outside his home by a solitary gunman. The attack came two months after the attempted shooting of the chargé d'affaires at the US Embassy in the city. In March that year, an Israeli diplomat was fatally shot by a young woman in the lobby of his Paris apartment, and in a brutal episode in August, six people were killed and twenty-two were injured when a grenade was thrown and attackers opened fire inside a busy restaurant in Paris's Jewish quarter.

As he waited for his travel documents from the Libyan Embassy, Duty Man chose not to share with Ryan why the IRA leadership was especially keen to send him to Tripoli. If his reticence was a deliberate ploy, he had met his match. Ryan had long learned that it was far more productive to wait for a person to reveal their motivations than ask them directly. For him, the measure of a man's character could almost always be gleaned by the simple act of patience; a person's motivations would invariably be unmasked in time by their own deeds or words. He deployed the same principle when it came to Duty Man. 'He gave me no idea whatsoever why he was being sent over, we never even discussed it and when we chatted, we did so about everything else except what business he had in Tripoli. Eventually the meeting was arranged and we went out for the supper with the Libyans.'

The restaurant chosen by the Libyan intelligence officials was somewhat formal, but discreet. Its heavy entrance door had not even closed behind the four men when the maître d', with little fanfare, graciously directed the group to a table located at a back corner of the establishment, beyond the path of meticulously dressed waiters shuffling plates to and from a kitchen that worked in near silence.

If Patrick Ryan had made an assumption that during the supper Duty Man would attach a higher value to listening as opposed to being heard, he was very much mistaken. It soon became excruciatingly apparent that Duty Man had much to share with those on whom he depended to green-light his visit to Libya. Yet the real revelation came when Duty Man confidently made pronouncements about a transformational change in priorities for the republican movement, a new direction that Ryan had not anticipated. 'He came alive, he waxed on, talking about peace, about the war coming to an end and the two Libyans were sitting opposite us, taking it all in.'

As Duty Man spoke, Ryan made sure that his body language gave the impression he was transfixed by what his comrade was saying, when, in fact, his gaze was fixed on the two men tasked with sizing up the IRA man. Neither man asked any questions, they merely gave Duty Man the floor, or, as Ryan saw it, enough rope to hang himself. 'While he was rabbiting on about peace and politics, I sat looking across at the Libyans and I could see their faces turning whiter and whiter. I could see that this was not going down well.'

Duty Man's political pronouncements reflected, in part, what had become tangibly attainable in the wake of the 1981 IRA hunger strikes – electoral success. At this time, the political ambitions of Sinn Féin were gaining traction within the republican movement. At its 1981 Ard-Fheis, the party decided to contest Westminster, Leinster House and Stormont elections on an abstentionist basis. The IRA's Easter message in 1982 indicated that political development was an imperative,[3] and in October the following year, Sinn Féin candidates took five seats in the new seventy-eight-member Assembly for Northern Ireland.

Gerry Adams, then the vice president of Sinn Féin, took the Belfast West seat, but made it clear that his election and that of his fellow party members would not stop the IRA's campaign of violence. 'The IRA have said that while the British army is in Ireland they will be there fighting,' he said.[4] Martin McGuinness also claimed a seat in this election, but he was far more direct in his pronouncement that Sinn Féin's political success would not in any way diminish the IRA's campaign of violence. 'We don't believe that winning elections and any amount of votes will bring freedom in Ireland,' he told a BBC documentary team the following year. 'At the end of the day, it will be the cutting edge of the IRA that will bring freedom.'

At the restaurant in Paris, Duty Man omitted to stress that the IRA's 'cutting edge' would continue in parallel with polling. Ryan read the room and attempted to discreetly temper his guest's candid assertions about the republican movement's political ambitions. 'I gave him a couple of kicks on the shins under the table, but I may as well have been kicking wood – he didn't take any notice.'

Ryan's attempted intervention could not erase the impression that had already been formed. By his own words, Duty Man had declared an enthusiastic aversion to the IRA's armed campaign and was seemingly too engrossed by the tempo of his own voice to notice that his supper companions, as well as Patrick Ryan, had hardly said a word. 'The supper must have lasted over a good hour and a half, and he took up three-quarters of that preaching politics and peace, and I was silent apart from the couple of kicks on his shin to try and get him to cop on, because I knew that the last thing the Libyans wanted to hear was the word "peace".'

It was three decades on from his studies in the seminary, but Ryan remembered how he had observed Duty Man's ilk before – characters who rated their own assertions far above those of others. During his training in the seminary, Ryan would sometimes watch other young novices converse with an arrogance that blinded them from seeing what was directed towards them in plain sight: withering looks of disdain from the person with whom they were attempting to ingratiate themselves. In Ryan's experience, actively listening to a person of power, irrespective of how much actual regard or otherwise he had for the individual, was a fail-safe demonstration of respect.

The long supper was brought to an abrupt end by the two Libyans, who had heard enough. 'They stood up and took me aside. "Pat," they said, "you come to see us in the Embassy tomorrow morning and this man is to stay here."' Ryan followed his instructions to a tee. 'The next day, the same two Libyans took me for a coffee and they started laughing. They said, "You can tell your man that we listened carefully to everything he said and weighed it all up and our conclusion is, and we are sending you back to tell him, that because he is such a good politician, it is obvious to us that he would be far better employed in Belfast than Tripoli."'

The message to Duty Man was met with silence. 'He said nothing; sure what could he say, he had to go back home.'

In Paris, Duty Man had failed to win over those he needed to impress. It was not enough to turn up in arrogance or ignorance and expect a free pass; he needed the approval of the Libyan intelligence officers in order to be granted a visa to travel to their country. The mistake he made was not seeking advice from Ryan on how best to handle himself in their company. 'Had he told me the road the leadership was going down, I would have briefed him on what to say, but, more importantly, what not to say. Peace was the leadership's decision; whether I approved or disapproved didn't matter because, when I represented them, my views were put to one side. But had I known their new tack, I would have advised him on what to say so he could get himself as far as Libya. What he did after that would have been his own business.'

In the City of Lights, Ryan was in the dark about how some on the IRA Army Council would take the news that their man had been deemed a no-go. 'He went home and must have told the leadership that I stopped him from going to Libya, but it couldn't have been further from the truth, I had no interest in stopping him.'

One month later, Ryan was to find out who had been personally incensed by the failure of Duty Man to travel to Libya: Martin McGuinness. At the duck pond in St Stephen's Green, Derry's 'blue-eyed boy' was a man metastasized by rage, betrayed only by his face, which was transformed into stone-faced, spittle-flecked anger.

'One of the previous times I'd met McGuinness, I handed him a good sum of money and he said, "Paddy you are the only one that is really helping at present."' Such platitudes of appreciation had dissipated. 'Now here he was, up right in front of my face, accusing me of stopping their man. I was there to do a job and I did it honestly.'

Ryan, though taken aback by McGuinness's temper, was too controlled to match his wrath. Then, before he could say anything, the three men were forced to turn their gaze towards the ducks, giving the impression of being intrigued by them. A group of schoolgirls buffered by two teachers was approaching; their laughter and excited chatter relieved the tension momentarily. Once they were out of earshot, the men's conversation resumed.

'How did Éamon get on?' asked Martin McGuinness.

Patrick Ryan knew the significance the Libyans attached to Éamon McGuire. Their gratitude went beyond an effusive praise; in a gesture they had not made towards any other IRA emissary Ryan had brought to their country, the Libyans sought to reward McGuire in monetary terms for his time and effort. Their appreciation was evident in the thick bundle of dollars handed to Ryan, the only stipulation being that the cash was specifically for McGuire and not the IRA.

'I told McGuinness that the Colonel and company were extremely pleased with McGuire's efforts, so much so that they gave me a large sum of money to pass on to him and that was when McGuinness said, "Where is it?" I said, "I have it." He says, "That's our money."'

For Ryan, it was a matter of principle.

'I said to him, "It's not your money and you're not getting it." McGuinness saw red over that as well and he said to me, "McGuire is not getting that money." I said, "That's grand."'

The second man, who up to that point had remained silent, now uttered his first words to Ryan. 'If you would like to leave, you can go now,' he said. His intonation of the word 'leave' was, in Ryan's assessment, quite deliberate: he wasn't referring to Ryan walking away from the Green; he was referring to Ryan's role on behalf of the IRA.

Patrick Ryan had already decided his next move. 'To say I was angry would be putting it mildly. I was so angry I could have killed them both. They were completely out of order in that meeting with me in St Stephen's Green. I was savage, but I don't show my anger, I never react, I go away and think about it, and then I decide what is the best thing to do. So I said, "Hold on, give me an hour to think it over."'

He left the park and walked towards the north-west corner of St Stephen's Green, past the bronze and stone statue of Wolfe Tone, one of the founders of the Society of United Irishmen in 1791, a group that embraced Catholics, Protestants and Dissenters in its aim to remove English control from Irish affairs. Their failed rebellion of 1798, however, resulted in the 1801 Act of Union, which actually brought Ireland under tighter British control.

It was not a day to ruminate about Irish revolutionaries. To strangers, Ryan may have given the impression of being a *flâneur*, wandering the streets of Dublin city with no particular destination or purpose, but instead he was deep in his own thoughts. It was clear to Ryan that McGuinness had asked for the meeting to show him the door, but he had no intention of walking away from the IRA on other people's terms. 'I came to the conclusion that these two lads were on a sell-out. I came back and said, "Just leave it as it is for the moment, my thinking is not finished."'

Ryan was, however, finished with the two IRA men. 'I was done with the IRA leadership. The deal I had originally agreed was that I offered my services freely, but that they could be withdrawn at any time. In St Stephen's Green I made a decision; I wasn't going to go back to Libya on behalf of a leadership and outfit that to my mind was selling out, I couldn't do that. I went back to Europe. I had a job to do for the Libyans.'

In Benidorm Ryan prepared for his next assignment, this time on behalf of the Libyan regime: a spying mission on the Italian island of Sicily. Strategically located just south of the Italian mainland and at the centre of the Mediterranean, Sicily had for centuries been at a crossroads of history, coveted by invading armies aiming to dominate the Mediterranean basin. Such was its importance that, in 1943, Sicily became the first part of Europe to be reclaimed by Allied forces after they drove the German and Italian forces out of North Africa during the Second World War.

In the 1950s the US Navy obtained permission from NATO to establish a presence on Sicily. For instance, the loading of US patrol and anti-submarine aircraft had begun to overcrowd the British Royal Navy Air Station in nearby Malta, so land for a United States Naval Air facility in Sigonella in eastern Sicily was made available under an agreement with the Italian government. It was a separate US Navy installation on the island that Libyan intelligence tasked Patrick Ryan with spying on – the Augusta Bay Port Facility, which provided logistical support to ships operating with the US Naval Fleet. 'They were most interested in submarines and I was sent to spy on the comings and goings of the port, and collect as much information as possible.'

Libyan intelligence had anticipated that Ryan would require an occupation to give him the appearance of an 'Irish man abroad' and presented their plan as a fait accompli. 'I was to run a little shop and up the road around two miles there was a church and me being a great Irish Catholic, I could go up there every morning, and that could be my initial look-out point until I could figure out other ways of gleaning the information I was tasked to collect.'

Ryan had listened to what was being proposed before sharing a prediction of his own. 'When we were finished, I said, "I am happy to progress the plan, but I am telling you now, I will never reach Sicily. I have your interests at heart, but you are infiltrated right up to the roots of your hair. My opinion is, before I have left this building it will be as good as already in the hands of your enemies." They laughed me out of town.'

As he boarded a plane in Germany bound for Milan, Ryan recalled the mirth his statement had caused; how his contacts were convulsed by the prediction he made with an absence of intended humour. He had decided that Germany, a less obvious route to Italy, was his best chance of circumventing any persons who may have been tipped off or following him, but his counter-security measures were in vain. 'I landed in Italy and, as I was about to go through passport control, I was confronted by Italian soldiers with sub-machine guns and they said, "You are going no further." They would give me no reason why.'

Patrick Ryan's endeavours on behalf of the Libyan regime were at an end. 'Italy taught me a lesson. I told the Libyans before I left that I'd never get as far as Sicily, and it turned out to be correct. I came to the conclusion that to do any more for them would be a suicide mission.' He never again travelled to Tripoli.

'I returned the money I was holding for Éamon McGuire to the Libyan Embassy in Paris. I handed it back to my contacts along with Martin McGuinness's comment, "McGuire is not getting that money." The Libyans didn't say anything.'

Patrick Ryan's ventures on behalf of the IRA had come to an end, of sorts. In St Stephen's Green he had privately vowed that his dealings with the leadership of IRA were over, a personal pledge made with some provisos – he would continue to gather intelligence for potential IRA operations on the European continent on his own initiative, or on the quiet word of others in whose interest it was to disrupt the operation of British military bases there.

'I stayed in Europe and any place I could lend a little hand quietly behind the scenes for the IRA, I did, but I was only a shadow in the background.'

EIGHTEEN

THE RYAN AFFAIR

Even from a distance, Patrick Ryan could see that the jogger approaching him on Poniente Beach in Benidorm was out of breath. He recognised him as the American he sometimes chatted to when their paths crossed when leaving the beach after their separate morning runs. It was always the same pitter patter of pleasantries as they walked across the sweep of golden sand gleaming in the early morning light, often leading to one or other marvelling at the impeccable work carried out by the town workers who cleaned the beach every evening.

The closer he was getting to the American on 7 March 1988, the more Ryan anticipated that he was running towards trouble. Aside from the man's blotched-red face and escalating wheeze, his arms were flapping indignantly like an impatient seagull trying to rid itself of excess water on its feathers. Suddenly, the man stopped jogging and looked like he was about to keel over from a cardiac arrest.

When Ryan eventually reached him, he recognised a look of fear on the man's face. 'He was completely terrified. There was nothing at all wrong with his heart, he had just worked himself up into an awful nervous state.'

It was the morning after the shooting dead at point-blank range of three unarmed IRA members on active service – Mairéad Farrell,

Seán Savage and Daniel 'Danny' McCann – by members of the British Army's Special Air Service (SAS) in Gibraltar, a British territory occupying a narrow peninsula of Spain's southern Mediterranean coast. Ryan had listened to Spanish radio news reports of the action taken by the elite counter-insurgency unit of the British Army. Many of the details had yet to emerge, but one element of what had happened that Sunday afternoon in Gibraltar was incontrovertible – the SAS knew the IRA's plans in advance.

On the beach in Benidorm, the jogger who stopped to catch his breath was clearly on edge and shared his concerns with Patrick Ryan. 'I was looking straight at the American man when he came out with the line, "These bloody IRA are every place and now after Gibraltar, I can't get out of fucking Spain quick enough." He was in a state of panic.'

Ryan was indifferent. He had known that the tiny British territory had long been on an IRA wish list of prestige targets. 'I knew that Gibraltar was always on the cards, I didn't know when it might actually happen, but, ultimately, it didn't surprise me that they were gunned down because the whole thing was so loose. I was convinced that there wasn't a move they could make during that time without the Brits knowing because they were infiltrated at every level.'

As far back as November 1987, MI5 were aware of intelligence that pointed to preparations for an IRA attack in Gibraltar.[1] Such was the level of detail being gathered that, on 20 February 1988, Siobhán O'Hanlon, a member of the IRA's active service unit, was observed at the La Línea border crossing between Spain and Gibraltar and kept under surveillance as she conducted a reconnaissance of Gibraltar, as well as the intended target, the ceremonial Changing of the Guard, involving up to fifty soldiers and bandsmen. After crossing back into Spain, she was being listened to when she phoned Danny McCann, telling him excitedly, 'Everything went great today!' On 24 February, however, she noticed that she was under Spanish surveillance, so she returned to Northern Ireland and dropped out of the active service unit.[2]

Despite O'Hanlon being compromised, and likewise McCann as a result of her phone call to him, the IRA operation went ahead. When McCann, Savage and Farrell crossed into Gibraltar from Spain on 6 March 1988, after being seen meeting at Málaga Airport two days earlier, all three were under surveillance.

That summer Patrick Ryan also came under surveillance in Belgium, at the request of British Security Services.[3] By June 1988 Ryan was no longer the main link between the IRA and the Libyan regime but, nevertheless, he continued to lend a hand behind the scenes to IRA active service units in Europe. He had settled into a life of shuttling to and from different cities from his Spanish base in pursuit of whatever opportunities he deemed were worth following up on. 'Benidorm was an ideal place to operate from. I had the routine of my swimming, great neighbours who I often helped out fixing their electrics, and I had also cultivated an English couple, whom I used to meet at times for dinner. No one had any clue what I was up to and why would they? As far as they were concerned, I was apolitical.'

As Ryan prepared to leave Spain late that month for a trip to Belgium, he was approached by a stranger. 'I was waiting in the sunshine with my suitcase, about to get on a bus in Benidorm, when I got a tap on the shoulder from a Spanish man in or around his early thirties. I was fluent in Spanish at that time and he said to me, "Are you getting on that bus?" and just walked away. I took it as a warning from some friends in Spanish intelligence not to go, but I was going to Belgium and that was it.'

Meanwhile, in the Netherlands, security preparations were at an advanced stage ahead of the impending visit in July by Queen

Elizabeth II, in celebration of the ties between the British and the Dutch. The royal visit was timed to mark the 300th anniversary of the Glorious Revolution of 1688, which brought the Dutch Protestant Prince William of Orange to the British throne as William III; the very William whose victory over the reigning Catholic king, James II, at the Battle of the Boyne in Ireland in 1690, marked a significant turning point in Irish and British history. Among its many consequences, William's success on the banks of the River Boyne in County Meath secured the Protestant ascendancy in Ireland for generations to come.

Forged in the crucible of sectarian street fighting in County Armagh in 1795, then Ireland's most populous county and where the number of Protestants and Catholics were roughly equal, the first lodge of the Orange Order was founded to defend 'the King and his heirs so long as he or they support the Protestant Ascendancy'. The Twelfth of July parades, the Ulster Protestant tradition when Orangemen march to commemorate the victory of William of Orange or 'King Billy' at the Boyne, were, in 1988, a near two-centuries-old celebration of a Protestant victory over Catholics. Any IRA disruption, or worse, during the Queen's visit to Amsterdam in 1988 would almost certainly further inflame sectarian tensions in Northern Ireland, a society already beset by violence.

In the Dutch capital, security fears were already heightened given what had unfolded that summer when, in the first IRA attacks in the country in almost a decade, separate car-bomb and gun attacks on 1 May left three off-duty British servicemen dead. In both incidents, the British soldiers had been in civilian clothes relaxing amid the off-base nightlife of Dutch border towns.

The first attack took place before 2 a.m. in the town of Roermond, when IRA gunmen opened fire at close range with a machine gun on three men sitting in a parked car, killing twenty-year-old Ian Skinner.

Half an hour later, in Nieuw-Bergen, about thirty miles north of
Roermond, a booby-trap bomb under a car outside a discotheque
exploded, killing twenty-two-year-old Millar Reid and twenty-one-
year-old John Baxter. All three men were RAF members based at
RAF Laarbruch in West Germany.

Twelve hours later the IRA issued a statement in Belfast admitting
the attacks. 'We have a simple statement for [Prime Minister] Thatcher
– disengage from Ireland and there will be peace. If not, there will
be no haven for your military personnel and you will regularly be at
airports awaiting your dead,' it said.[4]

The IRA had demonstrated in brutal terms that the loss of some of
its most experienced operators in Gibraltar had not halted its ability
to launch attacks on the European continent, a land mass where
border controls were relatively relaxed compared to the patchwork
of police and army checkpoints across Northern Ireland.

Shortly after his arrival in Brussels, Patrick Ryan had cause to
suspect that his movements were being monitored. 'I was getting
taxis to and from Lucie Ninane's house, to the home of the friend of
hers in Uccle who lived near the British diplomat, and what stands
out in that world tells its own tale because a couple of times running
the driver was the same fellow, and that said everything; they were
gearing up to make a move on me.'

On the evening of Thursday 30 June, police from Belgian's
anti-terrorism unit arrested Ryan at the Uccle house, where they
also recovered material including technical information on how to
assemble bombs, along with equipment for making remote-control
detonators and a large quantity of cash.

'They'd surrounded the place, came in and said the usual, "Put
your hands up and lie down." They made the first night uncomfortable
for me, put me in some kind of, well it wasn't a room at all, it was
only a big slab of marble, but nothing of comfort.'

In an account recorded by the British Consul in Brussels, entitled 'The Ryan Affair', stamped 'Confidential', it was documented that he was detained because 'the Belgian authorities began to panic, fearing that Ryan was planning a terrorist outrage in Belgium, possibly connected with the impending visit of the Queen to the Netherlands, and insisted that he be arrested'.[5]

In custody, Ryan denied he had any plans to attack the British monarch. 'It was the first question that was put to me after being arrested and I knew of course that she was going to visit Amsterdam, but I had no plans to do anything.' The Belgians, according to British officials, had made a 'mistake ... all London had asked was that the Belgians keep an eye on Fr. Ryan as they felt his visit to Brussels was operationally significant. However, the Belgians believed that there were guns in the garage of the house where Fr. Ryan was staying and, as a result, they had decided to move in and arrest him.'[6]

No guns were found. Patrick Ryan was charged with illegal entry and possession of a false passport and remanded in custody for one month.

Behind the scenes, British security officials remained adamant that they had never asked their Belgian counterparts to arrest Ryan, only follow him day and night. With the arrest, they felt that an opportunity to identify his network in Brussels had been missed. The Belgian security authorities, according to Sir Peter Petrie, then Britain's Ambassador to Belgium, had made a 'hasty move' in arresting Ryan, 'as opposed to simply shadowing' him.[7]

When news of the arrest broke on 5 July, some British newspaper headline writers went big on juxtaposition, describing Patrick Ryan as a 'Terror priest', 'the Devil's Disciple', 'the IRA's Godfather' and the 'Provos fix-it priest'. In Belgium the development was widely hailed as a major coup for the country's security forces in the struggle against terrorism. However, the tide soon began to turn; Brussels' early triumphalism was replaced by scepticism when further reports began to question if it was possible to charge the former Irish priest for more than simply travelling under an assumed name with a false passport.

The Belgian authorities realised that they had a problem; an absence of evidence to take 'this hot potato off Belgian hands'.[8] An early hope that Ryan could face charges for the 1979 murder of André Michaux, the Belgian banker shot dead in Brussels in a case of mistaken identity, soon began to evaporate.[9] At the same time, British authorities had not requested Ryan's extradition and there was no certainty that they would do so; even police delegations who made the trip to Brussels from Switzerland, Germany and the Netherlands failed in an attempt to find evidence linking Ryan to IRA attacks on the European mainland. Such was the concern in Brussels that Albert Raes, Director General of the Belgian Sûreté, the State Security Service, reportedly rang a British official 'with a personal plea that HMG should request extradition' and suggested that failure to bring Ryan to justice would 'undermine the credibility of anti-terrorist cooperation'.[10]

The clock was ticking. Unless more charges were forthcoming, the Belgians doubted their ability to hold Patrick Ryan for long.

At that point, officers from the anti-terrorist branch at Scotland Yard, along with Metropolitan Police forensic staff, were given full access to the material seized by the Belgian police, which they assessed over two months. In the meantime, Ryan was remanded in custody in monthly intervals on charges of using a false passport and, later, additional explosive charges, while security and, later, judicial authorities in both Brussels and London worked on the case. Eventually, the Crown Prosecution Service believed there was sufficient evidence for charges to be brought against Ryan in Britain, including conspiracy to murder and offences under the Explosive Substances Act 1883. 'These relate to his activities in the 1970s when he was apparently involved in obtaining switches for use in PIRA bombs ... There is no evidence to link him to terrorist crime in Northern Ireland.'[11]

In mid-September the British government formally sought the extradition of Patrick Ryan in respect of a number of charges: conspiracy to murder persons unknown with persons unknown on diverse dates between 1 May 1975 and 1 July 1988; conspiracy with persons unknown to cause explosions between February 1986 and June 1988; possession of explosive material in June 1982; and possession of explosive substances in June 1988.

Back in Tipperary, news of Ryan's detention had, at first, caused little alarm within his circle of contacts, including Marcus Fogarty. 'We were not unduly worried, but when the Brits looked set on extraditing him, it was game on. I remember meeting the Padre's [younger] brother Joe down the town, and he says to me, "Well, what about himself?"'

The 'Fr Paddy Ryan Justice Committee' was set up under the chairmanship of Joe, who, among a number of measures, urged people to petition the Belgian Embassy in Dublin to stop the extradition. 'Paddy is one of our own. SEND HIM HOME', read one of the handwritten placards Joe Ryan held aloft in Dublin.

The newly formed group also included Eamon O'Brien. 'I was involved in the Dublin '68 Committee, set up to promote debate and discussion on the conditions that existed in the six counties for both unionists and nationalists; that's how I started working on the campaign. The charges they put to Father Ryan – conspiring with people unknown to murder people unknown on a date unknown – how could a person fight a case like that, and what's more, if they could do that to a priest, they could do it to anyone.'

At a European level, the campaign was co-ordinated by Richard Behal, the Irish republican who often broke bread with Ryan around

Lucie Ninane's dinner table in Brussels. 'I was back living in Ireland, but I went out to visit Father Paddy in prison. He was in good enough form but, by God, he was determined to get out. I told him that I would do what I could.'

By 1988 Behal had severed his links with Sinn Féin. 'I was not a member of any political party, so I could work away with my contacts from various solidarity groups. Behind the scenes it was made very clear that if the Belgian authorities were to extradite him to Britain, they would incur the wrath of Catholic civil rights people from all over the world, who would see Patrick Ryan as the first priest politically persecuted in western Europe.'

Despite the lobbying, momentum was beginning to build in London's direction and according to British officials, 'it was clear that the IRA were beginning to recognise that the case against Ryan was serious and extradition a real risk'.[12]

In court on 3 November, Ryan sat in silence as the four separate extradition charges were read out. Ever watchful, he observed an individual whom he believed was tasked with bringing him to London. 'The Brit that was sent over to escort me home was sitting in his seat and as I was passing by, he says, "We'll be seeing you in London soon." I gave his ear a gentle tug and I said, "Yes, but just remember there is a fair chance you won't be."'

Ryan had already decided on his next move. 'I had a fair idea at that stage that the Belgians were going to cave in, so I went on hunger strike.' The age-old Irish republican tactic was announced at a press conference by his brother Joe, who had travelled to Brussels by then to lobby for his release. In a statement read on his behalf by his brother, Patrick Ryan said that the hunger strike was not an attempt to put pressure on the Belgian authorities but 'to highlight the plight of Irish people on trial in England today and the injustices of the English system as it applies to Irish people'.[13]

'He is in a good state of health,' Joe Ryan added, and went on to explain that his brother had taken a keen interest in events over the border after his return from missionary work in Africa and had decided to 'throw in his lot with the nationalist movement'.[14]

A hunger strike guaranteed one certainty; Patrick Ryan would become frailer with each passing day.

On 8 November British authorities stressed to their Belgian counterparts that a hunger strike was a 'very powerful IRA propaganda weapon ... and the legal timetable was now of critical importance'.[15] However, for another seven days the British Embassy was largely in the dark: 'neither the Justice cabinet nor the Public Prosecutor's Office were able to give us any hard news. Although we were reassured that Ryan was in good health and not suffering from the effects of hunger strike. He was continuing to take liquids: he even gained weight at one stage.'[16]

On the thirteenth day of Ryan's hunger strike 'the case took a new twist';[17] the Belgian Commissioner for Refugees rejected an application by Ryan for political asylum but advised that the extradition order should be refused and that, instead, the prisoner should be deported to the Republic of Ireland. The development prompted the British Home Secretary to forward an urgent telegram to Belgian's Justice Minister appealing for a swift decision. 'Now that PIRA terrorism has spread to the European mainland, it seems to me especially important to demonstrate our joint determination to see that those accused of serious criminal offences are brought to trial,' said Douglas Hurd. 'I well understand the difficulties surrounding this case but I do urge you to make an early and favourable decision.'[18]

In parallel, the spectre of a Catholic priest dying on hunger strike was continuing to play out in real time. Georges-Henri Beauthier, Ryan's Belgian lawyer, released a statement claiming that Ryan's health was 'precarious' because of his age – fifty-eight years old. In an open letter to the press, Ryan himself stated that he was ready to continue the hunger strike 'to its inevitable outcome, if necessary, rather than submit myself before a British tribunal', adding that he did not recognise the validity of British tribunals 'to pronounce against me for doing my patriotic duty'.[19]

On Friday 18 November, British officials believed they were close to a positive breakthrough. As well as being given assurances that they would be informed, unofficially, twenty-four hours before the extradition decision was announced, they were also asked if they could make practical arrangements to move Ryan over a weekend, leading to a confidence that Ryan would soon be extradited.

The logistics were put in place; British Embassy staff, the RAF and the Metropolitan Police were all on standby in case a decision emerged over the weekend.

In Saint-Gilles Prison, Patrick Ryan, who was aware that an extradition decision was coming ever closer, remembered the life-long lesson his mother had passed down to her children – that any effort to keep an enemy at bay was a risk worth taking. He turned the screw by going on a thirst strike on Thursday 17 November and let it be known in explicit terms that he would rather take his last breath in a Belgian jail than be extradited to Britain. 'The medic said to me, "Patrick, we are doing all we can for you, but seeing that you are not drinking any liquid you'll do yourself damage and while we can give you an injection every day to help, we can't go beyond the four days." I told him, "That's alright, if I start to fade out in the next day or two do not resuscitate me." I was heading for Tír na nÓg.'

Back in Ireland, those lobbying for Ryan's release from prison advised his brother Joe to up the ante. 'As part of the strategy to build the pressure, Joe rang Rossmore and ordered ten graves,' says Eamon O'Brien. 'It was a way of letting the Belgians and the British know, because someone was bound to be listening, that should Father Paddy die on their watch, we were going to build the biggest monument ever seen for an Irish nationalist martyr.'

By his doctor's estimation Ryan was getting weaker, but the Belgians had still not made a decision. On the morning of Friday 25 November British officials still believed, based on indications from 'virtually all the Belgian officials involved', that Ryan's extradition would be granted; an impression compounded when a senior police commander, on hearing that a decision had been taken, reportedly ordered extra security around British establishments in Brussels because 'he understood it to have been a decision to extradite Ryan to the United Kingdom'. The stage looked set for Ryan to be flown to London on an RAF jet.

As per Belgian law, the Justice Minister had the final say on extradition. A secret opinion had already been handed to him from the special court who heard Ryan's case. It accepted that the British extradition request was in order and recommended to the Minister that it should go ahead. However, in this case, Melchior Wathelet, described by a British official as the 'golden boy of Belgian politics',[20] opted to share his responsibility with the Belgian Prime Minister and his Cabinet colleagues during the coalition government's weekly meeting. That government went against the recommendation of the court and decided to repatriate Ryan to Ireland.

In Saint-Gilles Prison, Ryan got a visit from his Belgian lawyer. 'There was a knock on the door, I was free to go.' In Dublin, Taoiseach Charles Haughey called an emergency meeting of ministers and officials to sanction the Belgian request to repatriate Ryan. The Irish had received a tip-off at 3 p.m. that Friday afternoon that the Belgians had refused to extradite the prisoner to the UK.

At a diplomatic level, despite assurances that they would informally be given twenty-four-hours' notice of Ryan's departure,

British officials were among the last to be told. When the Belgian Foreign Minister eventually spoke to the British Ambassador later that day, he confirmed that, after a 'long and difficult debate', the Belgian government had decided to send Ryan back to the Irish Republic on that basis that, according to Belgian law, the charges against him were not precise enough to allow for extradition. The Foreign Minister rang again an hour later to say that he was 'embarrassed and sad', adding, amongst other details, that it was his understanding that Patrick Ryan was already in transit from Saint-Gilles to a Belgian military plane. Furthermore, a C130 of the Belgian Air Force had been charged to file a flight plan avoiding British airspace over fears that the plane may be forced to land on British soil.

In London the decision of the Belgian government not to extradite Ryan was described by a Foreign Office official as 'pusillanimous', their means of executing it 'deceitful' and their subsequent attempts to explain it 'mendacious'. The Belgian cabinet had appeared unwilling to take a decision until 'put in a corner by the foreseeable escalation of Ryan's hunger strike'. The personality of Belgian Minister for Justice Wathelet, 'all brains and no guts', was also highlighted as one reason for the unexpected decision, another possibility being 'that Belgian Ministers were simply afraid' of IRA reprisal attacks.[21]

The Belgian government continued to deny that the decision had been entirely political, aimed solely at removing a problem from Belgian soil. 'We've had three IRA attacks in Belgium,' said the Belgian Ambassador to Britain, Jean Paul van Bellingham. 'We've had a bomb on the Grand-Place of Brussels, underneath the podium where a British band was to play; we've had a Belgian banker shot down by mistake in Belgium; we've had a British sergeant shot in Ostend. We're not at all afraid of them.' A British official described the outcome as 'a collective act of passing the buck – in this case to the Irish Government'.[22]

The plane carrying Ryan left at 8.55 p.m. After twenty-two days on hunger strike, he was homeward bound. 'I was put in a bed on a four-engine tank transporter with a number of special forces, a doctor and a nurse on board. They were afraid the Brits would force the plane down so, escorted by two fighter planes, they flew clear of British airspace. They were letting the Brits know that they were not going to have their way.'

When the military plane touched down shortly before 11 p.m. in Dublin Airport, the 'Provo priest' was back on Irish soil, a free man. Ryan's supporters, who were waiting in the main arrivals hall, were jubilant. 'He would have got down on his knees and kissed the ground, except that he was too weak to get up again,' said Tom Ryan of his cousin's return to Dublin, citing an image that resonated with Irish Catholics who had witnessed Pope John Paul II descend the stairs from the plane and kiss the ground on arrival at Dublin Airport at the start of his papal visit in 1979.[23] Dublin Airport authorities later installed a plaque on the airport apron: 'This is where his holiness Pope John Paul II first touched Irish soil on the occasion of the first ever visit by a Pope to Ireland.'

Patrick Ryan was well enough to leave the Belgian Air Force C-130 Hercules aircraft on foot and walk into a waiting ambulance that left Dublin Airport at high speed with emergency lights flashing until it reached the Blackrock Clinic, a private hospital on the south side of the city. On arrival, Ryan walked through the clinic's double doors unaided. 'There were five or six personnel waiting for me with a stretcher, and I ran up the stairs ahead of them all.'

But British officials still had a card to play. That Friday evening they sent a fax to the Attorney General's office in Dublin requesting the extradition of Patrick Ryan from Ireland.

NINETEEN

'THE BIRD HAD FLOWN'

The darkness impeded the search for the mangled wreckage of the car in County Tyrone. Barney Lavery and his thirteen-year-old granddaughter Emma Donnelly were on their way home, after dropping an elderly neighbour off from bingo night on 23 November 1988, when they drove past a van parked in the gateway of the unmanned RUC station in the village of Benburb at the same time that the massive IRA bomb in the van exploded, blowing their car through a hedge and into a field beyond. The blast was heard eight miles away in Armagh city.

It took forty minutes for those who rushed to the scene to find the car, which an eyewitness said looked like it had been crushed mechanically,[1] and what remained of sixty-seven-year-old Barney and his beloved granddaughter.

'A wise and Christian gentleman and a young girl full of promise,' became the IRA's twenty-second and twenty-third 'mistakes' of 1988;[2] men, women and children, Protestant and Catholic civilians, who died violently at the hands of the IRA in so called 'blunders'.

In the aftermath the IRA said it called police to warn of the attack, while the RUC said it received two warnings but did not have sufficient time to clear the area. 'It takes a lot of time and the time limits on this bomb, there's no way we could have achieved that and obviously the intention was to kill the security forces on arrival,' said Chief Superintendent Adrian Ringland, the RUC divisional commander in charge of the investigation. 'Two completely innocent people driving past have been killed because of this.'[3]

On Friday 25 November the village of Benburb stopped to bury its dead. Shops closed and hundreds lined the streets as the funeral corteges from the Donnelly and Lavery homes joined together at the main street before pausing for a moment's silence outside the RUC station where the bomb had detonated. Freezing fog shrouded St Jarlath's Church as the auxiliary Bishop of Armagh, Dr James Lennon, a friend of Bernard Lavery's since their school days, told the grief-stricken congregation that the IRA's 'excuses are hollow, bordering on the obscene'.[4] The following day newspapers carried photographs of distraught teenagers from the Naomh Mhuire camogie club, to which Emma belonged, crying bitterly for a friend they would never see again.

Many of the front-page headlines that Saturday, however, were focused on the ongoing saga of Patrick Ryan, who had spent his first night in Dublin's Blackrock Clinic after the Belgian government repatriated the hunger striker to Ireland. 'There was nothing at all wrong with me, I'd lost some weight but that was all. On the Saturday morning there was a flurry of tip-offs saying that a hit team was coming for me. I left the clinic for a couple of hours, but it was only scaremongering, so I returned for another night.'

In Dublin, Ryan was free to come and go as he pleased; there were no grounds for gardaí to arrest him and Ireland's then Attorney General, John Murray, had only just begun to examine the British extradition warrants and was expected to need a week or so to come to a decision on the substance of the case.

Just as the British authorities feared he might, on Sunday 27 November Ryan signed himself out of the clinic and immediately went to ground. 'The message came back from the 'RA that I was to keep my head down, that I had nothing to worry about.'

That day the British Ambassador to Ireland, Sir Nicholas Fenn, contacted Irish government officials to convey that his 'hope' that the extradition case could be processed quickly remained unaffected by the fact that 'the bird had flown'.[5] The consternation caused by Ryan's sudden departure was amplified by reports that gardaí had not been tasked to mount a surveillance operation on the clinic and only learned accidentally that he had left. The priest, wanted by British authorities and described in a London newspaper headline as the 'Devil in a Dog Collar', had effectively disappeared.

The British Prime Minister was furious. When Margaret Thatcher took her place at the dispatch box during Prime Minister's Questions on Tuesday 29 November, she was barely able to contain her anger and dropped all pretence of diplomatic language about the Irish government and Attorney General, criticising them in particular for failing to secure the arrest of Ryan.

Spurred on by her backbench MPs, Thatcher said the warrants for Ryan's extradition were obtained and transmitted to Dublin straightaway on Friday night, together with all the additional documentation required. 'Despite this, no action was taken by the Irish Attorney-General to serve provisional warrants or to endorse the original warrants. The failure to secure Ryan's arrest is a matter of very grave concern to the Government. It is no use Governments adopting great declarations and commitments about fighting terrorism if they then lack the resolve to put them into practice,' she said.[6]

In a raucous House of Commons, Tory backbencher Michael Mates was the first to put a question to the Prime Minister about Patrick Ryan: 'Further to what my right hon. friend has said, will she please make the strongest representations today to the Irish

Government about their abject surrender for short-term political gain when one of the most wanted terrorists has been let free?' he asked.

Thatcher hardly took a breath. 'As I said earlier,' she replied, 'the Irish Attorney-General's failure to secure Ryan's arrest is a matter of very grave concern to the Government. I entirely agree with my hon. friend that, although the Government of the Republic of Ireland make fine-sounding speeches and statements, they do not always seem to be backed up by the appropriate deeds.'

The die was cast; the Prime Minister did not disassociate herself from the claim by Mates that Patrick Ryan was one of Ireland's 'most wanted terrorists'. These words would come back to haunt her.

On 13 December Ireland's Attorney General announced his decision on the validity of the British extradition request for Ryan. He turned it down on the grounds that Ryan would not get a fair trial in Britain. John Murray said he took the unusual step of issuing a statement about his decision because of the considerable importance of the case and a desire not to 'allow speculation to replace fact'. In his seventeen-page explanation, Murray accused members of the House of Commons of making statements there about the case whose 'tone, tenor and contents ... carried an assumption or inference of guilt'. While accepting that there was sufficient legal evidence to justify Ryan's extradition, he said that the prejudice and hostility against him in Britain was 'irredeemable' and no judge or jury could be expected to ignore it. Murray also said that references to Ryan in British newspapers and on radio and television had consisted 'of attacks on Patrick Ryan's general character, often expressed in intemperate language and frequently in the form of extravagantly worded headlines, and also assertions of his guilt of the offenses comprised in the warrants and, indeed, assertions of his guilt of other offenses in respect of which no charges have been brought'.[7]

In Dublin the British Ambassador to Ireland, unlike the experience of his Foreign Office colleague in Belgium, had been given advance warning of the decision by an Irish government official. On hearing the development, Sir Nicholas Fenn said it was 'the worst possible outcome', describing the statement that Ryan would not receive a fair trial in Britain as 'untrue ... offensive ... gratuitous ... provocative'. In his note to the Foreign Office, marked confidential, Fenn urged restraint: 'Ryan is lost to us,' he wrote, 'what we say now must be calculated to maximise our influence in that process so that we can salvage something from the wreck.' He wrote that a 'major row' would benefit only 'the men of violence and the opponents of the Anglo-Irish agreement' and added: 'When the dust has settled, Ireland will still be here, and we shall still need the understanding of its people and the co-operation of the government if we are to achieve our objectives in Northern Ireland. For all these reasons I strongly recommend that our reaction should be measured.'[8]

The Prime Minister's reaction was relatively muted when compared to her earlier comments. Her voice strained with emotion, Thatcher told the House of Commons that her government 'repudiates utterly' the suggestion that Ryan could not get a fair trial in Britain, and described the decision as 'a great insult to all British people'.

'The Prime Minister can repudiate as much as she likes,' said Neil Kinnock, the Labour Party opposition leader. 'She is faced with the fact that Patrick Ryan will not be extradited to Britain and it is primarily her fault. I understand that the Prime Minister is very disappointed; that feeling is shared by many others, including myself. But she is also culpable.' In words that would later be echoed by their target, he concluded, 'She blew the possibility of extraditing Patrick Ryan.'[9]

Back in Tipperary, where he was lying low, Patrick Ryan was gleeful. 'I was still officially "missing", so I gave the press conference my brother Joe had arranged for that day a skip, but it couldn't have gone any better for me and any worse for Thatcher because, on account of her own words, she blew it.'

TWENTY

A VERY WICKED MAN

A British monarch put Killarney on the tourist map. When Queen Victoria visited the County Kerry town in August 1861, it made the area one of the most fashionable places in Europe to visit. Although the Queen had visited Ireland on two previous occasions, in 1849 and 1853, her visit in 1861 was the first time that Kerry was included in her itinerary.

In Killarney, the royal party was taken to local sites, such as Ross Castle, Muckross Abbey and Torc Waterfall, while the Queen's ladies-in-waiting were taken to a viewing point that overlooks the Lakes of Killarney, known henceforth as Ladies' View in honour of the pleasure expressed by the group when they visited.

The royal visit came at personal cost to Henry Arthur Herbert, the owner of Muckross House, who was given six years' notice to prepare for the Queen's stay at his spectacular mansion on the shores of the lakes of Killarney.[1] Such was his extravagance during the refurbishment of Muckross that his son lost his inheritance. The estate was put up for auction by the Standard Life Assurance Company in 1899, then withdrawn and later sold that year to Arthur Edward Guinness.

Patrick Ryan appeared to be on a winning streak when he visited Killarney in the summer of 1989. By then, there had been no visits to the Republic of Ireland by a reigning British monarch since 1911, when King George V visited what was then a united island, part of the United Kingdom of Great Britain and Ireland, but Killarney was bustling with American tourists on a trip back to the 'auld sod' in search of their Irish roots.

It was in Killarney that Ryan purchased a raffle ticket and won a return air ticket to the US. 'The luck of the Irish' was how a British official described Ryan's win in a letter to the Crown Prosecution Service in London: 'The question [that] now arises is whether in the event of Ryan visiting the United States, we should seek his extradition from that country.'[2]

In June 1989 Ryan was still a wanted man in Britain, as well as the subject of a red Interpol warning, which meant that he was likely to be detained if he travelled outside Ireland, pending instructions from the UK wherever he came to notice. The reply from a Home Office official confirmed that ministers 'would wish to leave no stone unturned in attempting to secure the extradition of Ryan to the UK'.

Ryan had not travelled to Killarney to admire the scenery; he was campaigning as a candidate in the 1989 European elections. He had made the announcement at a press conference in a hotel in Cashel in April, his first public appearance almost five months to the day since he signed himself out of Dublin's Blackrock Clinic on his repatriation from Belgium.

Dressed in full clerical garb, he told the large number of reporters and supporters that he was running as an independent candidate in the five-seat Munster constituency primarily on an anti-extradition ticket. It was 'an issue above and beyond politics', he said, insisting that his candidacy was not designed to embarrass the Irish government. He also 'thanked God for bringing me through a difficult time', adding that he denied all charges against him, as well as membership 'past, present or future' of the IRA.[3]

The development prompted a few reporters to seek out some of Ryan's contacts in Europe, including Lucie Ninane in Brussels. 'I am certain Patrick never planted a bomb,' she said in a television interview recorded in her home where Ryan used to stay. 'He had never killed anybody with a machine gun,' she continued. 'He helped them with his intelligence, with his knowledge.'[4]

Ryan was the first priest to contest an election in the state's history and the Catholic hierarchy disapproved. Archbishop Clifford of Cashel accused him of abusing his priestly status, claiming he was a priest who 'is now using clerical dress as a passport to acceptance by the electorate'. The Pallottine Fathers, the order to which he belonged, urged him to withdraw his candidacy and cease all activity connected with the campaign, but their priest was not for turning. On the campaign trail, Ryan said his difficulties with the Pallottine Order amounted to no more than a 'canonical hiccup'.[5]

Ryan's candidacy added to the diplomatic jeopardy in relations between the Irish and British governments, but his ambition to bring about a diplomatic showdown fell short when he failed to win a seat in the election. 'The gardaí, the Catholic Church, the British and Irish governments were all gunning for me, but I still got over 30,000 votes – that frightened the living daylights out of them all.'

Had he been elected as a member of the European Parliament, Ryan would have had to return to Brussels, from where he'd been sent home only the previous year. 'I wanted to be elected so I could have a couple of words with the woman who failed twice to extradite me. If I had ever met Mrs Thatcher, my parting shot would have been, I wish you well ma'am, but I'm sorry we missed you at Brighton.'

Ryan's facetious expression of regret masked a frustration over the IRA's failure to assassinate the British Prime Minister and her cabinet. 'We had the whole lot of them in a nest, and the Brighton bomb was supposed to kill them all. And as for Thatcher, she was within a cat's whisker of being wiped out.'

Ryan had a personal interest in the bomb that failed to kill Margaret Thatcher in Brighton, because it included material that he had provided to the IRA. 'The Brighton bomb included my Memo Park component. And I also had a hand in the Hyde Park bomb; didn't they say they found something when they searched the grass after the blast?'

The IRA bomb attacks in Hyde Park and Brighton had launched separate and intensive police investigations. A crucial discovery in 1984 in ancient woodland would help to unlock aspects of both cases. In January that year, police dug up an IRA arms cache in Salcey Forest, a remnant of a medieval royal hunting forest, seven miles south of Northampton. The location was unwittingly given away by two IRA operatives during a Special Branch surveillance operation. Among the material found were timing units set to run for about twenty-four days. Each long-delay timing unit was numerically labelled, and crucially, one number was missing.

The significance of the discovery only became apparent several months later in the wake of the IRA's long-delay bomb at Brighton. Police investigators were armed with two vital pieces of information – the precision of the timing units found at Salcey and the fact that one was missing from the haul – so they worked back through the hotel guest register to find out who had checked in some twenty to thirty days before the bomb exploded. An unknown 'Roy Walsh' had done so and had left a forensic trace; a palm print on the hotel registration card for Room 629. Months of painstaking forensic examination of prints in police records from Northern Ireland and England eventually found a match: Patrick Magee. The evidence went on to form a critical part in the prosecution case against him. He was convicted of the IRA Brighton bombing in 1986.

The Salcey Forest arms cache also included material forensically connected to the circuit board found in the grass of Hyde Park after the remote control-detonated bomb exploded there. When the fragment from Hyde Park was forensically examined, the 'artwork' of the circuit board was identical to that of another example found in the Salcey Forest dump.[6]

There was more. Given the type of bomb and the fragments of the circuit board that were found, forensic experts believed a particular type of switching device had been used to detonate the bomb – an FX401. In June 1989 a television documentary broadcast 'evidence' linking Patrick Ryan to the Hyde Park bomb. 'In Salcey Forest, Nottinghamshire, in 1984 a complete decoding unit for a bomb was found in an IRA arms dump,' said the programme reporter. 'That unit contained an FX401. Its batch number was 8131. The circuitry of the bomb [found here] exactly matched the fragments recovered from the Hyde Park bomb.' An FX401 was one of the two types of switches Ryan had asked the Englishman he had met in Tripoli to purchase for him. Batch number 8131, the programme alleged, matched the batch number purchased by that Englishman in Consumer Microcircuits in Essex in January 1982.[7]

The fifth anniversary of the Brighton bomb fell on 12 October 1989. That same day, Ireland's then Director of Public Prosecution (DPP) announced that there was insufficient evidence with which to prosecute Patrick Ryan in the Republic of Ireland, despite previous statements from the Attorney General that there was a case to answer. For a time, it looked like Ryan might have had to face a trial in Dublin's Special Criminal Court. Four witnesses indicated to British authorities that they would consider giving evidence against Ryan – a Swiss shopkeeper, relating to Ryan's purchase of Memo Park timers in Geneva; a London businessman, who claimed that he met Ryan in Tripoli in the early 1980s; and two continental police officers. Later, however, it appeared less likely that the witnesses wished to travel to Dublin, citing security concerns.

Reaction to the DPP's decision was relatively muted in London when compared with the fury unleashed by Dublin's refusal to extradite Ryan. In a briefing note prepared for the Foreign Secretary ahead of an informal meeting with his Irish counterpart, the 'line to take' included, 'Grave disappointment at this outcome. Although innocent before the law, Ryan is known to be a very wicked man with serious terrorist connections.'[8]

In January 1990 Patrick Ryan was dismissed from the Pallottine Fathers. He no longer had permission to offer Mass or administer the sacraments. According to a statement from the Catholic Press and Information Office, 'there is no such thing as a freelance priest'.[9]

'I was a *persona non grata*, but I didn't care, my nationalism was more important to me than the Catholic Church. My work for the IRA, if we're to judge it by Thatcher's rage, was effective. The only regret that I have was that I wasn't more effective; that the bombs made with the components I supplied, didn't kill more. That is my one regret.'

EPILOGUE

Patrick Ryan never changed his mind about the decision he made during the ill-tempered meeting with Martin McGuinness and the other senior republican in St Stephen's Green; he viewed the leadership of the IRA as a lost cause and, as the 1990s unfolded, he also decided against setting up a breakaway group. 'You see, when I came home that time from Brussels, with the level of support I had here, I could have started up another outfit, and I thought about it for a while, but the Brits knew too much and it was a waste of time. I came to the conclusion that the 'RA were so infiltrated, right at the decision-making level, that it was only lambs to the slaughter; fellas were getting killed for nothing, so I pulled back.'

Six years after his repatriation to Ireland from Belgium, Ryan faced criminal charges in court, albeit over matters unrelated to his IRA activity. In April 1994 he was convicted of handling stolen property and ordered to pay IR£10,000 compensation after he was found guilty of handling a stolen caravan and other property.

By then Ryan had long dispensed with the Roman collar he was always photographed wearing at the time of his European election candidacy and had made connections with some of Ireland's most notorious criminals, including Martin Cahill, commonly known as 'The General'. 'When I'd go into the General's house, himself and the missus would vacate their own bed and insist that I sleep there for the night. He'd say, "Paddy if I knew you thirty years ago we'd own half the country."'

Martin Cahill was a ruthless and prolific criminal, notorious for masterminding and carrying out burglaries and armed robberies in Dublin from the mid-1970s onwards. 'He'd say to me, "Paddy, when the 'RA started that war there were plenty down here who didn't know how to steal a car. We showed them and we couldn't teach some, so we stole the cars for them, and when they needed petrol, it was us who provided it. On and on and on it went, we gave them mountains of money until we got tired of giving them it and because I wouldn't give them any more, they began to dislike me." That is what the General said to me.'

Cahill was on bail for kidnapping charges when he was killed by the IRA in a Dublin suburb in August 1994, just weeks before the declaration of its first ceasefire. 'The IRA shot him dead because they were about to make an onslaught on more of the up and coming "generals" and they wanted to set him up as an example – that is what was going on.'

In the decades after his return to Ireland, Patrick Ryan operated on the fringes of society. His reputation, which he was content to trade on at times, saw all manners of plots put to him down the years.

'I was approached by a farmer, fighting with another over land. He wanted the other fella dead so that the acres would fall like cherries off a tree into his hands and asked would I do the necessary. I said I'd think about it. But I met him months later: "Well Patrick, did you do your thinking and what conclusion did you come to?" An old farmer he was, so I said, "Look, at your age and mine it doesn't matter too much, as your sons will get the land. I have a plan. I will get two revolvers, ten rounds in each and seeing on your own admission that it's your two sons that are going to benefit, I will give them a weapon each with the cartridges and let them go down and kill the farmer." He says, "Pat, you're not thinking at all. Sure, if my two sons killed that man," and he paused, "wouldn't that be a mortal sin?" There he was, a respectable pillar of society who if he saw me in broad daylight coming up the street would cross over to avoid me. That's human nature at its best or worst. We are all flawed entities.'

ENDNOTES

ONE: THE SHOWDOWN IN RHODES

1 *The Times*, 28 November 1988.
2 Margaret Thatcher, *The Downing Street Years* (HarperCollins, 1993), pp. 379–83.
3 Christopher M. Andrew, *The Defence of the Realm: The Authorized History of MI5* (Penguin, 2010), p. 704.
4 *The Irish Times*, 13 May 1986.
5 *The Times*, 13 October 1984.
6 Ibid.
7 Thatcher, *The Downing Street Years*, pp. 379–83.
8 *The Guardian*, 10 May 1986.
9 David McKittrick, Seamus Kelters, Brian Feeney, Chris Thornton, David McVea, *Lost Lives: The Stories of the Men, Women, and Children Who Died as a Result of the Northern Ireland Troubles* (Mainstream Publishing, 2004), p. 1123.
10 *14 Days*, BBC One Northern Ireland, 2013.
11 Frank Dunlop, *Yes, Taoiseach: Irish Politics from Behind Closed Doors* (Penguin Ireland, 2004), p. 209.
12 *The Irish Times*, 23 June 2011.
13 https://c59574e9047e61130f13-3f71d0fe2b653c4f00f32175760e96e7.ssl.cf1.rackcdn.com/841D9F8CE5374D5297D784D4440520C9.pdf.
14 *The Irish Times*, 24 December 2014.
15 Conor Brady, *The Guarding of Ireland* (Gill & Macmillan, 2014), p. 161.
16 *The Irish Times*, 29 December 2017.
17 Paddy Hill, Gerry Hunter, Johnny Walker, Hugh Callaghan, Richard McIlkenny and Billy Power spent sixteen years in prison for the IRA's murder of twenty-one people in the November 1974 bombing of Birmingham's Tavern in the Town and Mulberry Bush pubs. They were finally released in 1991 after their murder convictions were quashed.
18 State papers. Meeting between the Taoiseach, Mr Charles J. Haughey and the British Prime Minister, Mrs Thatcher, at the European Council, Brussels, February 1988.

19 State papers. Meeting between the Taoiseach, Mr Charles J. Haughey and the British Prime Minister, Mrs Thatcher, at the European Council, Hanover, 28 June 1988. The RUC (Royal Ulster Constabulary) was the Northern Ireland police force, from 1922 to 2001.

20 Unless otherwise indicated, all quotes from this meeting between Haughey and Thatcher are taken from: State papers. Meeting between the Taoiseach, Mr Charles J. Haughey and the British Prime Minister, Mrs Thatcher, at the European Council, Rhodes, 3 December 1988.

21 The National Archives of Ireland, *European Control of Terrorism: Extradition*, Reference: 2018/68/15.

22 www.margaretthatcher.org/document/107401.

23 Dáil Éireann debate, Wednesday, 7 December 1988: European Council in Rhodes: Statement by Taoiseach.

24 *The Irish Times*, 28 December 2019.

25 During the Gulf War, Belgium turned Britain down when it requested ammunition for its forces there.

26 Thatcher, *The Downing Street Years*, p. 414.

TWO: A MOTHER'S LOVE

1   A narrow country lane.

2   *Seanchaí*: storyteller.

3   John Bowman, *Ireland: The Autobiography: One Hundred Years of Irish Life, Told by Its People* (Penguin Ireland, 2016), p. 323.

4   Dáil Éireann debate, Tuesday, 21 January 1919, Declaration of Independence, www.oireachtas.ie/en/debates/debate/dail/1919-01-21/8/.

5   Seumas Robinson, Bureau of Military History (BMH) Witness Statement (WS) 1721, p. 24.

6   Dan Breen, BMH WS 1739, p. 22.

7   Karen Harvey, *The Bellews of Mount Bellew: A Catholic Gentry Family in the Age of the Penal Laws* (Four Courts Press Ltd, 1984), p. 56.

8   G. McIntosh, 'Acts of "National Communion": The Centenary Celebrations for Catholic Emancipation, the Forerunner of the Eucharistic Congress', in J. Augusteijn (ed.), *Ireland in the 1930s: New Perspectives* (Four Courts Press, 1999), p. 87.

9   https://www.gov.ie/en/press-release/678fc-digitisation-of-the-1926-census/.

10 Daithí Ó Corráin, 'Catholicism in Ireland, 1880–2015: Rise, Ascendancy and Retreat', in Thomas Bartlett (ed.), *The Cambridge History of Ireland. Vol. IV: 1880 to Present* (Cambridge University Press, 2018), pp. 726–64.

11 John Kelly, *The Graves are Walking* (Faber & Faber, 2013), p. 83.

12 Address by President Mary McAleese on the Occasion of her Visit to Grosse Ile, 11 October 1998.

13 Asenath Nicholson, *Annals of the Famine in Ireland*, edited by Maureen Murphy (The Lilliput Press, 1998), p. 182.

THREE: MISSION TO AFRICA

1 Excluding Ruanda-Urundi, which went to Belgium.

2 Éamonn Ceannt, Seán MacDiarmada, Con Colbert, Michael Mallin – CBS North Richmond St; Patrick Pearse, William Pearse – CBS Westland Row; Edward Daly – CBS Roxboro Road; Seán Heuston – CBS O'Connell School, John MacBride – CBS Westport; Michael O'Hanrahan – CBS Carlow.

3 *The Catholic Advocate*, Vol. 6, No. 52, 28 December 1957.

4 www.gaa.ie/news/remembering-michael-cusack-175-years-after-his-birth/.

5 *The New York Times*, 7 January 1935.

6 Commission on Emigration and Other Population Problems, Reports: 1948–1954 (Stationery Office, 1955), p. 137.

7 Kate Lynch, '"For a splendid cause": Irish missionary nuns at home and on the mission field, 1921–1962', PhD thesis (University of Nottingham, 2012).

8 *Time*, 15 December 1961.

FOUR: OUT OF AFRICA

1 *BBC Six Ten*, 28 January 1964.

2 Bob Purdie, *Politics in the Streets: The Origins of the Civil Rights Movement in Northern Ireland* (The Blackstaff Press, 1990), p. 177.

3 www.rte.ie/archives/exhibitions/1378-radharc/355627-radharc-in-derry/.

4 www.cso.ie/en/media/csoie/census/census1961results/volume6/C_1961_VOL_6_T29.pdf.

5 Enda Delaney, *The Irish in Post-War Britain* (Oxford University Press, 2007), p. 91.

6 Taoiseach Mr Jack Lynch TD, 13 August 1969.

7 Letter from A. Peacocke, then Inspector-General of the RUC to General Officer Commanding, 14/8/1969, PRONI HA/32/2/55.

FIVE: THE SCULPTOR AND THE COLONEL

1 Aircraft Accident Report, 17 November 1972.

2 Ibid.

3 Patrick Bishop and Eamonn Mallie, *The Provisional IRA* (Corgi, 1988), p. 41.

4 Brian Hanley, *The IRA: A Documentary History* (Gill & Macmillan, 2015), pp. 150–1.

5 Desmond Long 'The Provisional IRA in Munster 1969–1974', MA thesis (University of Limerick, 2010). All quotes from Denis McInerney in this chapter are taken from this source, unless otherwise stated.

6 'Missionary turned to republican cause', *The Independent*, 29 November 1988.

7 Ibid.

8 Fr Phil Barry, interview with author, 9 December 2022.

9 *The Guardian*, 29 November 1988.

10 Tom O'Sullivan, interview with author, 14 August 2021.

11 *The Irish Times*, 4 September 1999.

12 *The Irish Times*, 29 January 1965.

13 Ibid.

14 Ronald Bruce St John, *Libya: From Colony to Revolution* (Oneworld Publications, 2017), p. 151.

15 Central Intelligence Agency, Research Study: 'International and Transnational Terrorism: Diagnosis and Prognosis', April 1976.

16 Aircraft Accident Report, 17 November 1972.

17 *L'Action-Québec*, 20 November 1972.

18 Marcus Fogarty, interview with author, 18 November 2022.

19 https://api.parliament.uk/historic-hansard/commons/1972/nov/29/northern-ireland-rocket-attacks.

20 Ibid.

SIX: 'A BOOT UP THE TRANSOM'

1 Sean Boyne, *Gunrunners: The Covert Arms Trail to Ireland* (O'Brien Press, 2006), p. 149.

2 Ibid., p. 154

3 Andrew, *The Defence of the Realm*, p. 623.

4 *The Irish Times*, 5 October 2017.

5 Long, 'The Provisional IRA in Munster 1969–1974'.

6 Brendan Anderson, *Joe Cahill: A Life in the IRA* (O'Brien Press, 2003), p. 159.

7 *The Irish Times*, 3 March 2001.

8 Andrew, *The Defence of the Realm*, p. 623.

9 Anderson, *Joe Cahill*, p. 160.

10 *The Irish Times*, 1 October 1984.

11 *The Irish Times*, 30 March 1973.

12 Des Long, interview with author, 13 August 2021.

13 Marcus Fogarty, interview with author, 18 November 2022.

14 *The Irish Times*, 30 March 1973.

15   *The Irish Times*, 3 April 1973.

16   Ibid.

17   Anderson, *Joe Cahill*, p. 161.

SEVEN: THE SLEEPERS

1   Peter Rogers, interview with author on dates in 2020 and 2022.

2   Press conference, Dublin, Monday, 24 January 1972.

3   Ibid.

EIGHT: OUR MAN IN TRIPOLI

1   *The New York Times*, 6 December 1973.

2   George Heitmann, 'Libya: An Analysis of the Oil Economy', *The Journal of Modern African Studies*, Vol. 7, No. 2 (July 1969), pp. 249–63.

3   https://www.bbc.co.uk/news/world-africa-12688033.

4   Cited in *The New York Times*, 21 April 1973.

5   'Libya and Irish Terrorism', The National Archives (Ref. No. FO 973/368), June 1984 (citing Parisian press conference, November 1979); see also 'Death of Press Gallery Member – Libyan Support for IRA: Motion (Resumed)', Seanad Eireann, Vol. 117, 25 November 1987.

6   https://api.parliament.uk/historic-hansard/commons/1974/jan/30/libya# S5CV0868P0_19740130_HOC_36.

7   *The New York Times*, 20 February 1974.

8   Ed Moloney, *A Secret History of the IRA* (second edition: Penguin, 2007), p. 9.

9   Shane Paul O'Doherty, interview with author, 13 December 2022.

10   *The Irish Times*, 22 April 1975.

11   Ibid.

12   *The Irish Times*, 15 November 1974.

13   Ibid.

NINE: ON THE MOVE

1   *The Irish News*, 14 June 1975.

2   McKittrick et al., *Lost Lives*, p. 547.

3   *The Irish Times*, 17 June 1975.

4   Marcus Fogarty, interview with author, 18 November 2022.

5   Peter Rogers, interview with author, 27 August 2022. All quotes from Rogers in this chapter are from this source.

6   The last execution in the Republic of Ireland took place on 20 April 1954. In 1964, under Charles Haughey as Minister for Justice, the death penalty was

abolished for 'ordinary murders'. From then on, only the murder of a garda or a prison officer carried the death penalty. The death penalty was abolished in statute law in 1990 when it was replaced by a forty-year mandatory sentence for capital murder.

TEN: SWISS TIMERS

1 Joe Duffy and Freya McClements, *Children of the Troubles: The Untold Story of the Children Killed in the Northern Ireland Conflict* (Hachette Books Ireland, 2019), p. 12.
2 *The Irish Times*, 27 June 1970.
3 Duffy and McClements, *Children of the Troubles*, p. 11.
4 http://news.bbc.co.uk/onthisday/hi/dates/stories/june/26/newsid_2519000/2519711.stm.
5 *The Irish Times*, 11 December 1970.
6 Ibid.
7 Kieran Conway, *Southside Provisional: From Freedom Fighter to the Four Courts* (Orpen Press, 2014), p. 35.
8 George Styles, *Bombs Have No Pity* (William Luscombe, 1975), p. 83.
9 A.R. Oppenheimer, *IRA: The Bombs and the Bullets. A History of Deadly Ingenuity* (Irish Academic Press, 2017), p. xvi.
10 *The Irish Times*, 22 July 2002.
11 Urban, *Big Boys' Rules*, p. 207.
12 Ian Jones, *London: Bombed Blitzed and Blown Up. The British Capital Under Attack Since 1867* (Frontline Books, 2016, ebook).

ELEVEN: BENIDORM

1 *The Independent*, 27 May 2002.
2 www.superyachttimes.com/yachts/brave-goose-of-1972.
3 'Voyage Man', interview with author, 2021.

TWELVE: CHRISTINE

1 Irish National Archives, Father Patrick Ryan: extradition. Ref: 2019/102/12.

THIRTEEN: 'A MAJOR CALAMITY'

1 https://voices.britishschool.nl/2018/09/13/stories-from-the-archives-the-story-of-sir-richard-sykes/.
2 https://voices.britishschool.nl/2019/11/21/gwen-and-the-outbreak-of-war/.

3 Jane Ewart-Biggs *Pay, Pack and Follow: Memoirs* (Weidenfeld & Nicolson, 1984), p. 177.

4 McKittrick et al., *Lost Lives*, p. 663.

5 Kate Ewart-Biggs, *Desert Island Discs*, BBC Radio 4, July 2022.

6 *The Irish Times*, 8 September 1976.

7 *The Irish Times*, 22 July 1976.

8 Andrew, *The Defence of the Realm*, p. 650.

9 AP/RPN, 23 February 1980.

10 Roy Jenkins, *European Diary, 1977–81* (HarperCollins, 1989), pp. 389–90.

11 Ibid.

12 Cartledge, 'Protection of UK Head of Mission in Brussels', 19 February 1979, PREM 16/2244; Lever (FCO) to Cartledge (PM/PS), 'Bomb attacks in France and Possible Threat to British Targets in Belgium', 12 February 1979.

13 https://wikileaks.org/plusd/cables/1979STATE075366_e.html.

14 http://news.bbc.co.uk/onthisday/hi/dates/stories/march/22/newsid_2543000/2543867.stm.

15 https://hansard.parliament.uk/commons/1979-04-04/debates/710619fb-077d-4b6b-979a-89a9faf7d4cf/SirRichardSykes.

16 http://content.time.com/time/subscriber/article/0,33009,916726,00.html.

17 *The Guardian*, 23 March 1979.

18 Mike Weston, interview with author, 19 December 2022.

19 *The New York Times*, 24 March 1979.

20 There is some disagreement as to how this is spelled, so I have gone with the spelling Ryan uses.

21 Richard Behal, interview with author, August 2021.

22 Jenkins, *European Diary*, p. 410.

23 India Hicks in 2019 BBC documentary *The Day Mountbatten Died*.

24 www.bbc.co.uk/news/uk-northern-ireland-32748199.

25 *The Irish Times*, 27 August 2004.

26 Thatcher, *The Downing Street Years*, p. 56.

FOURTEEN: LION OF THE DESERT

1 *Radharc*, 'Blessing the Aer Lingus Fleet', 15 September 1962.

2 Margaret Thatcher, speech in Belfast, 5 March 1981.

3 Margaret Thatcher, House of Commons, 5 May 1981.

4 *The Irish Examiner*, 30 December 2011.

5 *The Irish Times*, 21 March 2017.

6 Éamon McGuire, *Enemy of the Empire: Life as an International Undercover IRA Activist* (O'Brien Press, 2006), p. 318.

7 *The Sunday Times*, 8 October 2006.

FIFTEEN: SWITCH AND SWITCH

1 Letter to the Speaker of the House and the President of the Senate, Enclosure 2, pt. III, 2 PUB. PAPERS: JIMMY CARTER 2290, 2294 (29 December 1979).
2 *The Washington Post*, 7 May 1981.
3 *The New York Times*, 21 August 1981.
4 Iwan Morgan, *Reagan: American Icon* (I.B.Tauris, 2016), p. 205.
5 www.reaganlibrary.gov/archives/speech/remarks-board-uss-constellation-coast -california.
6 Ronald Reagan, *An American Life* (Threshold Editions, 2011), p. 291.
7 *The New York Times*, 11 December 1981.
8 *The Irish Times*, 11 December 1981.
9 www.cia.gov/readingroom/docs/CIA-RDP84B00049R000200360010-5.pdf.
10 *This Week*, Thames Television, 'Holy Terror', June 1989.
11 Ibid.
12 Ibid.

SIXTEEN: HYDE PARK

1 https://horse-canada.com/horses-and-history/sefton-beloved-survivor-of-the-1982-ira-bombings/.
2 https://reparations.qub.ac.uk/assets/uploads/Young-v-Downey-judgment-161220.pdf.
3 *The Telegraph*, 28 February 2014.
4 *The Sun*, 12 December 2019.
5 https://reparations.qub.ac.uk/assets/uploads/Young-v-Downey-judgment-161220.pdf.
6 https://www.judiciary.uk/wp-content/uploads/2019/12/APPROVED-JUDG MENT-Young-v-Downey-18.12.19.pdf.
7 Ibid.
8 Ibid.
9 Press Association, 1 December 2019.
10 Brigadier A.H. Parker Bowles, 'The Hyde Park Bombing – Recollections', *Household Cavalry Journal*, 2007/8, p. 66.
11 https://reparations.qub.ac.uk/assets/uploads/Young-v-Downey-judgment-161220.pdf.
12 Parker Bowles, 'The Hyde Park Bombing – Recollections', p. 66.
13 https://reparations.qub.ac.uk/assets/uploads/Young-v-Downey-judgment-161220.pdf.
14 *The New York Times*, 21 July 1982.
15 https://reparations.qub.ac.uk/assets/uploads/Young-v-Downey-judgment-161220.pdf.

16   The Household Cavalry Journal, 2007/08.
17   https://www.judiciary.uk/wp-content/uploads/2019/12/APPROVED-JUDG
     MENT-Young-v-Downey-18.12.19.pdf.

SEVENTEEN: THE DUCKS OF THE GREEN

1   *Kildare Observer*, 24 October 1907.
2   *The Irish Times*, 18 April 2009.
3   https://cain.ulster.ac.uk/othelem/organ/ira/ira130406.htm.
4   http://news.bbc.co.uk/onthisday/hi/dates/stories/october/21/newsid_2489
    000/2489349.stm.

EIGHTEEN: THE RYAN AFFAIR

1   Andrew, *The Defence of the Realm*, p. 740.
2   Ibid., p. 741.
3   The National Archives, FCO 33/10117: Extradition requests between the UK
    and Belgium: Patrick Ryan.
4   *The Irish Times*, 2 May 1988.
5   The National Archives, FCO 33/10117: Extradition requests between the UK
    and Belgium: Patrick Ryan.
6   Irish National Archives, 2018/68/15: European control of terrorism: extradition.
7   The National Archives, FCO 33/10117: Extradition requests between the UK
    and Belgium: Patrick Ryan.
8   Ibid.
9   Ibid.
10 Ibid.
11 The National Archives, CJ 4/7614: Extradition of Father Patrick Ryan from
    Belgium.
12 The National Archives, FCO 33/10117: Extradition requests between the UK
    and Belgium: Patrick Ryan.
13 *The Irish Times*, 4 November 1988.
14 Ibid.
15 The National Archives, FCO 33/10117: Extradition requests between the UK
    and Belgium: Patrick Ryan.
16 Ibid.
17 The National Archives, CJ 4/7615: Extradition of Father Patrick Ryan from
    Belgium.
18 Ibid.
19 *The Irish Times*, 25 November 1988.

20 The National Archives, CJ 4/7615: Extradition of Father Patrick Ryan from Belgium.
21 FCO 27 January 1989, National Archive file.
22 The National Archives, FCO 33/10117: Extradition request between the UK and Belgium: Patrick Ryan.
23 *The Guardian*, 29 November 1988.

NINETEEN: 'THE BIRD HAD FLOWN'

1 *The Irish Times*, 25 November 1988.
2 Ibid.
3 BBC, 23 November 1988.
4 *The Irish Times*, 26 November 1988.
5 The National Archives, CJ 4/7614: Extradition of Father Patrick Ryan from Belgium.
6 https://api.parliament.uk/historic-hansard/commons/1988/nov/29/engagements.
7 The National Archives, CJ 4/7615: Extradition of Father Patrick Ryan from Belgium.
8 Ibid.
9 https://api.parliament.uk/historic-hansard/commons/1988/dec/13/engagements.

TWENTY: A VERY WICKED MAN

1 *Irish Daily Mail*, 14 June 2018.
2 The National Archives, CJ 4/7615: Extradition of Father Patrick Ryan from Belgium.
3 *The Irish Times*, 29 April 1989.
4 'Blood Money', *The Cook Report*, ITV, September 1989.
5 *The Irish Times*, 19 May 1989.
6 https://www.casemine.com/judgement/uk/5a938b4060d03e5f6b82bcd3.
7 *This Week*, Thames Television, 'Holy Terror', June 1989.
8 The National Archives, CJ 4/7615: Extradition of Father Patrick Ryan from Belgium.
9 *The Irish Times*, 11 January 1990.

ACKNOWLEDGEMENTS

Some lives span pivotal stages of Irish history and mirror contradictions born out of a fervent belief in militant Irish nationalism; in telling Patrick Ryan's story, I have always been mindful of the lost lives and the broken hearts left behind.

The research for this book consumed a great deal of time, taken up with chasing down shadows, and I wish to thank the sources who spoke to me on condition of anonymity.

To my agent, Lisa Moylett, thank you for your kindness and generous encouragement throughout the writing of this book. I am indebted to my editor, Zoe Apostolides, whose insights and advice transformed the telling of this story – thank you. I would also like to thank Wendy Logue in Merrion Press, for her wise editorial guidance, and Conor Graham for his patience. I wish also to thank my colleagues in the BBC for their support.

On a personal note, I wish to thank the friends who helped me along this path, in particular Geraldine and Moon. My sisters and brothers-in-law, were as always, a tonic and support during this endeavour. To my parents, thank you for everything.